J. G. Dehner sj

# Sex, Priests, and Power

## Anatomy of a Crisis

Also by
A. W. RICHARD SIPE

*A Secret World: Sexuality and the Search for Celibacy*

# Sex, Priests, and Power

## Anatomy of a Crisis

A. W. RICHARD SIPE

BRUNNER/MAZEL *Publishers* • NEW YORK

We gratefully acknowledge the sources listed below for permission to excerpt material for use in this volume.

pp. 32 & 36, reprinted with permission from the *Diagnostic and Statistical Manual of Mental Disorders, Fourth Edition.* Copyright © 1994 American Psychiatric Association.

pp. 52, 53, 54, & 55, reprinted with permission from *The Cardinal Sins* by Andrew Greeley. Copyright © 1982 Warner Books/A Bernard Geis Associates Book.

pp. 164, 165, 166, 182, 188, & 189, reprinted with permission of St. Martin's Press, Inc., from *Sin and Fear: The Emergence of a Western Guilt Culture* by Jean Delumeau. Copyright © 1990 Jean Delumeau.

pp. 175, 176, & 177, reprinted with permission from "Charisma of Celibacy: A Priest's Personal Story of Liberating Discovery," in *Tablet,* by Didascolos. Copyright © 1994 The Tablet Publishing Co., Ltd.

Library of Congress Cataloging-in-Publication Data

Sipe, A. W. Richard
    Sex, priests, and power : anatomy of a crisis / A. W. Richard Sipe.
       p.     cm.
    Includes bibliographical references and indexes.
    ISBN 0-87630-769-1
    1. Celibacy—Catholic Church. 2. Catholic Church—Clergy—Sexual behavior. 3. Sex—Religious aspects—Catholic Church. I. Title.
BX1912.9.S575   1995
253'.2—dc20                                  94-45136
                                                      CIP

*Published by*
BRUNNER/MAZEL, INC.
19 Union Square West
New York, New York 10003

Manufactured in the United States of America

10 9 8 7 6 5 4 3 2 1

To Father Virgil O'Neill,
who by his courage, charity,
and awareness of the divine
in all life, taught me
the service, privilege, and the
pain of loyal dissent

# CONTENTS

# FOREWORD

The 1990 Canadian film *Jesus of Montreal* featured a priest who is *only human*. Unwilling to surrender the social esteem and the political and material benefits of priesthood, he nevertheless maintains a sexual relationship with a much younger woman. His bad-faith representation of church authority while violating his vow of celibacy ultimately—through a series of circumstances—results in the death of "Jesus." This priest is one fictional representative of the actual effects of the ancient tradition of celibacy in the lives of countless Roman Catholic clergy and laypeople.

At the end of the twentieth century the stabilized power of the Catholic Church is more evident to many people than its sensitivity to human pain. Examining the requirement for a celibate priesthood and the church's sexual doctrine, Richard Sipe describes, by examples and figures, the evidence for an appalling amount of suffering, both by priests and by those to whom they relate sexually. Sipe's figures are estimates; they may even be conservative estimates. Whether or not they are exact is not the issue since figures never give an accurate reading of human pain. Sipe estimates that approximately 2% of those vowed to celibacy achieve it. Since 1960, twenty thousand priests have left the active priesthood in the United States, the majority to marry. At any one time, 20% of priests in good standing are involved in sexual relationships with women; 8% are experimenting sexually, approximately evenly divided between heterosexual and homosexual activity; about 30% of priests have a homosexual orientation. About 50% of both homosexual and heterosexual priests practice celibacy.

In the context of the Roman Church's prohibition on all forms of sexual activity for its ordained priesthood, a conspiracy of secrecy maintains the privilege and social esteem of the priesthood while

ix

permitting sexual activity. Moreover, since *any* and *all* sex is forbidden, there is no discussion of criteria for moral responsibility in sexual behavior. Given this situation, abuses are inevitable. A number of priests use their power and position to seduce women, children, and men who are led to expect from their priest the care of a loving father. Certainly, sexual abuse is not specific to Catholic priests, but its occurrence among a clergy pledged to celibacy and service to others strikes the North American public as a particular travesty when they read of such incidents in the daily newspaper.

How did the *celibate/sexual system* analyzed in the following pages originate? Why did some highly intelligent and resourceful historical people adopt a practice that is the source of the high levels of human pain Richard Sipe describes? Although it is seldom useful — or even accurate — to identify a single historical villain, it *is* instructive to reconstruct the social and institutional circumstances in which a practice originated. When those historical situations have been considered fairly and in sufficient detail, the productivity of the practice in question for its society of origin can be understood. More importantly, it is also possible to see that a practice that made sense in the context of its society of origin can have destructive and painful effects in a vastly changed contemporary society.

A full description of the institutionalization of the Roman Catholic Christianity in the fourth-century Roman Empire is beyond the scope of this brief introduction. Two aspects of the rapid advance of Christianity during the fourth century are, however, important to contemporary discussions of celibacy. These are (1) the centrality of control of sexuality to emerging formations of institutionalized power; and (2) the recognition of the practical usefulness of sexual regulation and/or abstinence for gathering and maintaining spiritual energy.

A groundbreaking book, Samuel Laeuchli's *Power and Sexuality in the Early Church,* explored — when other historians of Christianity were largely treating their field solely as a history of theological ideas — a dramatic preoccupation with issues surrounding sexuality at the beginning of the fourth century. Using as his evidence the *canons,* or rulings on practices, of the A.D. 309 Council of Elvira, Laeuchli demonstrated that church leaders recognized — whether consciously or unconsciously — that establishing authority in matters of sexuality was intimately connected to establishing and maintaining institutional power. A bit later, the ecumenical Council of Nicaea also legislated both sexual and institutional practices with equal attention. It is remarkable that a church that moved, during the course of one century, from persecuted sect to official religion of the Roman Empire should expend so much attention on regulation of sexuality both among clergy and laity. By the 380s, when Catholic Christianity became the religion of the Empire, the professionalization of a Catholic clergy involved the demand that clergy maintain a practical and symbolic separation from secular society.

The universalization and institutionalization of celibacy testifies to its importance at a particular moment in history when leaders of a recently marginalized and persecuted church felt the need for gathering social power. With the most massive persecution of Christians ever in the West—the Diocletian persecution—still in living memory, the Constantinian Peace of the Church offered the opportunity for the irreversible establishment of Christianity. Toward the end of the fourth century, Christian leaders rejoiced in the establishment of a Christian Empire. For a religious body whose experience in the Roman Empire had been vulnerability and necessary secrecy, power represented, first of all, permanent relief from persecution and execution. Secondly, it is important to remember that in the late-classical world, power was understood not primarily as *power over*, as a modern people tend to think of it, but as *power to* accomplish the fundamental necessities of providing food and protection to unimaginably precarious societies. In this historical context, celibacy took on a very different value than it has in a wealthy and powerful Church that has had, for many centuries, the ability to legislate belief and practice and to punish dissidents. The statements on celibacy of an Augustine or Jerome must be understood in this social context if we are to be fair and sensitive historical interpreters.

Secondly, the first legislation of clerical celibacy occurred in a society enamored with asceticism as a method for achieving what Michel Foucault has called the "care of the self." Fascination with a "self" constructed by disciplined practices—especially of diet and sexuality—crossed religious and philosophical affiliations. In the context of this fascination with asceticism, a monk named Jovinian drew the vitriolic and verbose ire of both Augustine and Jerome by proposing that marriage provided a condition in which spiritual discipline and progress could be achieved equally with celibates. Clearly, asceticism was the ascendant mood of the moment, and not only within the Christian movement. By incorporating the ascetic ideal of philosophers, Roman religions, and the spectrum of religious groups that self-identified with Christianity, Catholic Christianity simultaneously strengthened both its respect in the eyes of secular society and its internal energy. Celibacy also provided the definition of what one historian has called "Christian overachievement," a way to differentiate between ordinary members and those who sought Christian perfection. Critical as twentieth-century people may be of the fourth-century social consensus on asceticism, it is difficult to see that a more relaxed Christianity would have achieved the institutional power with which the Catholic Church was able to modify some of the social calamities of the fifth century.

St. Augustine, bishop of the North African town of Hippo at the end of the fourth century, is commonly cited as the primary expositor and advocate of clerical celibacy. It is certainly the case that he articulated with remarkable power his own experience of compulsive youthful sexual activity as well as his resolution in celibacy of a sexuality that was destructive both to himself and to others. Augustine undoubtedly found relief and "freedom"—his word—in celibacy, but he was careful to say that this solution was both personal and God-given. He insisted repeatedly that celibacy should neither be universalized for all committed Christians, nor should it be admired as the result of intransigent will power. Augustine's followers, however, did not heed his cautions. Stimulated by the rhetorical beauty of his descriptions of his own conversion to celibacy, they claimed celibacy as the "higher way." Ignoring his insistence that sexual abstinence is a *gift*, not the result of a teeth-gritting willpower, celibacy developed into a requirement for all Catholic clergy.

A more precise understanding of Augustine's analysis of the root of sin may help to demonstrate that contemporary concern over priests who abuse their power and indulge their sexuality are not unique to the twentieth century. Augustine's word for the cause of sin was *concupiscentia*. Although modern interpretations of concupiscence tend to confine the meaning of the term to sexual lust, late-classical authors understood it to entail irreducibly the three lusts endemic to human nature—lust for sex, power, and possession. No single lust—if it were possible to separate them for purposes of analysis—has the destructive potential of the closely woven combination of lusts. It was *concupiscentia*—the interconnected lusts, not sexual lust in isolation—that Augustine labeled "original sin." Strikingly, Augustine understood the whole human race—both perpetrators and abused—as "victims." He insisted that the appropriate reaction to the ubiquitous evidence of original sin is empathy. After discussing children and adults' compulsive pursuit of the socially designated objects of sex, power, and possession in his *Confessions*, he marveled, "And no one is sorry for the children; no one is sorry for the adults; no one is sorry for both of them" (*Confessions* I:10). Similarly, Sipe is empathetic with priests as well as with their partners and victims. Yet he deplores the systemic ignorance and — to use the ancient word — *concupiscence* that creates so much suffering. What he advocates is exposure and discussion of the interconnection of power, sexuality, and secrecy on which the celibate/sexual system is built.

Sipe focuses here on the male priesthood of the Roman Catholic Church. In order to fully understand the operation of the celibate system, a similar study of women celibates needs to be done. Sensitive to both the ideological sexism that maintains the celibate system and to the treatment of actual women who become priests' friends and lovers, Sipe does not presume to generalize his findings to women members of religious orders. A study of female celibacy could be expected to reveal both some similarities with male celibates and some startling differences. It is to be hoped that this book will stimulate and encourage such a study.

*Sex, Priests, and Power: Anatomy of a Crisis* can be understood as part of a massive contemporary project of revision and reconstruction within Christianity. Many Christians are presently recognizing that some central affirmations of Christian faith have been either ignored or too slenderly developed to merit a place in mainstream Christianity. When one considers the strong affirmations of human bodies implied in the doctrines of creation, the Incarnation of Jesus Christ, and the resurrection of the body, it seems odd that management of one of the human body's most intimate functions, sexuality, has not been considered a crucial part of one's *religious identity.*

It would be simplistic to blame the inclusion of philosophical ideas in Christianity for this. *All* the religious and philosophical movements of the centuries in which Christianity was being formed struggled to define the role of the body and sexuality in religious practice. Moreover, it does not solve the problems of the present merely to identify the historical origin of ideas that live and have their effects in the present. Augustine is frequently and unfairly blamed for distorted sexual doctrine because he worried about and addressed, with the conceptual tools available, issues of sex and the body. The relative silence of Christian authors prior to and contemporary with Augustine and their own inadequacies in addressing sexuality have, ironically, guaranteed their immunity from twentieth-century criticism.

Finally, Sipe admires celibacy, not as legislated and institutionalized, but as a personal "quest of spiritual relationship and religious reality based on unflinching self-knowledge and radical truth about one's innermost desires." As a *sexual orientation,* those who have the gift, and have undertaken the hard work of self-knowledge required for productive celibacy, he says, evidence "an interior freedom and integration that unite their individuality and their service." Those who are gifted with celibacy are, in Sipe's word, "awesome." And, in his studied opinion, they are rare. The goal and spirit of this book, then, is not the overthrow of an institution that damages people, but scrutiny of a destructive strain within a church that *could be so much more powerful for healing and blessing* if it were willing to examine and revise its celibate/sexual system. It is a book that exemplifies and advocates what therapeutic programs call "tough love," the ruthless honesty and relentless analysis that exposes the self-deception of an individual or an institution in order to heal, not to destroy.

MARGARET R. MILES, PH.D.
*Bussey Professor of Historical Theology*
*Harvard Divinity School*
*Harvard University*
*Cambridge, Massachusetts*

# PREFACE

*The faith in the order of nature which has made possible the growth of science is a particular example of a deeper faith. This faith cannot be justified by any inductive generalization. It springs from direct inspiration of the nature of things as disclosed in our immediate present experience.*

Alfred North Whitehead
*Science and the Modern World*

*When men have harnessed the winds, the waves, the tides and gravity, they will harness for God the energies of love, and then for the second time in the history of the world, man will have discovered Fire.*

Pierre Teilhard de Chardin
*The Evolution of Chastity*

The Catholic Church is writhing, like Laocoön, in the grips of a crisis of epic proportions. The form and the substance of the struggle are sexual. A majority of people neither believe nor practice the official church teachings about sex; many priests and bishops do not believe what they teach, and others reject the celibate practice that is so intimately intertwined with their claim to power and cultural identity.

In 1960 when I began studying the practice, process, and achievement of priestly celibacy, I had no sense of crisis or any idea that my explorations would lead me inexorably to the vortex of a critical contest that engages moral doctrine and religious discipline.

The parameters of the conflict are not limited to a relatively few men who may or may not practice the celibacy they profess. The power of Catholic priests and the sexual reasoning of Christian tradition have implications for life on this planet, including the issues of population growth, gender and racial equality, and understanding the nature of human sexuality. The salient questions are not about theoretical preferences, venerable traditions, or sacred opinions. The questions are practical struggles for truth, which affect people's lives and the future of the planet.

This book is not an attack on an important religious practice— celibacy —much less on a church or religion. It is an invitation to dialogue about issues that have profound effects on people. It is an effort to analyze the function and structure of a system that exerts real power in an area of existence vital to human service, happiness, and productivity: sexuality as it is understood by the celibate/sexual teaching and practice of the Catholic Church.

This work invites anyone, from whatever discipline, to engage in concerned discourse on the nature and meaning of human sexuality, its ramifications for human existence, and the future of life. The search for truth and life is not a finished ordeal.

But this work is not polemical. I do not offer crisp definitions of terms like reality, nature, healthy, normal, mature, and so on, because each discipline entering dialogue will have its own definitions as discussion impinges on the territory of each person's perspective. I trust discourse to help each of us move elegantly from one language game to another.

Those who wish to denigrate religion, religious practice, or celibacy will find no ally in these explorations if they follow my arguments to their conclusion. Equally, those who wish to use the moniker *celibate* or *religious* as a cover for the abuse of children, women, or men or as a means of sexual control or domination will find no consolation in these pages.

Since 1988 the writings of Edward O. Wilson, more than any other thinker, have influenced the direction and development of my explorations of the celibate/sexual system of the church. Prior to that time my efforts were centered on individual considerations. When I finished the first 25 years of study in 1985, I was content that I had found answers to the questions, What is religious celibacy? How is it practiced by those who profess it? What is the process of celibate identity? What is the structure of personal celibate achievement? Those observations were published in 1990 under the title *A Secret World: Sexuality and the Search for Celibacy*.

My focus was always practical: an effort to understand and assist the individual priest in his striving for religious service and integrity by way of a seldom-discussed and little-explored physical pathway—celibacy or sexual deprivation. Margaret Mead, in 1966, gave me good advice: while not challenging my basic psychotherapeutic method, she encouraged me to forsake a narrow psychoanalytic frame of reference for a simpler ethnographic record, described by Spradly and McCurdy as "not merely an objective description of people and their behavior from the observer's viewpoint...[but] a systematic attempt to discover the knowledge a group of people have learned and are using to organize their behavior" (1972, p. viii).

In this present study, two questions led me beyond simple description of individual celibate practice and to the doorstep of Wilson and the consideration of coevolution: Why does celibacy persist as a personal and cultural entity (specifically in religious culture)? And how are celibacy and sexuality connected to the power system of the Catholic Church? This preliminary analysis of the function and structure of the celibate/sexual system of the Catholic Church is only a modest beginning and an introduction to questions about the genetic and cultural dynamics of this phenomenon. Throughout, I have been guided by six principles that Wilson articulates clearly and cogently—which in my estimation prove practical and useful to the exploration of theological and psychological development and complement the profound contributions of Father Pierre Teilhard de Chardin.

First, all human behavior must be understood in the context of evolutionary reality and as cultural adaptation.

Second, biology must be taken seriously. Most religionists have not taken evolutionary biology (and molecular biology) into account in explaining human sexual behavior or in their pronouncements about sexual ethics. Most moral doctrine on sex is based on a deficient perception of human nature.

Third, the scientist can be seen as a mythmaker. Wilson, the scientist, calls himself a storyteller—that is, one who tells a story based on fact, a product of his imagination passed through the crucible of rigorous testing in the real world. This perspective is eminently coherent with the theological enterprise. Religious myth untempered by human reality begets irrational cult and anti-intellectual fundamentalism. Religious story not subjected to the crucible of reality becomes magic and superstition. The human reality of sex and the spiritual dimensions of love make sexuality an inevitable area of interest for religion and science, both of which are concerned with the origins, nature, and future of life.

Fourth, knowledge makes us free; there is ultimately no such thing as dangerous knowledge. For the religious person, this sentiment is evocative of Christ's statement, "the truth shall make you free." And there is a solid theological tradition that holds that ultimately there can be no contradictions in truth. Truth is one. The problem is not truth, but those who—whether in the name of religion or science—claim for themselves complete and exclusive access to it.

Fifth, some people find the idea of scientific materialism inimical to religion. I do not; in fact, I believe that it is a stance that can purify religion of magic and superstition and bring to religious understanding a credibility worthy of human dignity and congruent with progress in knowledge of sexual nature, life, and love. Philosophical dualism is no longer viable as a basis for religious understanding. Monism must account for religion and the spiritual.

Sixth, Wilson's writings reflect an awe in the face of life and demonstrate a capacity to identify with all humanity and all living things, qualities that exceed any exclusionary boundaries that dogma or sect can erect. That stance is a *sine qua non* for anyone who would claim validity for the spiritual.

These considerations have guided and inspired me as I have struggled to explain my observations of the celibate/sexual system of the Catholic Church.

The sexual questions facing religion are not new. The evolutionary perspectives and biogenetic knowledge now available to us are new, however. Augustine and his contemporaries were deprived of such truth when his synthesis was ossified into systemic power after the fifth century. In this lies the crisis: how to respect and account for earlier understanding and explanations at the same time as we become fearlessly self-critical and free ourselves of bias in order to integrate discoveries that demand a new synthesis based on a more accurate definition of human sex and nature.

I offer this study as a step toward that goal.

*Rome, Italy*
*April 3, 1994*

# Acknowledgments

The priests, of every rank, who shared their experiences and observations of the celibate/sexual system merit my deepest gratitude and admiration. Their radical self-honesty and heroic self-disclosure make this their book. I am privileged to be a chronicler.

This book is one piece of a larger research project on *Celibacy in Literature and Life.* Dr. B. C. Lamb and Dr. Harris Gruman, scholars in comparative literature, have offered insight and direction to every phase of its development. Gregory Guri-Glass, Ph.D., epidemiologist and statistician, and Margarita Guri-Glass, Ph.D., expert and sensitive advocate of the abused, have offered their expertise in evaluating elements of clerical crisis. Marianne Benkert, M.D., serves as the loving psychiatric gyroscope of our team.

W. E. B. Sipe, Eliot House Harvard, is a relentless searcher for sources and a thoughtful devil's advocate. Andrew Jezic, J.D., Chip Welch, Esq., and Mike Ryan, M.S., have contributed to the understanding of the legal, criminal, and social service dimensions of clerical abuse. Jeanne Miller, Andy Kagan, Father Tom Economus, and Mr. and Ms. Dennis Gaboury have spoken powerfully to the pain of victimization by the trusted, and eloquently to the hope of survival and recovery. They represent a thousand unnamed voices who give testimony to the symptoms of the current crisis in the churches. Fred Berlin, M.D., and Peter Fagan, Ph.D., of Johns Hopkins Medical School are models of good sense and therapeutic wisdom in the diagnosis and treatment of sexual problems and abuse. Their example provides hope, leadership, and encouragement to those of us working in the field.

J. F. Powers refreshed my spirit with hospitality and wit several times during the painful labor of writing. He understands. Kathleen Norris inspired and encouraged me in ways that extend far beyond the production of this book. Edward O. Wilson extended a gracious reception and kind encouragement to a convergent thinker. I am also indebted to the late Chris Mooney, S.J., for the gift of conversations and use of his unpublished notes on theology and evolution. Terrance Dosh and Fintan Kilbride suggested sources and provided access to a network of information. Dick Benson of the Menninger Foundation has inspired me for a quarter century.

Mark Tracten of Brunner/Mazel goaded me into writing this book; I am now beginning to appreciate his efforts and instincts. Bernie Mazel remains a hero to me; I am honored to have his reactions and advice about my labor. Natalie Gilman has the tough job of editing and production; I treasure her skill and her friendship. Janja Lalich copyedited this book with the sensitivity of an author. Patricia Wolf assured final refinement. My skilled and informed readers, E.B., M.B., C.S., J.G., W.S., M.G., E.K., J.M., M.N., and S.H. have all added to the refinement of detail and clarification of content. Delene M. Carlee typed more versions of the manuscript than either of us care to count. Only the love I have for each of the above and the support I experienced from them made endurable the pain involved in facing the content and the progress of this study. Thank you.

# Part I

# Symptoms of
# the Crisis

# 1

# PRIESTS AND CHILDREN

*People always refuse to see beyond the individual fault. But after all, the transgression itself is only the eruption. And the symptoms which most impress outsiders aren't always the gravest and most disquieting.*

Georges Bernanos

*The sexual abuse of children is found with uncanny frequency among school teachers and child attendants . . . and fantasies of being seduced are of particular interest, because so often they are not fantasies but real memories.*

Sigmund Freud

The man sitting across from me was a member of the American hierarchy, but the only hint of his office was the modest episcopal ring on his right hand. We spoke for a long while about priesthood and the church. After a brief lull in the conversation, he shattered the silence with a quiet reflection, almost as if he were talking to himself: "The thing that pains me about the organization to which I belong is that it is rotten from the top down."

I was caught short, even shocked. This kindly man before me was not some disgruntled or disaffected cleric. He loved his priesthood and his church. In the obvious anguish he expressed he was not distancing himself from the church of which he was a part or from the church that was a part of him. His reflection was all the more powerful because he was not pointing fingers. There was no sense of vindictiveness or recrimination—just deep personal pain.

I have thought long and hard about all of his observations. At one time I even wondered if the word *rotten*, or even the whole reverie, was a momentary Freudian slip of the ecclesiastical mind. I asked myself if it was a bit like a dream production, true but

3

private. Yet I realized that he knew what he was saying when he gave me permission to quote him. He rejected the rottenness of secrecy, the misuse of power, the cover-ups, the duplicities to salvage image, and any refusals of the celibate/sexual system to assume responsibility for its behaviors and its deficiencies—for itself—for what it truly is.

When asked why the American bishops were having such a difficult time dealing with priest sexual abusers, another bishop responded, "Undoubtedly part of the problem is that some of the bishops themselves are abusers." When reminded that he was speaking on record and not merely on background, he repeated, "Undoubtedly part of the problem is that some of the bishops are, themselves, abusers."

Such are clues to the anatomy of a crisis. These men and others who care about their church have helped me clarify the context of the issues discussed in this book as well as the thesis that unites them all.

That thesis is straightforward: The scandal of priestly sexual abuse of minors, although real and significant in itself, is primarily a symptom of an essentially flawed celibate/sexual system of ecclesiastical power. Analysis of the function and structure of the celibate/sexual system demonstrates that it is based on a false understanding of the nature of human sexuality and primary Christian experience. Maintenance of the system develops, fosters, and protects sexual abuse and violence. To expose the system is to confront Catholic Christianity with the most profound crisis of its integrity since the earliest centuries of its existence.

Sex has always been problematic for the Roman Catholic Church. In 2,000 years no Christian church has developed an adequate theology of sexuality—that is, no one has worked out an overarching, comprehensive, and integrative understanding of the nature and place of sexuality within the scheme of salvation and theological system. Religious pronouncements on sex are ordinarily moralistic and marked by rhetorical, polemical, and highly charged emotional overtones designed to compensate for the essential lack of substantive foundation.

This theological deficiency is highlighted and underscored by the current crisis of sexual confidence in which the Catholic Church finds itself. We will not solve the problem of sexual abuse by clergy without addressing in an honest and essential way these unsolved questions fundamental to religious integrity and the practical spiritual striving of men and women.

It would be futile to analyze the sexual trauma that has recently burst upon world consciousness via the exposure of the sexual abuse of minors by clergy without realizing that this phenomenon, so well documented in the media and courtrooms, is ultimately part of a theoretical system of unaddressed questions and, more immediately, a practical product of the religious system itself. To address the problem of sexual trauma in the church in any narrower context runs the risk of self-deception and certain failure similar to applying a bandage to a cancerous lesion.

Eventually, the church must submit its consideration of sexuality to the realities of evolutionary, molecular, and anthropological biology (that is, scientific perception), along with historical, sociological, and poetic speculation (that is, mystical perception). Failure to take account of scientific discoveries, especially in the areas of physics and biology, renders theological pronouncements on human nature and God noncredible.

In short, the Catholic Church has not yet incorporated enough knowledge of physical nature generally—and human sexual nature specifically— to develop an adequate theology of sexuality. This state of affairs affects both theory and praxis. In his 1991 Dudleian lecture at Harvard Divinity School, Edward O. Wilson spoke eloquently on the need for religion to develop a natural philosophy to reevaluate its teaching because "our profound impulses are rooted in a genetic heritage common to the entire species. . . . The role of religion is to codify and to put into enduring, poetic form the highest moral values of a society consistent with empirical knowledge." Wilson has also written, "In order to search for a new morality based on a more truthful definition of man, it is necessary to look inward, to dissect the machinery of the mind and to retrace its evolutionary history" (1978, p. 4).

The idea that theology needs to reconcile itself with nature is not new. Allister Hardy of Oxford University has long been interested in questions of spirituality and science and has cast that interest in the broadest ecological context: life.

> The decline in religion is, I believe, in no small measure due to theology ignoring the possible use of the scientific approach to its problems. If properly used the method could be invaluable in helping a scientifically minded public to realize that a faith in spirituality was not contrary to scientific fact. (1966, p. 23)

The sexual crisis of the church cannot be adequately addressed in any narrower context.

## SCOPE OF THE CURRENT CRISIS

The media headlines are clear: "Twelve Priests Abuse Students," "Priest Abuses One Hundred Children," "Priest Heads Sex Club for Adolescents." The Roman Catholic priesthood is in crisis. It is obvious that the crisis is sexual. In this book I will go beyond the headlines to the real story behind the scandals of priests sexually abusing altar boys or other minors. The situation is far deeper and broader than most believers would like to admit, but a surprising number of church officials are aware of its true scope.

Cardinal Alfons Stickler, former director of the Vatican library, was quoted in the September 4, 1993, *Tablet* to the effect that the state of the church today is even worse than it was during the fourth century. That was a period when the sexual teaching of Christianity was solidified by such teachers as Saints Ambrose, Jerome, and Augustine.

Sex, pleasure, sin, and women were woven into a theological equation that solidified the celibate/sexual structure of the Roman Catholic Church and influenced every aspect of its development. Power was consolidated in sexual terms. That structure is crumbling under the weight of its own hypertrophy, if not corruption. Practical reality, scientific development, and spiritual awareness of the origins and meanings of sexuality, life, and love expose the inadequacy of the system to sustain its own stated goals.

Pope John Paul II, speaking to the officials of his own household (December 21, 1993, as reported in *L'Osservatore Romano*, December 22, 1993), decried the spread of "moral deviations of every kind. . . . Among those that are particularly painful are the sexual [deviations] which sometimes have involved, 'I say it crying,' members of the clergy." Sexual activity among presumed celibates is symptomatic of the dysfunction of the system.

Only an understanding of the function and structure underlying the symptoms will alleviate the spiritual crisis that threatens the integrity of a religious organization more severely than any other in 2,000 years.

*Anatomy*, the basic structure of an organism; *physiology*, the functions of the organism; and *pathology*, the dysfunction of a living organism are three interrelated avenues of understanding the *systemic nature* of a living organism. These metaphors are useful in approaching a celibate/sexual crisis that has ramifications far beyond the borders of one church and its believers—for the culture at large and for human existence and the preservation of life generally.

The sexual behavior of priests must be understood against the clear and unbending sexual moral doctrine of Catholic Christianity, namely: *Every sexual thought, word, desire, and action outside marriage is mortally sinful. Every sexual act within marriage not open to conception is mortally sinful. Sexual misbehavior constitutes grave matter in every instance.* No other area of moral life, including murder, is treated with this same moral rigidity. The majority of Catholics simply do not believe this teaching, nor do they think that natural law supports it.

Also, Catholic priests in the Latin rite are bound by the church law demanding perfect and perpetual chastity. Ecclesiastical power is reserved to males who promise adherence to this church law. The core of the public crisis facing the church is the dissemination of evidence that what is taught, expected, and professed sexually is in fact not always (or often) practiced even at the highest levels of the religious power structure. All of this is no surprise to cynics and the worldly wise both in and outside the church. The revolution is in the popular consciousness and the consequent decline of confidence in church authority and control. Neither the cynic nor the easily shocked is well equipped to understand the complexity or the importance of the current celibate/sexual crisis. Patience, compassion, and dedication to radical truth are necessary in anyone who would approach the situation adequately.

The antisexual stance of church theory has profound practical and political implications. The current crisis challenges, irrevocably, the Christian authenticity of that stance. More and more scholars see the official Catholic position on sexuality as both dangerous and false. If we can approach the original Christian perception of sexuality, there is hope of renewal and reform. There will be renewed self-discovery, personal honesty, and shared discourse about celibacy/sexuality. But interest in these forces threatens to tear apart the official prevailing understanding of sexuality and replace it with a celibate/sexual structure more in conformity with nature and authentic religious intent.

## CLUES TO CRISIS

There are five related areas in which the crisis in the Catholic Church is manifested: belief, practice, vocations, finances, and image. Large numbers of Catholics simply do not trust the authoritative teachings of the Vatican in matters of sexuality. Contraception, abortion, remarriage after divorce, homosexuality, and masturbation—all areas of strict prohibition according to Vatican teaching—are tolerated as acceptable behavior by lay Catholics in roughly the same proportion as by members of other denominations that generally have much more liberal attitudes toward sexual behavior. Even acceptance of the ideas of married priests and female priests is widespread among both the laity and the clergy.

Catholics are required by church law to attend Mass on Sundays and Holy Days of obligation. Regular attendance at Sunday Mass in the United States runs under 50%. Some studies say such attendance is actually only 28%. The Sacrament of Reconciliation, or confession, is much less frequently used by the average Catholic. Many priests avail themselves of this sacrament only rarely.

Richard Schoenherr has shown decisively that worldwide in the years 1965 through 1985 "without exception the priest to lay-person ratio has declined steadily over the entire 20-year period" (1993, p. 10). He has also pointed out that "the current clergy shortage is a distinct Catholic crisis" (p. 6). Some other denominations have a surplus of clergy. His study, *Full Pews and Empty Altars*, predicts that by the year 2005, there will be twice as many parishioners per priest as there were in 1975. Of course this means that Catholics who would like to attend Mass cannot, and will not be able to, in ever growing numbers.

In 1993, two archdioceses, Chicago and Santa Fe, declared themselves in danger of bankruptcy due, at least in part, to compensation paid to victims of clergy abuse. Dioceses and religious orders have also paid for legal expenses involved in defending priests and themselves in civil and criminal suits in connection with child abuse, as well as treatment costs for the psychiatric care of priest perpetrators. Compensation, treatment, and legal costs are estimated to have passed the half-billion mark between 1984 and 1994. Although some of this burden has been shared by insurance companies, they, in ever greater numbers, are finding ways to eschew liability (Wojcik, 1994).

Since 1990 the popular image of Catholic priests in the United States has been assailed more broadly and with more sustained negativity than ever before, even by the church's own members. Naturally, this reality is difficult for and unfair to conscientious and responsible clergy (Rossetti, 1994). The crisis of image has been compounded by church authorities who were slow, defensive, and even duplicitous in their public response as abuse by clergy became public and as other indications of trouble mounted. Even as late as 1992 one expert in the area described fully two-thirds of the bishops as either confused about the issue or unconvinced that there really was a problem of abuse by clergy.

Such patent denial only added weight to the already over-burdened image of priests as unreliable and effete authority figures. As one leader of the victims' movement said, "They [the bishops] don't realize they are no longer calling the shots. Power has shifted." Traditional tactics of damage control and scandal suppression are not working. The crisis is too big to be controlled by any known methods. But more importantly, bishops integral to the system are themselves part of the problem. They have yet to realize the pertinence of Walt Kelly's aphorism, "We have met the enemy and they are us."

• • •

Priests who have traditionally cared for the education and protection of children can appeal to the example of Christ himself, who "took a little child, stood him in their midst, and putting his arms around him, said to them, 'Whoever welcomes a child such as this for my sake welcomes me. And whoever welcomes me welcomes, not me, but him who sent me'" (Mark 9: 36–37).

For many priests, work with children and young people is a healthy and productive sublimation of their generative drive. They perform a parental function and become *father* in the best spiritual sense. Monastic and cathedral schools had centuries of experience in teaching young boys prior to the existence of medieval universities. The Jesuits, founded in the sixteenth century, took upon themselves the mission of educating the masses, not merely the sons of the noblemen and the wealthy. As a result, they had a profound influence on popular attitudes toward children.

Parents who entrust their children—both boys and girls—to the care of priests as teachers, coaches, club directors, counselors, pastors, or advocates presume that the contact will foster good character and growth in self-confidence, moral values, and spiritual and mental health. Those priests who use their positions of trust and the presumption of moral integrity as a cover for sexual activity with children destroy and pervert the meaning and reality of celibacy and ministry.

There is general disdain for those who take sexual advantage of children. Intuitively, the known child molester is treated as immature and perverse. Matthew's gospel account of Christ's tenderness with children is a unique and prophetic stance in early literature and adds an admonition against giving scandal to the young: "Anyone who is an obstacle bringing down one of these little ones who have faith in me would be better drowned in the depths of the sea with a great millstone around his neck" (Matthew 18: 5–7).

## HISTORY OF CLERGY ABUSE OF CHILDREN

In spite of all the good done by clergy for children there is an ancient awareness of the danger of and potential for the corruption of children. The *Didaché*, the oldest extant commentary on the gospels, dating from the early second century, clearly commands, "Thou shalt not seduce young boys" (Foucault, 1988, p. 232). The earliest church council for which we have any records, that of Elvira in 309, has 81 Canons, of which 38 deal with sex. The modern reader will find that some have a familiar and timely ring. Among those who are threatened with irrevocable exclusion—that is, they could not receive communion even at the time of death (*nec in finem*)—are "bishops, presbyters and deacons committing a sexual sin" (Canon 18), "those who sexually abuse boys" (Canon 71), and "people who bring charges against bishops and presbyters without proving their cases" (Canon 75) (Laeuchli, 1972, p. 47).

John Cassian (365–435), who developed a coherent doctrine on chastity (published in the English language 1993), wrote, "Let no one, especially when among young folk, remain alone with another even for a short time, or withdraw with him or take him by the hand" (Foucault, 1988, p. 233).

The Council of Trent (1545–63), called by popes to reform the church of its abuses, reveals how disassociated doctrine was from behavior. The council that staunchly reaffirmed the law requiring celibacy for priests had at the same time Pope Julius III, who was elected in 1550 and presided over the second session of the reform council (1552–54). This pope entered a sexual liaison with a 15-year-old boy he had picked up on the streets of Parma, and the pope made the young man a cardinal before he himself died in 1555.

Jean-Jacques Rousseau writes about an experience he endured at a retreat center in 1725 as he prepared himself for the sacrament of confirmation. He was 15 years old at the time he was sexually accosted by an older boy. When he complained to the prefect, he was told not to talk about it and that he was making too much of it. The superiors said it was a small matter; they themselves had had such experiences; and his talk was compromising the honor of the Holy House (1955, pp. 61–62).

The atmosphere and the experience of scores of boys at the Franciscan Seminary at Santa Barbara, California, must have paralleled those of Rousseau. In December 1993 an independent board of inquiry revealed that 12 priests of 44, or one-fourth of the total faculty at the minor seminary, had been sexually active with the students, boys between the ages of 11 and 17, over a period of 23 years from 1964 through 1987. If even the lowest estimates of victims per offender—that is, 10 youngsters—prevailed in this case, it would mean that as many as 120 of the 950 students enrolled over that period might have been sexually approached. In response to an inquiry sent to former seminarians, "34 people came forward saying that they had in some fashion or other been abused—most, sexually abused, in varying degrees" (Stahel, 1994). No one on the panel of inquiry thinks that all of the abused have declared themselves (Stearns et al., 1993).

The Marquis Donatien de Sade lived for a time with his priest uncle, a man who kept a mother and daughter as mistresses in his household. This same priest was arrested in Paris (May 26, 1762) in a brothel (Lever, 1993, p. 58). The priest introduced his young nephew to sex in his rectory. There is also speculation that the later, more notorious Marquis de Sade was introduced to whippings and sodomy by his Jesuit teachers when he studied with them between the ages of 10 and 13.

Rousseau and Sade are cited here not because of the scandal, but because of their frank and forthright description of part of the celibate/sexual atmosphere of their day. More importantly, they offer from their own lives some clues to a province more secret and hidden: the sexual development of priests who tend to abuse others sexually, some because of immaturity, others because of fixation or a paraphilia. "For Sade, as for Rousseau, 'normal' sex never yielded more than incomplete satisfaction, and their sexuality became fixed very early at an infantile stage. In both men, passive pleasure and happy humili-ation defined an erogenous zone beyond the limits of normality" (Lever, 1993, pp. 63–65).

The most notorious example of an American priest sexual abuser is James Porter of Fall River, Massachusetts. His history reads like pages from the life of L'abbe de Sade and his nephew. At the same time the ecclesiastical system responded to Porter's sexual activity with clear echoes of Rousseau's experience—denial, rationalization, coverup, and blaming victims. One priest who "saw" Porter rape a child defended him, when confronted by a parishoner, with the response, "Father is only human."

Father James Porter victimized 200 minors in the 12 years between 1960 and 1972 when he was active in the priestly ministry. Many of his victims report violent rape, cruel humiliation, and punishment that can only be described as sadistic. His seminary gave him a high recommendation at the time of his ordination as a "manly man" who promised to be a "manly priest" and a "leader" (Burkett & Bruni, 1993). In 1993 he pleaded guilty and was sentenced to 18 years in prison for a portion of his offenses. He is one of only a small fraction of priests who have been prosecuted by the law for abuse of minors. Until recently, clergy sex with minors has been treated as an internal church problem—one for the bishops, religious superior, or spiritual confessor to handle, out of public view, and with scant regard for the victims. Scandal was to be avoided at all costs. The image of the priest as celibately observant and sexually abstinent was never to be questioned openly. But history must not be forgotten! To remember the past is to know the possible present and future.

## WHICH PRIESTS ABUSE MINORS?

Although there is not one set personality type for priests who abuse minors, after reviewing 473 priests or histories of priests who have done so, I conclude that abusers can fit into one or more of four specific categories. Beyond that, other generalizations can also be drawn. Priests, after all, are self-selected into a system that forbids any sexual activity. The priesthood, therefore, can be a haven for those who have some fear of sex (including masturbation). The system is also highly authoritarian, where men enjoy both the advantages of submissiveness and positions of power or dominance conferred by ordination.

Seventy to eighty percent of priests who sexually abuse have themselves been abused as children, some by priests. Furthermore, a high percentage of those who later abused youngsters—whether or not they themselves were abused as children—were in effect given permission for such activity by a priest or religious superior who himself crossed the sexual boundary with the priest abuser during the time he was studying for ordination. Ten percent of priests report that they were approached sexually by a priest during the time of their theological studies.

For a shy, dominance-conflicted, sexually inhibited man with poor impulse control such silent and secret gratification from a superior within the celibate/sexual system offers bonding, release, and acceptance of rationalization all at the same time. The system thus strings a dangerous and tempting tightrope for the student priests rather than providing a solid and consistent foundation. The abusive priest can find himself compulsively drawn to a balancing act inconsistent with religious integrity and sexual responsibility, indulged in with peril to others and himself. These factors are coexistent across the following four categories: those predisposed by a genetic lock; those predetermined by a psychodynamic lock; those conditioned by a social/ situational lock; and, finally, those rooted in a moral lock.

*Lock* is the term I use to delineate the extreme end of each continuum. The term does not mean that men even at the heavily weighted end cannot ever control their behavior or that the behavior is impervious to any form of treatment or grace. Lock does mean, however, that given ordinary circumstances and nonintervention, these men will inevitably act out and sexually abuse.

The subsets of each category are those people who have a vulnerability (but not a lock) based in their genetic, psychodynamic, social/situational, or moral endowment, but they are less likely to cross appropriate boundaries unless mental or physical illness, trauma, or substance dependence influences personality regression and activates their latent potential for abuse. Also, the four factors may be interactive and reinforce or exacerbate one another. They may also be mitigated by other factors of character, circumstance, or grace.

## The Genetic Lock

In 1960 when I began collecting data on the celibate/sexual practice of Roman Catholic priests, I believed, along with most of my contemporaries, that psychosexual maturity was an approachable norm that would inevitably follow birth and growth unless some factors of nurture or environment derailed, delayed, or perverted that process. Since that time, the research of John Money and Fred Berlin at Johns Hopkins, among others, has convinced me that some of the priests I have seen fit a category observed and recorded among other sexual offenders: those whose object of sexual attraction is genetically determined much as are their gender, sexual orientation, and level of sexual drive.

Although future genetic, endocrine, and biochemical research may greatly refine our understanding of these men and their development and behavior, it is clear that our comprehension of sexual behavior will always have to consider biogenetic factors. The simplest way for me to grasp this reality—that certain people are genetically predisposed or preordained to sexual attraction to a certain age group—is by way of analogy to mental/ intellectual capacity. It is known from the time of their birth that certain persons will never attain so-called normal adult intellectual levels of function. The most fortuitous of circumstances, the greatest care and attention that, of course, these people deserve, can only assist them to function at their optimal intellectual capacity, which may be that of a 6-year-old. Unfortunately, in a less than ideal environment or worse, negative physical or psychological factors usually exacerbate the genetic limitation.

At first it may be hard to believe that certain persons are genetically determined and confined to a level of sexual development usually attained by a child or an adolescent. We would like to think that everyone has the capacity for an adult-to-adult sexually reproductive, physically, psychically, and spiritually satisfying and committed relationship—if they would only try or if we could only help them enough. It is not so.

Human nature has programmed into itself a biosexual diversity, the scope and objects of which we are only beginning to fathom. A certain number of men thus limited either knowingly or intuitively select the priesthood as the best place to live out their lives. Ideally, if they can embrace celibate development, their sexual drive will be redirected, and their energies can be used in socially productive ways. The problem is that neither sexuality nor celibacy is well taught to priests, nor is the latter commonly practiced or achieved by the clergy.

In spite of all of these handicaps, I know of priests who almost miraculously (certainly by special grace) have achieved celibate function when they are clearly locked at a level of sexual development, which, were they to be sexually active, would cause them to be true pedophiles or ephebophiles. The latter are men attracted to minors who have attained puberty.

If the genetically locked priest becomes sexually active, as is often the case, he will inevitably gravitate to minors who are the age level of his own lock or predetermination. His choice of sexual object will be influenced further by two other factors that are also genetically determined or influenced: sexual orientation and level of sexual desire. At the most extreme, these factors can conspire to produce the most driven and exploitative sort of person—a sexual predator who has multiple minor partners.

One priest in his late forties who exemplifies the genetic lock had been teaching in a high school since the time of his ordination 20 years earlier. His behavior followed a consistent pattern. He would select a sophomore student as a special friend, cultivate the relationship during the sophomore and junior years, and then end the relationship, or certainly the sexual aspects of it, in favor of the next chosen sophomore student with whom he would begin the cycle. The pattern was honed to perfection. The priest had the freshman year to look over and test out the chemistry of the upcoming sophomores while he eased out of the intensity of his present 2-year liaison.

When confronted and interviewed at length, the priest could not ever remember being sexually attracted to anyone other than a boy between the ages of 14 and 16. His deepest friendships and sexual fantasies were exclusively and naturally confined to boys in this very limited age range. After examining him extensively, I became convinced that this man, as long as he was active, would invariably seek out youngsters of this age no matter what the circumstances.

Knowledge of the biogenetic factors determining sexual orientation and object of sexual desire is not new. As early as 1985, in a report made available to American bishops, a priest psychiatrist wrote,

> I would say as a very careful "thinker" in this area and a person well aware of the scientific research in this area that the etiology of this disorder is most likely biological with a strong contribution of premature, early childhood introductions to sexual behaviors as being the environmental co-etiologic contributor. In simplest terms, it is highly likely that *in utero* a type of programming of the brains of all persons takes place that contributes to the later expression of sexual behaviors in humans. This includes sexual orientation (i.e., heterosexual, homosexual, bisexual), sexual energy level (i.e., libido . . .), and perhaps even erotic age preference (i.e., pedophilia *versus* preference for age-appropriate partners) (Peterson, 1985, p. 37).

Nature, of course, is not the only cause of sexual attraction toward minors. Sexual experiences, especially early, can be traumatic in impact. Victimization can also strongly influence subsequent adult psychosexual adjustment and can even anchor pedophilia in a person's psychodynamic character structure.

## THE PSYCHODYNAMIC LOCK

Another group of priests seems to have been treated more even-handedly by nature. Their genetic endowment does not appear to be the determining factor of their choice of sexual object. Rather, factors within early object relationships, often coupled with early sexual overstimulation and experiences, work together to lock these men at one level of psychosexual development or make them extremely vulnerable to regress to a sexual attraction to minors.

After all, it is part of normal development for boys to be affectively attracted to their own sex at a prepubertal stage of development. It is normal for adolescent boys to be sexually attracted to adolescent girls (and even boys). But these attractions most commonly mature, more or less evenly, and are integrated with intellectual, physical, and social growth over time.

Nevertheless, the path of integrated psychosexual development is not equally open to everyone. Psychic factors can be powerful enough to arrest someone at one stage of development and cause him to overvalue and overinvest in persons of a certain age as sexual objects. In males this may be coupled with overinhibition with, or denigration of, adult women as sexual companions.

Freud's theories, which I consider valid, if incomplete, are too well-known for me to belabor here. I am convinced that the biogenetic and psychogenetic factors that influence sexual behavior (nature and nurture) do not act in isolation from or exclusion of each other but interact along with cognitive factors (learning) to account for what we observe in men who sexually abuse minors.

A 52-year-old priest was confronted by the father of two daughters whom, under the guise of family friend and tutor, the priest had sexually abused over a 2-year period when the girls were 6 and 8 years old. He admitted the abuse, was sent for prolonged psychiatric treatment, and was then required to attend Sex Addicts Anonymous 5 days a week. A 5-year follow-up was mandated.

As a child and adolescent, the priest had been sexually abused on several occasions by an older relative. After he entered a religious order his novice master examined his genitals. He was then assigned to several parishes, schools, and the military chaplaincy from which he resigned because of a complaint of child abuse against him. He was convicted in a civil suit in one state but pleaded the Fifth Amendment about sexual activity in five other states.

It was clear that this man's development was arrested. He was extremely constrained and repressed, qualities masking a vivid sexual fantasy life. His pastoral life was an open door to a range of sexual interactions with minors from playfulness to meanness. He feared adult sex. His impulsiveness was childlike. He maintained an ingratiating social demeanor, even in midlife, giving him access to his victims' families. He also had a history of conflicts with adults and authority who threatened his dominance.

All indications pointed to a person psychodynamically locked in the mode of an abuser of children. Long after his sexual activity was known, this man held a position of power and responsibility in his order, which did nothing to locate or compensate any of the victims he abused over a period of nearly 30 years. Here we begin to see the symbiosis between the priest abuser and the system in which he can be supported and fostered.

Discussions about the relative importance of heredity and environment in determining behavior are age old. The argument continues in an attempt to trace the etiology of pedophilia and ephebophilia. Kinsey and colleagues (Kinsey, Pomeroy, & Martin, 1948) indicated that by the time boys are 12 years old, 38% of them have been involved in some form of sexual play, of which 22.7% is heterosexual and 29.4% homosexual. Obviously, not all of these boys grow up to be pedophiles or adults exhibiting aberrant sexual behavior. A certain amount of childhood experimentation is normal. But abnormal results multiply when the childhood experimentation involves an adult.

Experts concur that many adult men who experience erotic urges toward minors were sexually involved with adults when they were children. In treating the abuser one is often treating a former victim.

Likewise, a large proportion of priests who become either pedophiles or sexually active with adolescents were themselves victims of sexual abuse as children or adolescents — some by priests. It is worth remarking that many of these men do *not* become abusers, but the fact that many do points to the importance of one's early sexual experience and its relationship to the determination to become celibate.

One celibate, who kept his vow with great mental anguish, reported that in the course of his psychotherapy he had retrieved the memory of having been sexually abused when he was about 5 years old by an uncle who lived in his home. The priest realized how large a part these early experiences, and his subsequent reaction formation, had played in his decision to become a priest and thereby reject the overwhelming and confusing realities of sex.

Another priest was introduced to sexual play at the age of 8 by a cousin who was 16. The younger boy was not only intrigued by the sexual activity, but also flattered by his induction into a secret world and the special affection of an older boy whom he idolized. The younger boy curtailed his sexual activity, even masturbation, in midadolescence when he entered the minor seminary. He said it was then that he vowed never to be sexual with a child when he grew up. And he did not. He was, however, bothered for many years of his priesthood by the images of the genitals of adolescent boys, particularly the huge phallus he remembered his cousin possessing.

He did not act out his fantasies but was tormented by his feelings of sexual inadequacy.

Another priest, when he was a 15-year-old seminarian, once experienced anal intercourse with a 26-year-old priest, when he and other seminarians were on a summer pilgrimage to a religious shrine. The sleeping arrangements were haphazard, and he was assigned to a bed with the older man. Years later he recalled with both excitement and regret his one and only sexual contact with another person. With no other sexual experience with which to compare the contact, it remained a vibrant and troublesome thorn in his flesh.

Studies of priests have confirmed over and over again that the memory of an intense sexual episode early in life takes on a particular significance. The deprivation resulting from celibate practice often either enhances the memory or, in some cases, firmly fixates the priest's psychosexual development at a preadolescent or adolescent level.

## THE SOCIAL/SITUATIONAL LOCK

A third group of priests who abuse children does not fit standard psychiatric categories. This group is specifically clerical; it may have analogies in other populations, but the predominant lock is social/situational. These men can be basically healthy. They fit well into clerical culture. To do so, of course, they have to sacrifice their sexuality or suspend their psychosexual development. The celibate process that is meant to redirect sexual energy is *not* engaged.

What is this social/situational setting like? Intellectually, it demands conformity. Set answers rather than free inquiry are rewarded. Theologically, it is a man's world where God is Father, Son, and masculine Spirit. The ideal and only woman uniformly venerated is mother or virginal, both forbidden objects of sexual fantasy. Emotionally, it is a world in which men are revered and powerful (pope, bishop, rector), and boys are treasured as the future of the church.

It is clear that the institutional church fosters a preadolescent stage of psychosexual development. This is a period, typically prior to 11 years of age, when boys prefer association with their own sex. They avoid girls and hold them in disdain, often as a guise for fear of women as well as a protection for themselves and their own as yet unsolidified sexual identity. Externally, they generally deny sex rigidly while internally they explore it secretly. Their rigidity extends to strict rules of inclusion and exclusion. Control and avoidance are of primary concern.

The institutional church structure, although it surely includes individuals who have matured beyond it, is dominated by and entrenched in a level of functioning that cannot face the sexual realities of adolescence, let alone mature male and female equality and sexuality.

This is an atmosphere and culture in which some men who are not genetically or psychodynamically locked, and who otherwise would not do so, do get sexually involved with minors. Those men who are socially/ situationally locked are usually devoted to the institution. They play by the church's rules. In some instances, they are loving—often genuinely so—to their victims. These men can be overly narcissistic or exploitative; they fail to move either celibately or psychologically beyond the social/situational limits of their religious institution.

Because their behavior is sometimes a passing phase of their celibate/sexual growth and the number of their victims can be limited, these men do not tend to come to public or legal attention in as great a number as those who are compulsively driven. Certainly their behavior is not innocuous. However, in my interviews with both the priest abusers and their minor partners, now adults, I found that not all of the victims were equally regretful or resentful of the experience. Neither could all of the priests extricate themselves from their sexual pattern.

As candidates, these men cannot be screened out. They are instead products of the system. The celibate/sexual culture they so willingly absorb forms a psychological and moral field that makes natural the affective exchanges and love between the adult male (often the hero) and the boy or girl admirer. It fits. A boy thus involved sometimes grows up to be the priest involved.

One example of a man in a social lock was the chancellor of a diocese—that is, one of the bishop's chief advisers and legal experts—who committed suicide when confronted with his abusive behavior of 20 years prior. He had been a rigid legalist on the marriage tribunal, always imposing church law and defending church rights to the maximum. Although he maintained secret sexual friendships—five other victims declared themselves—he was modulated, discrete, and proper in all other respects. His psychological defense of splitting off his sexual life completely from his conscious adjustment to the system was shattered by confrontation with the reality of his sexual life.

More than a dozen suicides by priests facing public exposure of their sexual activity were recorded between 1990 and 1993. For the most part, men in a social/situational lock are more prone to suicide because of the inflexibility of their defenses and their previously successful adaptation to the system.

Another priest in this group was a 38-year-old man who had struggled successfully with his celibacy/sexuality, especially in the preceding 5 years of his life. Although he had had very limited sexual contacts, he concluded that his orientation was homosexual. His fantasies were consistent with this conclusion. The objects of his sexual excitation were always men approximately his own age. He struggled, most of the time successfully, to control his sexual urges.

An excellent athlete and good with youngsters, he had never been distracted by a conscious sexual attraction toward children or adolescents. One 12-year-old boy took a special liking to him and responded well to his guidance and influence. The boy had lived essentially half of his life "on the streets." Troubled, abusive parents with lives and problems far too complicated to handle, along with local social agencies, were more than content to let the young man fend for himself. He caused them no additional trouble. That he often supplied his own food and spending money and even sported new clothing was not of concern or even interest to them; they were relieved.

Some of the boy's resources came from pilfering, but soon he learned that he could make money, good money, by supplying sexual relief to men in certain sections of town. This became his secret source of livelihood. It was his job; he did not mix it with his other troubled activities in the streets or in school. He told no one about it.

He developed a strong bond with the priest in question. It was a truly affectionate bond, more than just hero worship. And the affection, healthy affection, was mutual.

One summer evening, after the priest had had a particularly hard day, the youngster came around and invited him to get an ice cream cone with him. Proudly, he said, "My treat." It was within this context that the boy said, "Father, you look real tired." The priest admitted he was exhausted and even a bit down. The boy—sexually wise beyond his years—said, "Father, I'll take care of you."

The priest was genuinely taken unaware and momentarily paralyzed by what followed: the boy deftly, and with an expertise garnered from years of experience, fellated the gaping priest.

It was at this point that the priest's social/situational lock became apparent. He could not confine his sexual activity to this single incident nor in the end to this one boy. He learned about the availability of a sexual outlet that he could not consciously imagine by genetic or psychodynamic pre-disposition.

Although some men in a social/situational lock mature slowly and finally do resolve their identification at more age-appropriate levels, there are others who are impelled to act out with individuals who are essentially on their same level of immaturity and who are directed at least in part by their same sexual orientation. In other words, not all homosexual contact between priests and adolescents involves a man who is of an innate homosexual orientation. Nor is all of the behavior compulsive or exclusive. However, it is always problematic—at least for the adolescent who is to some degree the victim of a generational transgression and a violation of trust.

Several of these factors come together in the following case example. A 30-year-old priest completing his doctoral studies was on vacation with his married sister and her family. His two nephews, 4 and 6 years old, were typically energetic youngsters and were most enthusiastic about the visit of their very important uncle. They demanded his time and attention, which he very willingly accorded them. He genuinely liked them but became increasingly aware of his own sexual excitement as they hung on him and showered him with their affection. Because he had been so immersed in his doctoral studies and therefore somewhat socially deprived for the preceding 3 years, he attributed his reaction to his recent sense of isolation. He did not act on his impulse to play with his nephews sexually, but he grew more and more concerned when his masturbatory fantasies began to include images of children.

He went to a psychiatrist, and during his treatment he recalled some repressed memories of having been sexually molested when he was 8 years old by a neighborhood boy 6 years his senior. In therapy he also worked through several other sexual issues. Subsequently, he did not act out any of his fantasies.

Unfortunately, not all priests who become aware of either the sexual opportunity or their inclination toward minors seek or desire restraint or responsibility. We must be careful and judicious in assessing the distinct and multiple causes of child abuse by clergy, but we must be careful not to psychiatricize the problem. There can be situational and moral dimensions quite distinct from any psychiatric consideration. Behavior that is immoral or antisocial does not by itself merit a psychopathological diagnosis, as Karl Menninger so eloquently reminded us when he questioned *"Whatever Became of Sin?"* (1973).

## THE MORAL LOCK

Another group of priests sexually abuses minors but does not deserve the benefit of psychiatric diagnosis. Nor do these men merit understanding as simple products of social/situational conditioning. They go beyond the limits of any institutional inadequacy. The category that defines them is clearly a moral one. They coldly, calculatingly, by design involve themselves sexually with minors because they want to. They choose it, not compulsively, indiscriminately, or impulsively. They divorce what they teach, what they require of others, from what they stand for in the eyes of others. In short, what they do is to make a moral choice—they commit a sin.

Let me say it even more clearly: what we are talking about is the category of evil, not illness. (Solzhenitsyn said, "Evil is not a division between groups of people, us and them. It is a line that runs through each human heart.") Psychiatry does not make sin obsolete. A priest in this group is not likely to seek psychiatric treatment. Nor is he likely to come to the attention of legal authorities. He is too calculating: he picks his partners carefully, often from within the celibate system or from those groups of youth who are least likely to complain. These men are satisfied with this life and adjustment.

These priests often prowl the halls of power and hold positions of responsibility. They are not so much victims of the system as they are those who sometimes make the system work. Historic and current examples from this group are available, even if they are rarely prosecuted. Just because men who represent these last two categories may also have character flaws and personality deficiencies, we cannot subsume them within the psychiatric pale any more than we can medically ignore men who have genuine psychiatric illness because their behavior also contains significant moral implications. We must keep the core *cause* of each group in focus and address it appropriately.

Men from each category are liable for criminal and civil litigation. The legal system has been extremely persuasive in forcing a response from church authority to the problem of sexual abuse by priests. In fact, the law has been the only force so far that has moved the church to any serious consideration of reform. However, neither the law nor psychiatry can reform the celibate/ sexual system of the church or address fundamentally the evil that exists within it and in some cases because of it. Bishops should lead this reform. By analyzing the defenses and resistances employed so far against change, we may understand the problem further and offer some hope for serious transformation.

A view into this realm of evil can be seen through the eyes of a priest in his thirties who was admitted to a psychiatric ward for severe depression. His response to treatment was slow, and the danger of suicide continued for an extended period. All of his progress was clouded by some mysterious secret he could not seem to share with anyone.

A fellow priest probably saved his life by encouraging the man to share with his psychiatrist what he had finally been able to address in the sacrament of confession. This troubled priest had been on the staff of the chancery office, the administrative structure that supports a bishop. The bishop cultivated the young priest and entrusted him with many of the sensitive and delicate affairs of diocesan business and ecclesiastical affairs generally. Little by little the bishop confided an increasing number of his personal affairs to the young priest, who was by then thoroughly devoted to his work and his bishop—the closest and most trusted friend this priest had ever had. They could even talk about sexuality.

It was only in this context that the bishop's request for the young priest to find and deliver to him a young male prostitute could be imagined or tolerated. This service became a regular part of the young priest's duties. The incongruity between the young priest's own moral standards and his personal devotion to his superior/boss forced him into a psychological corner. Depression was a substitute for death as the only passage out of his bind. The bishop experienced no such conflict.

We must face the difficult and distasteful fact that some bishops and religious superiors are sexual abusers of minors. Further, we must recognize that forces and systems beyond psychopathology influence and maintain this sad condition.

The current epidemic of sexual abuse is neither a new phenomenon nor limited to Catholic priests. But once I realized that priest abusers constitute one symptom of a deficient understanding of human sexuality and not merely an isolated problem of broken vows, the length, breadth, depth, and height of the celibate/sexual system opened up before me. As I explored the biological, psychological, cultural, historical, and theological dimensions of sexuality, the function and structure of a religious system of power based on gender and sexual control became ever more apparent. Indeed, such a reevalutaiton involves a paradigm shift with all its attendant struggles (Kuhn, 1962). The first step toward a new understanding is among the most difficult; when I recognized clergy sexual abuse as a symptom, I took that first step.

# 2

# CRIME, SIN, AND SICKNESS

*In the modern trend to deny the intrinsic sinfulness of anything connected with sex, there is frequently a [denial] of the fact that the sexual instinct is often exploited by aggressive, hurtful and destructive intuitions.... There is such a thing as bad sexual behavior...because it corrupts or destroys the personality of the participants.*

Karl Menninger

*Some assert that it is sufficient to know the principles; they are altogether mistaken. The principles are few and known to all, even those who have only an elementary moral knowledge. The greatest difficulty in this science of moral theology is the correct application of the principles to particular cases, applying them in different ways according to the different circumstances.*

St. Alphonsus

For many years a beloved, crusty, old Jesuit priest taught a course required for all first-year theologians at his seminary. He began the first class of each year by bellowing at the new recruits, "Vos estis spes ecclesiae" (literally translated: you are the hope of the church), and then he continued, "which means, you're not much, but you're all we've got." I have thought about that story repeatedly during the 20 years I have lectured to Catholic seminarians in their final years of training for the priesthood.

I think of my students with hope and have never imagined them as criminals, sinners, or psychiatric patients. Unfortunately, the sexual behavior of some priests focuses a legal, moral, or psychiatric spotlight on the priesthood itself, and the resulting notoriety brings the whole celibate/sexual system under scrutiny.

24

# CRIME

Sex with minors is a crime. Seduction of a young boy was punishable by death under early Roman law. However, in this country prior to the 1960s, child neglect or abuse received very little attention, public or private.

Recently, however, the legal system, supported by advocacy groups and the media, has been the moving force behind bringing the sexual abuse of minors to public awareness. The first state statute requiring professionals to report suspected child abuse was enacted in 1962. As early as 1978, twenty states required *any person*, not just professionals, to report suspected child abuse of any kind to appropriate state authorities, either social services or the state's attorney's office (Fraser, 1978, pp. 657–658).

Since 1989 several states have extended the statutes of limitation, which had been 3 to 6 years after the incident. The trend is to extend the time of civil claims to a period of years after the victim is able to remember the abuse.

Child abuse by priests and in the general population is a highly underreported crime. Most victims never reveal what has happened to them. William H. Reid wrote that "careful studies have indicated...that child molesters commit an average of sixty offenses for every incident that comes to public attention. These must not be thought of as situational or hidden in some other disorder...if they are to be understood completely and treated successfully" (1988, p. 24).

Schetky and Green quote Kinsey, Pomeroy, Martin, and Gebhard (1953): "24 percent of a population of 4,441 women had experienced sexual abuse during childhood" (1988, p. 30). Studies of female college students revealed a 19% incidence of abuse during childhood and adolescence, and 9% among male students. A 1986 federal study reported that 150,000 children were victims of sexual abuse nationwide. The 1990 figures classify 15% of annually reported child maltreatment as sexual abuse (National Child Abuse and Neglect Data System, 1991). Hunter (1990) quotes several authorities who conclude, "A review of several national studies puts the prevalence of sexual abuse in males at between 2.5 and 16 percent. If the rate of abuse is constant from year to year, then at least 46,000 to 92,000 boys under the age of thirteen are sexually abused each year in the United States alone" (p. 26). All studies record a two to three times higher incidence of abuse of girls.

The percentage of offenders in the general population is unknown and will probably remain so for some time because of the complex nature of the problem, the incestuous behaviors that are masked by familial ties, and the general reluctance of the victim to confront the abuser or the reluctance of the abuser to reveal himself.

## PRIEST OFFENDERS

Several accounts already record the extent, history, and struggles of the sexual abuse of minors by priests in the United States (Berry, 1992; Burkett & Bruni, 1993; Rossetti, 1990; Sipe, 1990a). It remains an ongoing saga. A quick review of the alleged priest abusers who have come to legal attention demonstrates the trend: 10 priests of a total of 97 in a Southwestern diocese; 9 of 110 in a Midwestern diocese; 7 of 91 in a Southern diocese; 15 of 220, and 40 in a diocese of 279 in the Eastern United States. One expert estimates that at any one time since 1989, three dozen priests are incarcerated for sexual crimes. Sixty Catholic priests and brothers were in prison on sexual abuse charges as of September 1994. Some of the victims coming forward are priests who were themselves abused as youngsters by priests—3 out of 33 victims in one Midwestern diocese.

The occurrence of sexual abuse by clergy has been found in every sector of the United States and Canada, and although this exposure has led to public awareness around the world, there is no reason to think of this as an American problem. The celibate/sexual system of Catholic clergy in the Latin rite is relatively standard worldwide in its dynamic, education, power structure, and function. Although different localities are more or less tolerant or sensitive to certain sexual behavior by priests, the system itself is universal.

There are clear indications that other nations are becoming aware of the frequency of child sexual abuse in their own local churches. On November 17, 1992, Dutch television aired a program on the victims of clergy sexual abuse in the United States. In the first days following the airing of the 17-minute segment, 300 viewers called the station alleging that they too had been sexually abused by priests in the Netherlands. In England, Australia, and Germany signs of this symptom of major crisis in the priesthood are emerging. On November 17, 1994, the Prime Minister of Ireland was forced to resign as a result of civil mishandling of a clergy sexual abuse case.

It is clear that some clergy of every rank from pastor to prelate, simple cleric to cardinal have had sexual relations with minors. The situation abides. The hierarchy of the church knows that sexual activity by priests not only exists but is relatively common. Bishops frequently ascribe to their private confidences and administrative decisions the quality of a confessional.

Confusion between confidentiality and secrecy remains. I can appreciate that many bishops have not solved this dilemma. *Confidentiality* is a private, personal, and privileged communication that must be protected at great sacrifice (not only out of professional duty) because it is in the service of (and necessary for) personal transformation and growth. It may also be necessary to protect due process. *Secrecy* is a stance that reserves access to knowledge in the service of power, control, or manipulation.

Secrecy is often rationalized as the only way to avoid scandal. However, bishops need not break confidentiality to pool their legitimate knowledge in the service of reform. They simply have to be motivated and honest. Today that motivation is being supplied forcibly by the courts and by the victims.

In 1976 I was convinced that I had enough data to estimate that at any one time 6% of Catholic priests in the United States were having sex with minors. Since 1985 I have reviewed an additional 1,800 accusations by adults who claim that as children they were sexually abused by priests. I also have seen the histories of nearly 500 priests who are known to have abused.

This further study convinces me that the celibate/sexual system as it exists fosters and produces, and will continue to produce, at a relatively stable rate, priests who sexually abuse minors. The numbers of victims who are coming forward 20 and 30 years after their abuse, whose accusations are being corroborated and substantiated, plus an analysis of the function and structure the celibate/sexual system of the priesthood, which follows in the later sections of this book, demonstrate the degree to which abusive sexual behaviors inhere in the system of priestly power.

Public exposure prompted by the victims' movement and litigation is validating my 6% estimate. The proliferation of state statutes and federal laws that required professionals to report suspected child abuse prompted my estimate 9 years before the completion of my study of the celibate practice of Catholic priests in the United States. One third of the priest abusers, or 2% of the priest population, can be classified as true pedophiles with a three to one preference for boys. This gender attraction is reversed in the general population. Two thirds of the priest abusers, or 4% of the priest population, become sexually involved with adolescents. Gender preference is distributed more evenly in this group.

However, same-sex preference is larger than in the general population of child molesters. These observations should not be confused with the question of the homosexualities in the celibate/sexual system. To some degree, at least, what is observed of the general population can be said of some priests: "Although it may appear that these men are homosexual because they are being sexual with someone of their own sex, it is important to remember that most men who sexually abuse children have a heterosexual (other sex) orientation when it comes to adults" (Hunter, 1990, pp. 33–34).

## LEGAL INTERVENTION

Some priests who abuse minors have been tried on criminal charges, found guilty, and sentenced to prison; some for life terms. Other cases have been tried on civil grounds, often because the statute of limitations has run out for criminal charges. Financial settlements for damages have already run into the hundreds of millions of dollars. And at least 600 of these cases are at some stage of resolution.

Not all grievances come before the courts.

The legal ramifications of clergy sexual abuse snap into focus when accused priests or bishops confront the judicial system in criminal and civil suits and when they face the demands and restrictions of canon law. Reporting laws have given victims a voice, and they have spoken, along with lawyers who have championed the cause of the molested. One conservative estimate suggests that between 1984 and 1994 more than 5,000 victims confronted church officials about their sexual experience with priests. Often in exchanges or negotiation of settlements outside of the judicial system, the church demands that victims relinquish all future claims against the diocese or religious order and maintain silence about the financial aspects of the settlements, if not about the entire matter. Sometimes part of the settlement monies are held in escrow to guarantee silence, with the money forfeited if the person reveals the amount of the settlement. Sometimes a special clause in the agreement pledges repayment of compensation if the victim speaks.

Wherever there are lawyers for the oppressed, there will be an equal number of lawyers to defend the rights of the accused and the property of the church. Even as its verbal messages about child sexual abuse by clergy have become more pastoral and humane, the greatest investment of time, energy, and money on the part of the American church as a whole has been in its legal efforts.

A headline and article in the *Wall Street Journal* (November 24, 1993) expressed well the state of affairs: "The Catholic Church Struggles with Suits Over Sexual Abuse: While It Pledges Compassion, Its Lawyers Play Rough Defending Lapsed Priests." Victims of abuse know that they are entering a brutal ordeal when they seek justice or compensation in court. They face intimidation, humiliation, and the accusation that they consented to the behavior and were not victims but willing and gratified partners.

The church has a lot of money and influence, but whatever happens in courts will never save the clergy from corruption. Most victims of clergy abuse do not want a legal battle. They want the assurance that what happened to them will not happen to others. Victims want to survive. Survivors want to heal.

Legislation requiring reporting of the sexual abuse of minors, the public outcry of victims and their families, plus lawsuits that exposed cover-ups by ecclesiastical authorities have converged to challenge traditional structures and traditional means of keeping the *church* free from *scandal*. Part of the problem for bishops is their felt need to protect their privileges and prerogatives as well as the church's property.

There are many legal fights still to be fought about access to a priest's personnel files, about what constitutes privileged communication, and about when the bishop has the duty to turn a known offending priest over to civil authorities. But the largest and most invested battles are over money. On April 30, 1993, Father James Provost, a canon lawyer, addressed the priests of Chicago. He said, in part,

> The bishop has a responsibility to safeguard the community's resources, its resources of personnel and its material resources. The bishop has to be concerned about the fact that he's going to be sued. One of the reasons why we have so much Catholic clergy showing up in these suits and not Baptists or Fundamentalists isn't that we're more involved in this kind of activity today, but that our bishops have a deeper pocket... people are after the cash.

Leaders of the victims' movement resent being cast as second-class members of the church who are out to "get the cash." Rather, they experience this role thrust upon them as a revictimization. They demand a reform that will ensure the safety of their children, and they see themselves on the side of truth and justice.

Civil and criminal lawsuits are bound to continue for some time as there has been no fundamental change in the celibate/sexual education system, and the functional and structural aspects of the system remain firmly in place.

## SIN: MORAL DIMENSIONS

The Catholic Church considers any sex outside marriage to be gravely sinful. Because priests are, by definition anyway, celibate, the church is reluctant to make official statements about priests' sexual activity. Papal statements on Catholic sexuality are usually directed toward lay-people, not the clergy. Thus far, the church has chosen not to address directly the underlying issues of priests' sexuality. Until it does, their moral development will remain undefined and unsupported.

Priests can and do find willing sexual partners of all ages. Sexual activity by a priest who publicly presents himself as celibate is a contradiction, a moral ambiguity, and a violation of religious power. Some church authorities tend to use celibacy as an excuse and cover for sex among their ranks. Some bishops in defense of priests who have been sexually active point to teenage girls and boys who have taken the lead and willingly been involved in a sexual relationship with a priest.

Ignorance and naiveté do not excuse a priest's violation of power and trust. These deficiencies must be prevented or accounted for by responsible church authority. The moral dimensions of the sexual abuse crisis must be discussed in their totality. The magnitude of the current crisis is epic and demands suitable moral discourse and response. Psychiatry and the law can only deal with the symptom-atology of the crisis. Moral education, formation, and reform must address systemic causes.

Certainly there are firm but fine lines between what is immoral, what is sexually abusive, and what is dissent from church discipline on celibacy for its priests. The question is this: why has the church been so sensitive and proactive in response to questions of dissent from sexual discipline (married priests, ordination of women) and so blind, defensive, and reactive when it comes to questions of frank sexual abuse? Law or psychiatry must not pretend that they can answer that question! Priests may be ordinary men, as stated in the 1972 Kennedy-Heckler study of the priesthood, but they do not exist in an ordinary social-moral culture. Theirs is a culture apart. It is an exclusively male world bounded by mandatory celibacy, where power, control, employment, and even financial reward are depen-dent on the exclusion of women and the appearance of a sex-free existence.

No one can say that this culture has nothing to do with the problem of child sexual abuse. Experience demonstrates clearly that cultural factors inherent in the celibate/sexual system are crucial and pivotal in some instances of sexual abuse not only of minors but also of adult women and men.

## SICKNESS

Anyone trying to assess the sexual behavior of a priest or clergyman with a minor must determine six things: (1) the age of the child or children who were abused; (2) the gender of the child, which may give some indication of the sexual orientation of the priest and the potential trauma to the victim; (3) whether the incident is isolated or part of a pattern; (4) whether the behavior is fixated or regressed; (5) whether the behavior is compulsive or addictive; (6) and, finally, the painful but necessary task of ascertaining precisely what behavior was indulged.

Kathleen Faller's handbook *Child Sexual Abuse: Intervention and Treatment Issues* (1993) is one guide to the understanding of sexual abuse from the child's point of view. All of the behaviors she outlines can be found among the priest offenders: from abuse that *avoids direct sexual contact*—like comments, exposing oneself, peeping, showing pornographic pictures or videos—or encouraging the child to expose himself or herself, or masturbate in front of the adult—to that which includes sexual contact.

*Sexual contact* can involve touching the genitals, buttocks, or breasts or inducing the child to touch the offender either directly or through the clothing. *Sexual penetration* of the vagina or anus with fingers or objects, oral sex, and penile penetration of the vagina or anus either in active or passive exchange have also been recorded.

Several priests have been known to have a *sex ring* where several priests share the same victim(s), and other priests have encouraged *group sex* and organized sex clubs for adolescents. There have been some scattered reports of *ritual* sexual abuse in which a priest participated. Priests who abuse adolescents frequently ply them with alcohol and even drugs as part of the experience.

Priest perpetrators commonly explained away these activities with excuses or rationalizations that they have educational value for the child or are helpful to the child, that the child derives sexual pleasure from them, or that the child was sexually provocative. These themes are also common in pedophilic pornography. Psychiatric experts explain how the rationalization can be maintained:

> When a person desires sex or falls in love, it is often easy to become convinced that the relationship is good and healthy and not harmful or wrong. Such self-deception may at times be easy for the pedophilic individual in light of the fact that sex with children, though wrong, may not in every instance be damaging (Gilbert, 1976). Some children may enjoy certain aspects of their sexual relationships with an adult, thus facilitating self-deception. (Berlin, 1986)

The sexual offender may be generous and very attentive to a child's needs, in all respects other than the sexual victimization in order to gain the child's affection, interest, and loyalty and to prevent the child from reporting the sexual activity.

In the United States the law makes no criminal distinction in its broad category of child molestation between the victimizer of an adolescent and the victimizer of someone who is younger. *Pedophilia*, on the other hand, is a specific psychiatric term, referring strictly to the sexual abuse of a prepubertal child.

By extension and analogy we can learn about sexual activities with adolescents by studying the more refined observations on pedophilia. According to the *Diagnostic and Statistical Manual of Mental Disorders* (DSM-IV), diagnosis of pedophilia requires

A. Over a period of at least 6 months, recurrent, intense sexually arousing fantasies, sexual urges, or behaviors involving sexual activity with a prepubescent child or children (generally age 13 years or younger).

B. The fantasies, sexual urges, or behaviors cause clinically significant distress or impairment in social, occupational, or other important areas of functioning.

C. The person is at least age 16 years and at least 5 years older than the child or children in Criterion A. (American Psychiatric Association [APA], 1994, p. 528)

Pedophilia can be either homosexual or heterosexual, but apparently in the general population, attraction to girls is twice as common as attraction to boys; many pedophiles are sexually aroused by both young boys and girls.

Experts in sex studies claim that pedophilia occurs almost exclusively in men. But as more information becomes available, certainly more women will be counted within this diagnostic category. Some researchers are speculating that 10 to 20% of abuse will eventually be attributed to women. They note that because people do not decide voluntarily what will arouse them sexually, there are great differences among pedophiles as to which partners and behaviors will appeal to them, as well as differences in the intensity of their sexual drive and their ability to resist sexual temptation, or even whether or not they decide the temptation *should* be resisted.

Sexual impulses can be either fixated or regressed. Fixated sexual offenders experience no erotic attraction toward adults and "manifest an arrest in their psychosexual development and maintain a primary psychological and sexual interest in young children who are prepubertal" (Schetky & Green, 1988). They are more likely to victimize boys than girls and generally first act on their impulses during their adolescence.

Regressed pedophiles are men who find both adults and children erotically appealing and tend to select female victims. Their tendencies emerge when they are adults and are usually triggered by a stressful sexual situation with an age-peer.

## TREATMENT OBSTACLES

The most important issue in considering the treatment of the child sexual abuser, especially among the clergy, is how the abuser treats himself—how he handles his sexual desires and whether or not he recognizes them as inappropriate.

Many priests do give in to their urges. Those priests who are locked psychosocially at an adolescent level of development fit emotionally with young people who are growing up. A growth phase for the young person is an ominous state for the priest. To him, it all feels so natural and can be temporarily acceptable to adolescent partners. Both the priest and his teenage friends are endangered by their sexual interaction, characterized by an unstable fluctuation between loss of control followed by overcontrol.

Luckily, some priests will recognize their urge as inappropriate, become fearful of the behavior it demands, and avoid compromising situations for years. A child who had been abused by his uncle became a priest, hoping that the vow of celibacy would keep him from repeating the behavior. A priest who, as a child, engaged in mutual masturbation with his adolescent cousin was tormented throughout his ministry by images of the genitals of adolescent males, but he did not act out his desires. A priest who, as a teenager, had been subjected to anal intercourse by an older priest on a church outing always remembered the incident with excitement and fear. Without other sexual experiences to reduce the impact of it, he found the memory intensified as the years passed.

At times priests who are sexually active with minors become greatly troubled by their sexual activity and concerned over their own loss of self-control as well as the damage they have inflicted on the children involved. Therefore, some of their activity comes to the attention of other priests through the confessional or psychiatrists through psychotherapy. Occasionally, a priest will seek help prior to acting out his desires. More often, however, the fits of guilt are all too fleeting, and the priest who so desperately wants a relationship cannot sustain the adult demands of either a psychotherapeutically or spiritually directed attachment that might offer him a modicum of insight or help in working through his problem.

Most active child molesters do not turn themselves in for therapy. Many try to conceal their activity from anyone else, and they try to seek anonymity by limiting their partners to persons who have no connection with their work or ministry. Others avoid confiding their behavior because they simply do not experience any guilt in connection with it. Some confide their sins in confession, which perpetuates a cycle of guilt and relief and seals their behavior behind the sacred wall of secrecy. Even colleagues who witness or know about the sexual behavior of a fellow priest deny their responsibility to victims by saying "Father is only human."

Likewise the system, which includes bishops and laity, must face up to the problem of abuse and neither deny nor minimize it.

Most times one or more people suspect that something in the priest-child associations is not right. Frequently bishops or superiors have an awareness on some level (sometimes direct), but are reluctant to intervene. Few people want to believe that the celibate/sexual system does indeed include sexually active child molesters. Denial on the part of the system is as inimical to the treatment and control of the problem as is the denial by the perpetrator that he has a problem.

Another reason that the sexual problem is easy to rationalize and deny, even when it is suspected or known, is that the priest may be very effective and talented in his ministry. He can have many friends and defenders. The abused are the isolated few.

I have witnessed cases in which abuse was verified and admitted, but the priest or prelate was so popular or powerful that even the civil authority refused to take action. All of this reinforces a secret system where truth is known, but fear of scandal protects and fosters abuse and scapegoats the victims. Increasingly, under the pressure of civil and criminal liability, church authorities have quickly required a priest to submit to psychiatric evaluation once someone registers an allegation of sexual abuse. Religiously sponsored facilities specializing in the treatment of priest sexual offenders have flourished since 1988. Several university centers such as Johns Hopkins and the University of Minnesota and private institutes like the Menninger Foundation and Hartford's Institute for Living frequently treat priests and bishops.

## TREATMENT MODALITIES

Basic to all treatment for sexual molesters is that the abuser must acknowledge his problem and want help. One trouble with most of the sexual activity of celibates is that it has been viewed by both the perpetrator and church authorities as an isolated act or sin that could be resolved by confession and a firm purpose of amendment. In some instances, the sexual activity of a priest is secretly considered part of a necessary or inevitable human failure. In cases of the sexual abuse of minors, a much more finely tuned assessment of the priest's total developmental history and personality structure is needed for effective interaction to help him come to grips with his sexual behavior. At the same time, we must not lose sight of the system in which he lives, moves, has his being, and carries on his sexual activity.

The evaluation of sexual offenders has become more sophisticated, involving psychiatrists, psychologists, and counselors who are specially trained or who have specific experience in evaluating and treating sex abusers. Since some priests are brought to treatment only under duress from superiors or threat of incarceration, intensive inpatient treatment is often required. The sex offender's specific treatment usually involves individual psychological testing and psychotherapy, and group psychotherapy along with supportive expressive therapies (i.e., art, drama).

Involvement and active support from the priests' diocese or religious order are usually required, and assurance of ecclesiastical monitoring and usually a minimum of 5 years of follow-up treatment are recommended. Few therapists consider individual, insight-oriented, outpatient therapy adequate to cope with the sexual offender attracted to minors. Some therapists feel that there is an essential addictive component to this group of patients.

In the course of treatment most specialized facilities now use a twelve-step model for addiction similar to that developed by Alcoholics Anonymous. This involves daily group meetings and open admission of one's own story. It considers sexual activity with minors a compulsive illness. The model was pioneered by psychologist Patrick Carnes (*Out of the Shadows* [1983] and *Don't Call It Love* [1991]).

Physical and psychological evaluations ordinarily precede any treatment; many abusers merit a dual diagnosis—alcoholism, depression, and character neurosis often accompany the sexual disorder. Standard therapy regardless of modality consists of 6 to 8 months of inpatient treatment plus a 6-month reevaluation for a period of 5 years. Supervised work placement in which the priest has no contact with minors is also recommended.

Depoprovera, a medication that lowers the testosterone level, is frequently used to help the abuser control his sexual behavior. It has proven successful, especially when used in conjunction with a twelve-step program or group therapy.

But even in the best of circumstances, compulsion requires multifaceted intervention. The transient incident of an adult-child sexual contact can be dealt with in spiritual direction or psychotherapy if it is genuinely a single incident and not part of a pedophiliac or addictive process.

Most experts are not encouraging about the course of pedophilia, and this observation can be extended to many priests who are attracted to adolescents. According to the DSM-IV,

> The frequency of pedophilic behavior often fluctuates with psychosocial stress. The course is usually chronic, especially in those attracted to males. The recidivism rate for individuals with Pedophilia involving a preference for males is roughly twice that for those who prefer females. (APA, 1994, p. 528)

Psychological and medical modalities—although promising for the treatment and behavioral control of offending priests who seek or are forced into treatment—cannot address the systemic problems that lead to the production of and fostering or harboring of sexually abusive men who are selected, trained, and cherished by that system.

## VICTIM VOICES

Victims and survivors of clerical sexual abuse have produced the most powerful witness to the inner workings of the celibate/sexual power system. Facts that were only whispered in confessionals are now spoken out loud and in public. Abuse victims who had reported offenses to church officials and been rejected and sometimes ridiculed and persecuted took their stories—often as a last resort—to the courts and the media.

Thousands of victims and survivors of clerical abuse in childhood began to tell their stories to each other. I believe that the groundswell of sharing long-held secrets from childhood—not on television or in courtrooms, but with a trusted friend or relative in the living rooms and back porches across the nation—forms the real force of the movement toward sexual reform in the church. Hundreds of thousands of people have said, "That happened to me too." The cloak of celibacy turns out to be the emperor's new clothes.

Some courageous victims and their families have led the fight for protection for their children. During 1990, considered to be the watershed year, we saw the convergence of victim voices and a shift in power away from church authorities who appeared confused, defensive, and downright resistive to the increasing numbers of people alleging abuse and instituting civil and criminal lawsuits against priests, dioceses, and religious orders.

Jeanne Miller of Chicago, the mother of a boy who was the victim of attempted abuse, began her quest for clergy sexual responsibility in 1982. She was the single most consistent and powerful lay voice in making the plight of victims and their families audible. She organized the Victims of Clergy Abuse LINKUP, inspired by the thousands of abused who contacted her in response to her book and television appearances. Victims held their first national meeting in October 1992. Miller's work, more than that of any other individual, was responsible for the policy established in 1992 to respond to allegations of abuse by priests in the Chicago archdiocese (Burkett & Bruni, 1993, pp. 238–251). Her work was accomplished at great personal sacrifice, but her organization represents about 4,500 victims of clergy sexual abuse. Father Tom Economus, a victim of abuse by a priest in his youth, is now national director of the LINKUP.

Also in 1991 Frank Fitzpatrick, a 42-year-old private investigator from Providence, Rhode Island, located the man who had abused him as a boy. Fitzpatrick's memory had been repressed until the year before. Like so many victims, his memories emerged with great pain, fright, and confused emotion. Fitzpatrick became a one-man movement to gather together other victims of Father James Porter. In 1993, 106 victims were compensated in settlements with the diocese of Fall River and insurance companies (Burkett & Bruni, 1993, pp. 3–25).

Fitzpatrick established *Survivor Connections*, a newsletter and database of priest abusers and their victims. On June 5, 1993, he was a part of the formation of the American Coalition for Abused Awareness (ACAA), which includes survivors of clergy abuse, survivor organizations, activists, and attorneys. Their goals are ambitious and clearly motivated by disappointment in the response they experienced from church authority.

Several other groups with national constituencies have also taken shape. Barbara Blaine of Chicago and David Clohessey of St. Louis, both victims of clergy abuse, organized the Survivors Network of Those Abused by Priests (SNAP). They have maintained an activist stance and have met with the head of the bishops ad hoc committee dealing with clergy abuse. Vincent Toomey of Washington, D.C., also heads a survivors group, Survivors of Catholic Clerical Abuse (SOCCA), inspired by the experience of his own abuse and the suicide of a young friend also abused by the same priest.

Dennis Gaboury, a victim of Father Porter, describes in chilling and horrifying detail his experience and those of his childhood friends and relatives (Gaboury & Burkett, 1993). The experience of abuse by the trusted and its aftermath can only be appreciated by listening to the victims—the survivors. Only they can describe adequately the real effects of this sexual crisis of the celibate/sexual system.

The physical effects on the child victim include the abuses endured in a sexual encounter itself, especially penetration in vaginal or anal intercourse, or the pain and scarring from a sadistic episode. Just as serious, however, is the emotional damage that the victims suffer. Women and men who report having been touched, fondled, or otherwise sexually violated by a priest when they were children can recall the overwhelming guilt they experienced about their own sexual feelings.

Sometimes the results of the abuse are irrevocably tragic. Suicide and attempted suicide by the victims of sexual abuse by a priest are common. At least 12 of Father Porter's victims tried to kill themselves. Some victims escape into the world of celibacy to avoid dealing with sexual episodes in the future. Some victims become abusers themselves; and sometimes the two responses overlap.

When priests are the abusers, "the effects," according to one priest, "are long lasting and go well into the adulthood. This is well documented, though it may well be difficult to predict the extent of the effects in particular cases. We are speaking not only of psychological effects but also the spiritual effects, since the perpetrators of the abuse are priests or clerics. This will no doubt have a profound effect on the faith life of the victims, their families and others in the community."

Father Stephen Rossetti has conducted studies showing the profound effect of priest sexual abuse on the family, parish, and diocese in which the abuse occurs. Special questions arise when the abuser is a priest. How will the child be able to perceive the church and clergy in the future as unselfish, loving representatives of the Gospel and Body of Christ? What happens to the child's perception of the sacraments as administered by the clergy? As an adult, will the victim come to view the hierarchy of the church as hypocritical and weak for not having prevented the abuse or putting a stop to it once it was discovered? Depending on how widely the situation is known among the child's family and acquaintances, how many other ancillary victims will there be for each abused child?

## MEMORIES TRUE AND FALSE

Integrating and healing memory is a part of life and growth. If we lose our memory we lose ourselves or at least part of ourselves. Many times sexual abuse in childhood is repressed by the victim only to be retrieved and remembered once the victim reaches an adult state of ego strength that can tolerate the trauma. Many victims of child abuse are diagnosed as suffering from posttraumatic stress disorder. Some of the adults now confronting priests and bishops with allegations of sexual abuse performed years earlier have recovered repressed memories either in or outside of a psychotherapeutic context. Most of the victims I have interviewed over a period of three decades demonstrated a variety of symptoms, and increasing numbers are moved to confront their abusers.

Sometimes in the process of psychotherapy, victims of childhood sexual abuse, who tend to develop depression, anxiety, and addictive behavior, recall the repressed memory of those events. In a great number of instances, these formerly repressed memories can be validated and corroborated. In some cases, the courts determine the validity but not the truth of the accusations.

But repressed memories do not surface only in psychotherapy. Several of Father James Porter's victims began to recall their abuse after reports of his activities became public. Porter admitted guilt to these allegations, confirming the accuracy of the repressed memories.

In 1993 a backlash movement developed, which centers in Philadelphia around the leadership of the False Memory Syndrome (FMS) Foundation. Under the care of certain psychotherapists, some patients have produced memories that cannot be validated and even under closer examination are proven to be false. One famous case was settled in the early 1990s. An Iowa bishop in his seventies was accused of sexual abuse by two women who had been his parishioners several decades earlier. Under the pressure of pursuing a civil case against the bishop, the women recanted their accusations, and blamed, and later sued, their psychotherapist for the production of their false memories. In March 1994 the man who accused Chicago's Cardinal Bernardin of sex abuse decided that his recovered memories of the abuse were "unreliable."

Dr. Paul McHugh, chair of the department of psychiatry at Johns Hopkins University, serves on the board of the FMS Foundation. He feels that the child abuse movement has taken on the character of a witch-hunt and claims that traumatic sexual events tend to be remembered rather than forgotten. McHugh's point of view must be heard and registered along with the false accusations noted already at the Council of Elvira. Cases must be evaluated on an individual basis.

Psychiatry is faced with the task of clarifying the working of the human brain, mind, and emotion—no easy task when it comes to sex and memory, fact and fantasy. It is not a new problem. Freud himself confronted and commented on it repeatedly (1905/1953, 1916/1963). Nothing is more harmful to the cause of victims' rights than false accusations. Justice is served by truth and accuracy alone.

Great strides are being made in understanding the brain function of memory. Dr. Elizabeth Loftus of the University of Washington is involved in some of the seminal studies that demonstrate that memories are encoded in different areas of the brain; retrieval of memories involves a complex process of reintegration. Most false memories that arise in psychotherapy are credited to suggestibility that has been imposed or enhanced by therapeutic techniques involving hypnosis or the administration of the drug sodium Amytal.[M]

McHugh's most important points should not be lost for those who care about determining the nature and extent of sexual abuse: the quest for truth should not have any trace of a witch-hunt; psychotherapy as a mode of healing must retain its scientific integrity and objectivity (1992, 1994).

## CHURCH RESPONSE

The problem of priest sexual abuse was addressed publicly for the first time at a meeting sponsored by the National Association for Pastoral Renewal held on the campus of Notre Dame University in 1967. All American bishops were invited to that meeting.

In 1983 Father Thomas Doyle, a canon lawyer on the staff of the Vatican embassy in Washington, D.C., was sent to investigate the diocese of Lafayette, Louisiana. Its bishop had known as early as 1974 that one of his priests was abusing children.

In 1985 Canonist Doyle, along with priest psychiatrist Michael Peterson and lawyer Ray Mouton, produced a report on the problem of child sexual abuse by priests and made it available to the bishops. The report, which accurately predicted the events of the next 10 years, was largely ignored or rejected by the majority of bishops at the time of its release.

The church's traditional preference for secrecy has been assaulted irrevocably by the facts revealed in press and courtrooms. The crisis has mobilized various dimensions of scandal and intense personal and public emotion. Catholic parents in the 1990s are more alert to the possibility of sexual abuse by a priest, an unthinkable or at least unmentionable notion in the 1960s.

Most people in the victims' movement have regarded the progress of the church as a whole as too little and very late. Prior to 1988, in the United States, Catholic Church authorities handled problems of child abuse in secrecy, by denial and rationalization. The offending priest was remonstrated, sometimes given time to make a retreat (repent), and usually transferred to a different parish or parochial assignment. Or else, he might be sent to one of a few psychiatric institutes under religious auspices.

Since 1988, under the pressure of lawsuits against the church, the picture changed. What has remained constant is that sexual activity by a priest with anyone *was* and *is* a violation of the church's requirement that priests remain celibate. The forced acknowledgment of a priest's sexual activities with minors is the thread that threatens to unravel the cloak of priestly celibacy.

At first, 1992 seemed to be a year of vindication for victims of clergy abuse when the Archdiocese of Chicago adopted a model plan for processing allegations of clergy abuse. The plan set up an independent board of evaluation, called for the immediate suspension of the accused priest's church function during the evaluation, and provided for psychiatric help for both the accused and the abused. Today, the plan remains incompletely and unevenly implemented.

By June 1992 the bishops were still handling the problem behind closed doors at their annual meeting. By this time the issue had blitzed the airways on every radio and television talk show from Larry King to Oprah Winfrey. Substantive articles continued in the *National Catholic Reporter, America,* the *Wall Street Journal,* the *Washington Post,* and other major news carriers. In 3 years more than 400 articles covered either particular priest offenses or the problem in general. Although some bishops and religious superiors have taken the

existence of priest abuse seriously, the official response of the church
has been slow and defensive.

Bishops are concerned with priestly morale and the pastoral care
of their people. Theirs is a difficult task since they are responsible for
both the priest abuser and the victims and must keep an eye on
financial claims against the church as well as the loss of image. These
are formidable challenges for men not accustomed to submitting to
public scrutiny.

Progress could be substantial with the establishment in 1993 of
a committee backed by the bishops. Bishop John Kinney of Bismarck,
North Dakota, has taken determined leadership of the ad hoc
committee. He defined his goals as follows:

> 1) show bishops the most effective ways to reach out to victims and
> to affected parishes and institutions; 2) show bishops how to
> promote the well-being of priests and how to prevent abuse from
> within their ranks; 3) create a national clearinghouse for infor-
> mation so that dioceses can learn from each other's experience;
> 4) show bishops how to educate Catholics about sexual abuse and
> thus create a "preventive environment"; 5) identify research
> projects to analyze the experience of those who work with abused
> and abusers. (Feister, 1994, pp. 32–33)

Most bishops now respond to the needs of the psychiatrically
needy and demand immediate psychological evaluation and treatment. They have heeded the advice of experts:

> Although it is not the pedophile's fault that he has the sexual
> orientation that he has, it is his responsibility to deal with his
> sexuality in a manner that does not put innocent children at risk.
> However, in order for him to be able to do this and to be held
> accountable by society, adequate treatment facilities must be made
> available, facilities where a person can seek out help without fear
> of stigmatization, ridicule, retaliation, or unwarranted disdain.
> Only under such circumstances can one expect an individual to
> talk candidly about the innermost aspects of his own sexuality.
> (Berlin, 1986, p. 22)

Further, the bishops' committee seems to be dedicated to more
careful selection of candidates for ordination, although screening, no
matter how sophisticated, will not eliminate predators encouraged by
the system.

According to Canon 1342 of church law, a priest against whom
criminal allegations have been made and supported, or even suspected of being supported, can be suspended from his duties without

a trial and by means of an extrajudicial decree. Such a suspension is now employed as a protection for potential victims as well as for the church.

Some dioceses are establishing lay boards to review how authorities have handled complaints against clergy. Although these are positive steps, they are symptom relief rather than system analysis and do nothing to readjust the power elements in the celibate/sexual system.

In August 1993 St. John's Abbey and University in Collegeville, Minnesota, established an Interfaith Institute to study sexual trauma in the church. It has a promising structure and agenda, since it is not limited to damage control or image repair. The institute has allied itself with the victims' movement and has as its primary concerns prevention, healing, seminary education, and the exploration of a theology of sex.

Change comes hard to a system that has enjoyed the privilege of feudal function and secret self-maintenance. Resistance to change is formidable even in the face of public exposure. One bishop told a priest, "There is no real problem. The devil is just persecuting the church in this way."

• • •

When one begins to grasp the implications of priest sexual abuse— that it is a symptom of a failed system of power and inadequate sexual doctrine—one can understand the confusion and fright of church leaders. The very structure of their existence is disintegrating. The more they analyze the symptoms, the more clearly the diseased function and structure of the system become apparent. Instinctively, some bishops know that they are witnesses to the demise of the celibate/sexual system of power.

As one examines the structure of the celibate/sexual system in which priests exist, one becomes acutely aware of how vulnerable many priests become, not because of their genetic or psychodynamic lock, but because of their situation and, for some, their lack of moral stability.

The church of the future will have to reexamine carefully its need for a theology of sexuality as well as its basic assumptions, many of which have been codified and accepted without question for centuries. It is a matter of survival.

# 3

# DISCOURSE:
# THE SEXUAL TOWER OF BABEL

*The beginning of wisdom is to get things by their right names.*

E. O. Wilson

*Discourse . . . requires the virtualization of constraints on action. This is intended to render inoperative all motives except solely that of a cooperative readiness to arrive at an understanding.*

Jürgen Habermas

A middle-aged pastor said, "It really saddens me that I am part of an organization that takes an issue like sex and is afraid to talk about it. . . . There's a saying in those twelve-step programs that you are only as sick as your secrets. The more [the Catholic Church] tries to hide, the less we address these sexual issues and problems, the more we try to stonewall people, the more it leaves us vulnerable" (De Nike, 1994, p. 22).

Several bishops told me that in the 1980s Pope John Paul II explicitly forbade them to talk about "contraception, abortion, homosexuality, masturbation, a married priesthood or women's ordination to the priesthood other than to defend the Church's official teaching." The moral paralysis such a policy engenders is demonstrated by the action of one bishop at a national meeting of diocesan vocation directors. These are priests, usually appointed by each diocese or religious order, who foster vocations to the priesthood in their respective areas. During one of the informal breaks, the conversation

44

turned to the possibility of women's ordination. A bishop in attendance, by eyewitness account, "red-faced and gasping, shouted out,
'The Pope has forbidden us to talk about this!'"

## NEED FOR DISCOURSE

If priests and bishops may not discuss even among themselves issues
vital to their sexual function and existence, how can they attain moral
responsibility?

Such is the anatomy of a crisis. The crisis that now exposes
priests who have had sex with minors raises questions and demands
moral discourse, ethical response, clear understanding, and accountability in areas of behavior, structure, doctrine, and teaching.

### BEHAVIOR

If religion cannot tell the truth about itself, it has nothing to say.
Hypocrisy—professing one thing and performing the opposite—is the
greatest moral violation. In approaching the crisis of clergy abuse,
truth must be the preeminent goal. Truth—wherever found, however
discovered, whatever it exposes—must be the agenda for any exploration of abuse by clergy. Anything that impedes unflinching directness, honesty, or clear unambiguous communication and confrontation of the facts will perpetuate the secret system in which abuse can
continue and flourish.

The sexual abuse of minors is only part of the problem. Four
times as many priests involve themselves sexually with adult women,
and twice the number of priests involve themselves with adult men.
Sexual involvement of a supposedly celibate clergyman with anyone
is a violation of trust. Litigation has forced child abuse to the fore,
but the sexual abuse of adults is no less a violation of celibate honesty
and trust.

All concerned citizens have a stake in the honesty of religious
leaders. They should be a moral and cultural resource. Religion needs
the help of all concerned women and men. Everyone is victimized by
a system that fosters or tolerates abuse. It is not unholy or unseemly
to be vitally interested in the performance of moral leaders. If religion
was taught anything by the German holocaust of the Jews it is that
standing by silently does not absolve one from guilt. Institutional
structures and behaviors are not above question or challenge.

## Structure

The celibate/sexual structure of the church must be discussed—openly, freely, energetically—and reevaluated. Sexual abuse by the presumed celibate most often involves a violation and abuse of power. Some observers have speculated that this issue is as central or even more central than the sexual elements. Victims of clergy abuse complain most vociferously about the undeniable experience of being revictimized by the ecclesiastical system.

Certainly celibacy is an issue in understanding abuse and the power structure of the church. The requirement of perfect and perpetual chastity and therefore celibacy for all of its priests is peculiar to the Catholic ministry. Anyone who has read my study of celibacy knows that I deeply revere this religious achievement, and that stance should be clear in these pages. But it would be simplistic to suggest that a married priesthood would by itself solve the sexual problems of the Catholic Church. Both Protestants and Catholics must search deeper levels of religious reality for answers to the current crisis. On the other hand, it is ridiculous to summarily dismiss the celibate tradition as one causative factor in some of the problems of Catholic clergy.

No seminary teaches celibacy/sexuality adequately. Most training programs value and foster naiveté and sexual immaturity. Emotional 13-year-olds support the system and vice versa.

Sexual abuse in any form—of children, of adult women or men—is a violation of celibate practice. Any member of the clergy, of whatever rank, who cannot distinguish between ideal and practice will, in one way or another, sooner or later, violate the process and achievement of celibacy, by denial, rationalization, or psychological splitting in his own behalf or that of another.

Celibacy is also a factor in the power system of the church and is intimately connected with its abuses.

Why is power reserved on the basis of gender? Why is celibacy irrevocably connected with religious power? There are no glib answers to this well-entrenched tradition, but the current sexual crisis in the church cannot be addressed adequately without squarely facing such questions in open discourse.

## Doctrine

Sexuality was the one area of moral teaching that was not examined by the Second Vatican Council (1962–65). Hopes for sexual reform raised by the council were dashed by the 1968 epoch-making encyclical *Humanae Vitae*. This statement, based on the church's traditional reasoning on sexuality, demonstrated one thing clearly: the sexual teaching of the church is not credible. We simply cannot afford to pretend that the Church's basic sexual teaching does not impinge on the behavioral crisis of priests. The encyclical elevates the moral and doctrinal questions to an urgency not experienced by the Catholic Church since the fourth century and the time of St. Augustine.

There are no easy answers, but we must discuss celibacy/sexuality and examine human nature and human sexual nature with greater diligence and humility. Edward O. Wilson's (1992b) observation is worth repeating: "In order to search for a new morality based upon a more truthful definition of man, it is necessary to look inward, to dissect the machinery of the mind and to retrace its evolutionary history" (1978, p. 4). Theologians must become partners with scientists to help each other clarify perspectives. Sexuality is not the only reality affected by noncredible moral pronouncements; all of theology is. No one has said it better than Jesuit theologian Christopher Mooney, "Insofar as theologians fail to take account of physics and biology, their interpretation of their own data as well as their models of God must inevitably lose credibility" (Gallagher, M.P., p. 630).

Left with a sexual doctrine they do find credible, priests resort too easily to rationalization and duplicity. The sexual crisis of the churches reveals moral leaders without a moral gyroscope.

The doctrinal problem of the church is based on the false assumption that it has grasped fully the sexual nature of humans and that its teaching about sexuality rests not only on revelation from God but also on "natural law." So far, church doctrine has failed to incorporate or acknowledge the rightful role of science in determining what is "natural." Wilson put it well in his Dudleian lecture at Harvard Divinity School: "The role of science is to test every conclusion about human nature remorselessly and to search for the bedrock of ethics—by which I mean the material basis of natural law" (1992b, p. 15).

John Cardinal O'Connor, archbishop of New York, unwittingly named the core of the problem of sexuality, celibacy, as well as of marriage, when he said, "In moral and spiritual matters I didn't create the truth. It is inherent in the *nature* of things." It is the question of sexual nature that has not yet been addressed fully.

The moral and spiritual truth of which Cardinal O'Connor speaks is not separate from biological, psychological, and social truth. None of these, as each impinges on the sexual, can be defined easily or apodictically. This does not mean that truth is relative. But the human brain, through which truth is apprehended, is not entirely developed yet, as Ludwig Von Bertalanffy (1971) stated:

[There is] the general human predicament. It is the dualism of man in a natural and a symbolic (or cultural) world. As I once expressed it, man's forebrain has developed splendidly, and this made possible the evolution from stone axes to atom bombs, from fetishism to physics. The brainstem of man, however, seat of emotions, instincts, animal drives, did not evolve but remained pretty much the same since the dawn of man and his ape-like ancestors. . . . Here is the reason that we have an almost superhuman intellect which created atomic physics and bombs, combined with the subhuman instincts of a savage or angry ape. (p. 118)

Although E. O. Wilson's theories of sociobiology (1978) are controversial, the questions he raises are important for celibate and sexual adjustment: just how genetically determined *is* a human being, not only in sexual but also social behavior?

Theologians will probably applaud Wilson's assertion that some sort of religious instinct is inborn (p. 175) — a view not far from some of St. Augustine's conclusions. They will also agree that love and sex in humans are biologically linked, as are certain temperamental differences between men and women (pp. 128–135).

Agreeing or not, moral and spiritual leaders, celibate or not, need to contend with the evidence that reproduction is not the exclusive and overriding purpose of sex among human beings. Love, fostered and supported by sexual consolation, bonds parents long enough to raise children; love and sexual consolation also bond others who can serve the community in positive but nonreproductive ways (Degler, 1991; Fisher, 1992)

[Natural laws] are biological, were written by natural selection, require little if any enforcement by religious or secular authorities, and have been erroneously interpreted by theologians writing in ignorance of biology. All we can surmise of humankind's genetic history argues for a more liberal sexual morality, in which sexual practices are to be regarded first as bonding devices and only second as means for procreation. (Wilson, 1978, p. 142)

Wilson links the growing evidence that homosexuality is biologically predetermined, or at least influenced, with the impulse toward altruism. Societies need individuals free of family obligation for special service to the community (p. 143).

At any rate, there is evidence that altruism among animals is genetically controlled. It increases the chances of survival of the group. There is great significance for the understanding of the nature of celibacy in determining how *natural*—genetically determined—is the capacity to make sacrifices, even to give one's life, for the good of others.

## TEACHING: ARCHAIC ANTHROPOLOGY

Regardless of the unanswered questions about the biological and social nature of celibate/sexual adjustment, it is clear that current Catholic teaching is based on an archaic anthropology.

What view of human nature is consistent with the church's teaching on sexuality? Dependence on an archaic anthropology calls into question the concept of human nature underlying all of the church's teachings on sexuality. Schematically put, the church's official teaching on sex is that all directly sought or welcomed sexual pleasure (thought, word, desire, or action) outside marriage is gravely sinful and that every act of sexual intercourse within marriage must remain open to the transmission of life.

How can this teaching be supported by the nature of sexual beings as known and experienced by thoughtful Christians? It imposes a system that makes grave sin inevitable and even necessary. There is only one way to demand intellectual assent, to justify such assertions, and to make the teaching coherent and internally logical: appeal to an outmoded anthropological model. I am indebted to Margaret Mead for the seed of this idea. In a private conversation in 1966 about psychoanalysis and anthropology, she said that Freud's oedipal theory makes sense only if we postulate a prehistory anthropology that assumes a life cycle of 12 to 16 years. Otherwise the oedipal threat has no reality base but is rather merely a psychic figment. Although I was involved in a study of celibacy and the church's sexual practice at the time, it took me nearly a decade to realize the importance of this observation for Catholic theology and sexual theory.

Sexual activity and interest begin in some form or other at birth; an infant discovers his or her genitals the same way he or she discovers other interesting appendages and cavities such as the nose, toes, fingers, mouth, ears, nostrils, and anus. There are special reactions in the genitals, also from birth (erection/lubrication), that enhance and command the attention of the infant and his or her peers and elders.

Socialization within the family matrix (clan) demands some channeling and restricting of behavior and instinct. The child must redirect its infantile sexual striving from its original object (mother, father) to one acceptable to the clan. At the point when childhood sexual activity (premoral) is submitted to understanding (the age of reason) and community responsibility (the formation of conscience), the person is ready for mature sexual involvement. In primitive humans, these activities coincided with physical sexual maturity and the capacity to propagate the species at approximately 5 to 7 years of age, thereby allowing enough time for the nurturance of children before menopause and senescence, which occurred from age 9 to 12. A long life of 16 to 18 years was the reward of the very hardy and lucky.

All of the church's teachings are consistent with this (*and only this*) understanding of human nature. Such a scheme leaves no room or need for sexual development outside marriage. Sexual practice and readiness are all accomplished in prerational, and therefore premoral, circumstances prior to the formation of conscience. (Choice of family size is not an option, but also not a question.) The scheme also requires that the marital state immediately follow the resolution of infantile psychosexual development (which at one time was probably the state of human affairs). Therefore, at the point when one is ready to leave father and mother (the resolution of the oedipal), one is ready to cling to a wife.

The church's teaching on human sexuality, in spite of its internal logic, is not credible because it is consistent only with this archaic anthropology. It has echoes of inherent truth, but its view of *human nature* is not validated as experienced and lived by reasonable and informed Christians today. The church's view of human sexual nature is quite literally underdeveloped. It is understandable that the official church would cling to an incomplete and outmoded sexual teaching at a time when there was no coherent and comprehensive rationale to substitute. However, in spite of current confusion and legitimate controversies in sexual studies and theology, the time has passed when clearly inadequate models can support official pronouncements. We can tolerate indecision while the church develops a theology of sex. But who can give credence to pronouncements that are clearly incredible?

The celibate/sexual system has been a factor in the spiritual development of Western culture. Likewise, it is part of the spiritual ecology of America, whether or not it is widely appreciated or acknowledged. The sexual crisis of priests needs an interested and informed general public in the hope of furthering a deeper understanding of and sensitivity to the struggles, the strengths, the passions, and the possibilities of this ancient practice.

Celibacy's vitality and life-giving potential are dependent not on its ritual but on its reality. Any reform or revitalization of a part of the ecosystem is dependent on the mobilization of other related parts of the system in the service of establishing balance. Bishops or priests alone cannot reform or revitalize the practice of celibacy. There is a mutual interdependence between married and celibate Christians. Each is enhanced by the achievement of the other as they seek to penetrate and master the common reality that generates and nurtures both — human sexuality. We must discuss these celibate/sexual issues openly.

## INTUITIVE PERCEPTION

What does it mean when a priest says, "I am celibate"?

Angela Bornemann, the editor of *The Jeffersonian* (Baltimore, Maryland), tells about a family priest friend, who has had a longtime girlfriend in spite of his continued priestly ministry. The questions about celibacy that the relationship raised prompted her to remember:

> I was probably six or seven years old at the time — being picked up and swung around, playful, to all appearances, by another priest at our school. What I didn't like was that he had one hand in my crotch. Maybe he was a sexual child abuser, maybe he just didn't realize this was not the proper way to hold a female child.
>
> I never told my parents about any of this. Even if I had understood the potential seriousness of the priest's actions, I doubt if anyone would have taken me seriously. Sexual child abuse by a priest just wasn't a topic for conversation back in the 1950s. (Bornemann, 1994, p. 6)

Bornemann also recounts a situation from her teenage years that gives her a perception — an intuition — about what celibacy means for those who claim it and to those who are taught to presume that "Father is celibate."

> I remember a particular priest who was the darling of the parish. A compelling speaker. A jokester. A former foreign missionary.
>
> The female students had another description of him. We nicknamed him "Father Dirty."
>
> He earned that moniker because he always wanted to discuss sins of impurity. Perhaps we were unfair. I only know that when the hair on the back of your neck suddenly goes up, when

you feel you're in danger when you're left alone with a certain person, it's probably because you are in danger. (1994, p. 6)

What is typical about this woman's experience and perception is that she had no words and no one to talk to at the times she suffered her observations.

The intuition of celibacy from the priest's point of view can be quite different. A 40-year-old priest was committed to a psychiatric hospital on the urging of his church superiors after he was picked up by the police on a morals charge. He was a highly visible pastor, and authorities wished to control scandal. His sexual history became clear: he had been sexually promiscuous during the previous 5 years. The psychiatric staff felt that he should be tested for AIDS and presented him with the forms for informed consent. The nurse presenting the forms for his signature said, "You understand why we are recommending this test?" The priest replied, "No, I don't see the necessity at all. I am a celibate."

This reaction was not merely the product of psychological denial or rationalization. It illustrates the use of the undifferentiated and undefined concept of *celibacy* as it is preserved within the celibate/sexual system; it is an unquestioned and unquestionable cover. *I am a celibate* obviates any discussion or definition and defies discourse on what celibacy really is.

I have begun to explore literature—biographies of celibates, novels of vocation, and novels by priests—to measure ethnographic and clinical observations about the function and structure of celibacy against intuitive perceptions. Literature, too, can clarify perception, hone intuition—raise the hair on the back of your neck, as Bornemann put it. Dr. Harris Gruman is associated with me in the analysis of vocational novels by Bernanos, Silone, Greene, Cather, and Lewis, among others (*Behind the Minister's Black Veil*, Sipe & Gruman, in press). Dr. B. C. Lamb is assisting in the analysis of 26 novels by priest-sociologist Andrew Greeley (*Reading Andrew Greeley*, Sipe & Lamb, in press). Greeley, who credits his productivity "to celibacy and hard work," is an invaluable witness to how celibacy functions through his intuitive and lived perception of the celibate/sexual system.

In one of his novels richest in this respect, *The Cardinal Sins* (1982a), Greeley exposes the system both in its range of behaviors and its presumptions and defenses. The story line of the novel is described in the author's note.

They were two Irish boys growing up on the West Side of Chicago, discovering themselves, awakening to desire, dealing with faith...then entering the priesthood. One rises to the center of power—the other remains a parish priest. Each must deal with the love of a woman—in his own way....A man of God is still a man. (p. 1)

In the same note at the beginning of the novel, Greeley validates the power of intuitive perception when he writes:

Unfortunately there is no real-life counterpart of Patrick Cardinal Donahue. Despite all his flaws and faults he is a much more effective leader than many of our current crop of crimson-clad princes of the Church. The student of the history of the Sacred College will perceive, I am sure, that many less worthy than he have worn the sacred scarlet during the last millennium.

He is a product of my imagination....The book, then, is story, not history or biography or (perhaps sadly) autobiography. It is nonetheless true. (p. 13)

The truth of the celibate/sexual system of the church is played out by the characters in word and action.

"Most of us keep our vows. No mistresses and no little boys" (p. 233) are words uttered by Pat Donahue, the protagonist who eventually becomes Cardinal Archbishop of Chicago. His observations would not be so remarkable were they not made to a woman to whom he repeatedly makes "violent and reckless" love (p. 247) and with whom he has a long-term sexual relationship. By the time he utters the statement he has also fathered a child with a married woman (pp. 188–189). Even as a cardinal at the height of his ecclesiastical power he tries to rape another long-standing friend (Ellen Foley) and declares, "I'm probably more of a homosexual than anything else" (p. 420). His sexual lapses are typically followed by paroxysms of guilt and a trip to the confessional to share his sin with a priest. The impulsive pattern of his encounters, however, do not change. His bisexual confusion is apparent already in his days at the seminary where as an adolescent he sneaks out to court women while he is infatuated with a fellow seminarian, Stan Kokoleck (pp. 82–84).

Power is the driving force of his life; sexual love is never fully integrated into his relationships. The future cardinal is described by his lover, Maureen, as a man who "would sell his grandmother's soul to get ahead in the Church....He chops his life into tiny compartments" (p. 212). Friends and associates describe him, perhaps unfairly but tellingly, as "sucking half the Cardinals in the Curia" (p. 220) and as a man who has never been able to keep his pants zipped (p. 221). Other priests who serve on his chancery office staff participate in cover-up, remain oblivious, or ignore the cardinal's private life and see him as "totally committed to celibacy" and magnanimously tolerant to priests who resign their priesthood, presumably to marry (p. 278).

Father Kevin Bennan, the lifelong friend of Pat Donahue, knows of his friend's escapades and even covers for him in the seminary and on several occasions afterward. Kevin participates in the system of secrecy equally with Pat. Kevin does practice his celibacy, but his character gives evidence that he has done so through consolidation of an adolescent adjustment structure (pp. 405–407). The culmination of Kevin's knowledge about how the celibate/sexual system works is summed up in the insight:

> Maybe we ought to make it optional. Yet I'd hate to see us lose it. The world, Catholic and otherwise, needs the witness of a few people who are living proof that you can intensely and passionately love members of the opposite sex without having to jump into bed with them. (p. 443)

Such a characterization of celibacy betrays a gross oversimplification by Kevin, a practicing celibate, with a tendency to caricature to the point of grotesque distortion, as if people in the noncelibate world jump into bed with every friend whom they love passionately.

Other characters in the novel make observations about the celibate/ sexual adjustment of priests and bishops. Ellen Foley attends parties in Chicago where priests come with their "dates." One priest describes the sexual antics of the bishop, Daniel O'Neil, who precedes Donahue in Chicago. He has a 25-year secret affair with a woman. He gets drunk, exposes other priests with whom he lives to "women's clothes in the bedroom across from" [the bishop's]. Another priest generalizes about bishops as "a collection of effeminate, prissy complainers without any guts" (p. 277).

Monsignor Martinelli, Donahue's powerful patron in the Vatican, who is eventually created a cardinal along with Donahue, is described by Donahue's lover as "an obvious fag" (p. 213); she similarly labels Pope Paul VI. The novel also includes references to real ecclesiastical personalities, such as Cardinal Baggio, Giovanni Benelli, Father Carter, S.J., John Krol, and Hans Kung. The total of the novel intuitively describes the function and structure of the celibate/sexual system.

In a personal afterword, Greeley explains his motives and conscious intent in expressing the "Truth" through his imagination:

> Stories have always been the best way to talk about religion because stories appeal to the emotions and the whole personality

and not just to the mind. Jesus told parables; the authors of the David and Joseph cycles and the Song of Songs in the Jewish scriptures, for example, also told stories. (p. 509)

He also poses six religious possibilities in his stories, which include God's love, human growth, and priestly creativity. Three other themes impinge directly on our theme and lead us to reflect not only on the power of the intuitive perception, but also on the need for clear definitions of celibacy and direct discourse on the subject.

3) The Church, while it often may be a whore (corrupt, lethargic, irrelevant), can renew itself and, on occasion, become again the fair bride (an image taken from St. Peter's first epistle).
4) The splendor of the priesthood persists despite the humanity of priests.
5) While celibacy is difficult for all priests and impossible for some, it is nevertheless a constructive and fulfilling way for some healthy and passionate men to live in the world. (p. 510)

## FEAR OF CLARITY

Some people fear direct discourse even more than intuitive expression. The workings of the celibate/sexual system will be clearly exposed if *celibacy* is defined and discussed. This is why discourse terrifies those who hide behind undefined celibacy as a shield, who maintain power at the price of the perpetuation of imprecision and duplicity at the sacrifice of radical self-honesty.

*Terror* is the word that best captures the church's reaction to any discourse on celibacy. More precisely, terror is the emotion that explains the assiduous avoidance of any significant discourse about celibacy and even the express command *not* to discuss that which they claim to hold in highest esteem. The terror emanates from an intuited threat to survival—not of celibate practice or achievement, but of a system of power and from fear of the exposure of noncelibate practice inherent in the function and structure of a system called *celibate* without discrete definition.

Clerical celibacy is a burning issue: not merely commanding attention in the popular arena, but burning in the sense of being dangerous—too hot to handle. Several of the best sociological researchers in the United States avoid work in the area because the topic is so polarized and politicized. They fear that if they venture into the celibacy preserve, they will be labeled *non gratae*, and other research funding will wither away. Their perception of danger is real.

Celibacy has long been the sacred cow of Catholicism, to be approached only in terms of the ideal. Like the untouchable cow, celibacy was to be acknowledged as sacred and special in spite of any of the practical or messy realities.

To question celibacy—simply to seek a clearer definition—is taboo. To ask, "How is celibacy really practiced by those who profess it?" has not only been discarded by many church authorities as unhelpful or unnecessary but also attacked with theological fury as doctrinally questionable and religiously disloyal.

A clear understanding of celibacy, of course, provides great advantage to those who truly strive to live it. Such an ideal cannot be lived without understanding, and there can be no understanding without discourse. What is lacking in the understanding of celibacy is not talk or opinion or even conviction but clear definition of the terms—therefore a primer for discourse—which could make productive a real exchange of ideas, sharing of knowledge, and debate about perspectives.

The two major deficiencies I mentioned previously—the failure to understand and embrace the true sexual nature of humankind, and the resultant lack of a theology of sex in any Christian tradition—have hindered a precise vocabulary for celibacy.

These lacunae have left celibacy without adequate foundations on which to construct solid definitions of itself. As a result, celibacy has remained generalized, idealized, romanticized, and most erroneously sacramentalized.

## CELIBACY AND SEXUAL ABUSE OF MINORS

There has been an ecclesiastical scramble to disassociate from celibacy the crisis of sexual abuse by priests. In their responses to the media, the bishops and the National Conference of Catholic Bishops have denied repeatedly any connection between the two. The official position is that, "it would be a tremendous waste of time and money to conduct such a study [on the relationship between celibacy and priestly sexual abuse]." That comes from one of the bishops' main psychological consultants in a 1993 lecture to the National Federation of Priests' Councils. According to this logic, priests abuse no more than any other group, and therefore it is reasonable to give specific instructions "not to study the nature and causes of sexual abuse [by priests]" (Fox & Berry, 1993).

Psychiatrist-priest James Gill hedges his bets a bit when he is quoted in the *Hartford Courant*: "There is no conclusive evidence that celibacy increases the incidence of pedophilia" (Renner, p. 6). But the Winter report (1990c) is unequivocal about the need for discourse and recommended that "Bishops across Canada [join] to address fully, directly, honestly and without reservation questions relating to the problematic link between celibacy and ministerial priesthood" (p. 35).

## CELIBACY DEFINED

Celibacy, the reality, need not be defended as a valid entity. It exists. It has been a valuable factor in the service of humanity and the formation of culture. It has always been, and persists, and will continue to do so quite independently of any determination of ecclesiastical law. To discourse productively, however, we need to think carefully about our definitions and not presume that when the words *celibate* or *celibacy* are used they describe *one* thing.

### CELIBACY: THE NATURAL PHENOMENON

Celibacy is not merely a supernatural phenomenon. Celibacy—that is, a nonreproductive, nonsexually active stance in the service of some group—can be a natural phenomenon. The celibate state is not dependent on the Catholic Church. It exists in *other cultures* in relationship to other religious beliefs—namely, Buddhist and Hindu; and it also exists independently of religious conviction or affiliation simply as one expression of human existence.

Celibacy exists in *other species*, especially in the organized insect societies, ants and bees, and even among the larger mammals—for instance, among lions, where some of the pride do not reproduce but rather devote their energies to the protection and care of their near kin.

We have so dichotomized flesh and spirit, divorced sex from spirituality, nature from supernature that we have forgotten that somehow it is all of one piece—all life and this existence of ours form a unity. Each of us has a place. Some humans have a natural predisposition to nonreproduction, to nonsexually active bonding and interaction with others.

### CELIBACY: THE STATE OF NONMARRIAGE

One of the most common definitions of celibacy involves the presumption of nonmarriage, but not the absence of sexual activity. Several years ago when I shared with a psychiatrist colleague the fact that I was studying celibacy, he immediately talked about the period of his courtship prior to marriage when he and his future wife were struggling to refrain from intercourse. He had no understanding that their intentions and even their self-discipline were directed toward marriage and preparation for it rather than celibacy.

Such imprecision and double-mindedness is not limited to seculars. One American bishop said at a 1990 assembly of bishops, "We're all celibate. None of us is a parent." (Even this, of course, is not true. Some bishops do father and have fathered children.)

Such rationalization is widespread and is perpetuated by maintaining a distinction between chastity and celibacy. A Vatican official stated that in his worldwide contacts he found that "the vast majority of priests do live their celibacy." But he defined a celibate as one "who is faithful to his option not to get married . . . he may on occasion be unchaste." The prelate (name withheld by request) went on in a very moving way to some humble self-revelation, "Chastity has always been a battleground for me, and I have always tried to fight the good fight (c'è chi vince e c'è chi perde)." He spoke repentantly about his own sexual compromises and his concern for the lack of charity involved in his sexual activity and concluded, "I have never been anything but happy in my celibate option even when I was losing the current battle for chastity." This statement is typical of the Italian clerical attitude toward celibacy.

This dichotomy between marriage and sexual activity, and between celibacy (nonmarriage) and chastity leaves great areas of imprecision where one can claim the rights and privileges of celibacy/ nonmarriage and at the same time enjoy a wide latitude of sexual exploration. The person remains a celibate, merely becoming a *sinner* or more simply *just human*.

## CELIBACY: THE IDEAL

Most frequently, ecclesiastical literature and spiritual writers address celibacy as an ideal. For instance, in the words of Pope John Paul II in 1992:

> Preeminent . . . is that precious gift of divine grace given to some by the Father (cf. *Matthew* 19:11; *I Corinthians* 7:7) in order more easily to devote themselves to God alone with an undivided heart (cf. *I Corinthians* 7:32–34) in virginity or celibacy. This perfect continence for love of the Kingdom of Heaven has always been held in high esteem by the Church as a sign and stimulus of love, and as a singular source of spiritual fertility in the world. In virginity and

celibacy, chastity retains its original meaning, that is, of human sexuality lived as a genuine sign of and precious service to the love of communion and gift of self to others. (Pastores Dabo Vobis #29)

Indeed, what an unassailably noble ideal celibacy is: characterized by complete devotion to God, free from all ambivalences, a living symbol of the universality and meaning of divine love, and complete availability and devotion to the service of humanity.

One does not diminish the grandeur of the ideal by pointing out that the ideal is not a reality in all who clothe themselves with the celibate mantle. To pose the ideal as if it were real is a gross deception. When an ideal is presented or articulated as if it were real, those striving toward the ideal suffer unnecessary alienation not only from themselves but also from the very goal they wish to approach.

## CELIBACY: THE CHARISM

Theologically, a charism is an unmerited gift of God. Such is the grace of celibacy and the perceived experience of the recipient of this divine favor. A man who presents himself for ordination to the priesthood is expected to be the object of this grace. The charism is distinct from the ideal just as it is separate from the law. After all, grace cannot be legislated. Neither can a spiritual gift thrive without cultivation. Life is a precious unmerited gift that cannot prosper without careful attention.

## CELIBACY: THE LAW

"Celibacy of the clergy" is defined in the 1906 edition of the *Catholic Pocket Dictionary and* [sic] *Cyclopedia* as "a law of the Church that forbids persons living in the married state to be ordained, and persons in holy orders to marry" (McGovern, p. 51) This is the complete entry.

Centuries of celibacy debates have nothing to do with the ideal of celibate love and service but rather revolve around the question of mandatory celibacy — a requirement for ordination to the priesthood. Canon law states its case clearly:

Clerics are obliged to observe perfect and perpetual continence for the sake of the kingdom of heaven and therefore are obliged to observe celibacy, which is a special gift of God, by which sacred ministers can adhere more easily to Christ with an undivided heart and can more freely dedicate themselves to the service of God and humankind. (Canon 277 1)

Pope John Paul II has also made it crystal clear that he endorses mandatory—that is, legislated—celibacy for any man ordained to the priesthood "despite all the difficulties and objections raised down the centuries." In 1992 he said he "does not wish to leave any doubts in the mind of anyone regarding the Church's firm will to maintain the law" that demands perpetual and freely chosen celibacy for present and future candidates for priestly ordination in the Latin Rite" (Pastores Dabo Vobis #29)."

It should be noted that the law is not simply a prohibition of marriage but a requirement of "perfect and perpetual continence"—that is, the law forbids any sexual activity. Again, it is deceptive to argue that just because one is bound by the law, one is ipso facto complying with the requirements of it.

In the course of 35 years, I have talked with scores of priests who maintain a celibate status in the church while having legal wives and families and civil marriage licenses to prove it. Others bound by church law are involved in long-term affective and sexual relationships, many of which have the characteristics of a marriage. The law is clear, but compliance cannot be presumed. In certain cultures, noncompliance is presumed until proven otherwise.

## Celibacy: A Culture

Because the law mandating celibacy is one of the defining parameters of the Catholic priesthood, many studies of priests confuse survey results about priest (celibate) culture with readings of celibate behavior or reality. For instance, one writer claims, "studies of representative samples of priests... [which] show that they are as mature and as capable of interpersonal intimacy as are married men of similar age and education" (Greeley, 1993, p. 45). Of course, such studies do not discriminate between priests who are practicing celibacy and those who masturbate, have mistresses, or are active in other sexual ways. *Celibate*—that is, priest—culture involves authoritarian alliances, economic bonds, societal privileges, and homosocial parameters, all of which have nothing to do with the reality of celibate practice. Members of the hierarchy can be sexually active and still maintain their offices, just as sexually active (noncelibate) priests can keep their ecclesiastical employment and privilege and their social association with the brotherhood while enjoying a sexually active life.

## Celibacy: Practice

In chapter 4, I outline my estimates of celibate practice, namely, that at any one time at least 50% (48 to 52%) of priests, bound by the law of celibacy and publicly claiming the identity "celibate," are in fact practicing celibacy. That is quite a remarkable assertion if one reflects on its implications. This claim does not mean that these men have reached an ideal, but in reality they are actively involved in the process of celibate achievement, by intention and behavior, free from gross rationalization, denial, or psychologically splitting their sexual energies.

The reasoning that many who are concerned about the church and its ministers use to defend the good name of celibacy is fascinating, if not enlightening. One religious superior who holds a doctoral degree in psychology was incensed at the claim of 50% celibate practice and insisted that 95% of priests practice celibacy at all times. He also asserted that "one or two lapses in the course of a year do not constitute being sexually active." The unsubstantiality of the rhetoric, let alone the logic, cannot hold up under even superficial examination. If one or two lapses in the course of a year can be discounted, why not three or four or even more? Is the cutoff simply subjective or circumstantial? Again, can one or two acts of pedophilia be counted as nonsexually active by a celibate? Similar activity by a person not labeled celibate certainly would be counted as the behavior of a sexually active person.

Similarly, a priest could impregnate two women in the course of 1 year, and using the criterion that one or two lapses do not count, he would still not be considered sexually active.

## Celibacy: An Operational Definition

After years of struggling with the issues of what celibacy is and how it is practiced, I settled on a seven-element operational definition: *Celibacy is a freely chosen dynamic state, usually vowed, that involves an honest and sustained attempt to live without direct sexual gratification in order to serve others productively for a spiritual motive.* This definition is in keeping with the spirit of gospel celibacy as articulated by St. Paul and is validated by the tradition of the Christian church. This operational definition cannot be subsumed under ideal, law, culture, or practice, nor does it obviate the need for discourse on the other categories. Each of the above uses of the word *celibacy* needs clarification and debate.

## CELIBACY: THE CELIBATE/SEXUAL SYSTEM

All of the concepts—ideal, charism, law, culture, celibate/sexual practice—as well as the operational definition of celibacy, are included in the concept of celibacy. Accurate definitions are crucial to any progress in the understanding of celibacy; equally important is the awareness that the differing meanings of celibacy are interrelated and interdependent at an operational level. Clarity demands both the precise definition of the different meanings of celibacy at the same time as we acknowledge that there is a celibate field that can be understood only by examination of the system in which it arises, sustains, and preserves itself and by measuring the effects it has on those who enter its sphere of influence. This study is an analysis of the function and structure of the celibate/sexual system.

Naturally, religiously motivated celibate practice will not be diminished by careful examination and debate, but deficits and dysfunction of the system will not be able to be generalized or rationalized away by one or the other of its diverse meanings.

The careful delineation of the usages and the meanings of celibacy has allowed me to analyze its distinctions and different valences. The current crisis that exposes the sexual activity of priests who are presumed celibate forces any interested student to question what celibate means when applied to priests who remain in good standing within the celibate/sexual system and maintain ecclesiastical power in spite of and sometimes because of sexually active lives. The task of getting celibacy accurately defined challenges all who care about spirituality and authentic tradition. Refined, accurate definitions of celibacy alone can demand and ensure accountability.

Keeping celibacy mysterious and part of a secret system fosters corruption. *Secrecy and accountability cannot coexist.* Vagueness and imprecision are enemies of truth. Open discourse on celibacy and an examination of the relationship of the celibate/sexual system to child abuse have great implications for a church that stabilizes its power around a reality it refuses to examine.

# 4

# PATTERNS OF
# CELIBATE/SEXUAL ADJUSTMENT

*Secrecy can mask reality. It may be that the current discipline that mandatory priestly celibacy is holding partly because a significant number of priests are in practice supported by hidden relationships, of many different kinds. People involved in spiritual direction and accompaniment are aware of this. There are difficult questions here of honesty, integrity and openness.*

Father David Standley

*I am not at all confident that celibacy is in fact being observed.*

Franjo Cardinal Seper
Archbishop of Zagreb

For the average person, sex is difficult to discuss openly, personally, and honestly. The current sexual symptoms affecting Catholic priests demonstrate over and over again the natural reluctance and aversion to talking openly about one's sexual experiences. If one's essential identity as a priest depends—at least in the eyes of the public—on not having a sexual life, that is, observing "perfect and perpetual chastity," public exposure or any public statements about one's sexuality become even more tricky and delicate. Priests encapsulated by such constraints have their own language and signs by which they share their sexual concerns, temptations, preferences, accomplishments, and failures. The system is sealed, bounded by confession, confidences, innuendos, and shared understandings, both verbal and nonverbal. Theirs is largely a secret world, hidden from the eyes and ears of outsiders and closely guarded and defended by mechanisms that are inculcated subliminally into the system. The elements protecting this secret world form a barrier of immense strength between private and public, with deep foundations anchored in unconscious mental mechanisms mixed with magic of childhood aspirations—where things are as we wish them to be—where fantasy instead of reality reigns supreme.

These barriers to fact, which constitute the secret system, cause the greatest problems for the person who truly wishes to be celibate. The process of celibacy is based on uncompromising self-confrontation and truth about one's self—radical truth—and about one's most intimate stirrings in relationship to self and others. This is why adequate language and discourse are so essential to the process. Celibacy/sexuality is not an area in which media sound bites and glib observations can capture the complex inner reality of a spiritual life.

When an American prelate faced television cameras in November 1993 to deny charges that he had sexually abused a minor 20 years earlier, he was faced with the dilemma of defending himself and exposing his celibate/sexual adjustment—a daunting challenge—when one reporter asked if he were living a sexually active life. Rather than a simple "No," the Cardinal said, "I am 65 years old, and all my life I have always lived a chaste and celibate life."

If this statement stands, given the official teaching this man publicly endorses, it means that he has never voluntarily entertained a sexual thought, word, desire, or action either during his developmental or adolescent years or at any time since his ordination to the priesthood. Such idealized virginal existence is hardly necessary for a good conscientious Christian. More, it is not believable. But developmental struggles or even failures in the pursuit of goals may become the kind of breaks of which Ernest Hemingway speaks when he says, "Life breaks us all and afterwards many are strong at the broken places."

A conscientious and actively celibate priest gives an example of the pressure of understanding the reality and the image of celibacy when private becomes public:

> A priest I know from [my] diocese was one of three who got into trouble for molesting boys over the summer. I was assigned with him when I was first ordained and felt for him. I cannot imagine the pain that he is going through. The other two I do not know. The priest I know fondled an 18-year-old at a party—a party held in the rectory for his being named a monsignor. Actually, it didn't surprise me. What did surprise me was that the kid ran off to the police that night, at two in the morning. The priest was drunk, and you would have thought that the kid would have let it go. It was all over the media.

Priests' sexual activity being made public may cause problems, confusion, wonder, pity, shame, or scorn, but that does little to help us understand what celibacy is or how it is practiced by those who profess it. The media provide a window into the secret world of celibacy/sexuality. The priest reporting the incident above says a great deal about the system through his own reaction, which reveals the tendency to accept the secret reality, excuse it, and hope others invited into the inner circle will understand, forgive, and keep silent about the humanity of the sexually active and drunken priest. Note that the priest gives less thought to the disillusioned victim. The serious student needs more than a glimpse to understand both the negative and positive workings of the entity. The reality of celibate/sexual practice and an accurate picture of its range of practice should be of prime concern to those who endorse and sponsor it as a mode of religious service and spiritual witness.

The selfless love—the profound altruism of which celibacy is meant to be a concomitant element and to which it is meant to be a witness and proof—is a matter of wonder and amazement to those who wish to believe in celibate service as a reality. And indeed celibacy is a reality, far beyond what skeptics and cynics can imagine. But celibacy is not a simple reality—or a celluloid rerun of *Going My Way*, the 1944 Academy Award–winning movie that portrayed human priests. One must turn back to Boccaccio, Chaucer, Rabelais, and Hugo, as well as to the saints and hagiographers, if one is to glean a fair and honest picture of the real pattern of celibate/sexual practice.

Observation and recording of data form the bedrock of any scientific understanding. When one observes a group—a culture—and records how that culture operates, the product is called ethnography. This seemingly humble and tedious work takes patience and a participant observer. Edward Sapir said that anthropology (and ethnography) does for a group what psychotherapy does for an individual—registers, reveals, and records the inner workings and structure.

To me the work of 34 years has been fraught with excitement, wonder, continuing challenge, and even awe. It came naturally. Whether by luck, destiny, or grace, I found myself asking questions in 1960 to which I assumed there would be ready and sure answers—somewhere. The more I sought, the less I found. Even today many within the celibate/sexual system refuse to look at themselves as part of a culture apart, as interesting, challenging, and with important implications about human behaviors, yet as distinct as any observed by Franz Boas or Edward Sapir. I owe psychoanalyst Leo Bartemeier and anthropologist Margaret Mead a deep debt for their encouragement and interest in my earliest fumblings and confirmation of an idiosyncratic mode of procedure where either instinctively or reflectively they knew conventional methods were inadequate to the task at hand—the study of sexuality within clerical celibacy. At face, it involves the study of that which does not, by definition, exist.

One thing is sure: anyone undertaking further study of the celibate/sexual system of priests must acknowledge that the *system* produces men who are celibate or sexually active in some kind of a relatively stable and predictable pattern.

In light of my observations, which included the celibate/sexual stories of more than 1,500 Catholic priests (during the years 1960–85) about whom I had enough data to evaluate their celibate/sexual pattern or development, I made estimates of the pattern of celibate/sexual adjustment of priests in the United States. Priests who shared their celibate/sexual development during periods of 5, 15, and a few now for 34 years form the backbone of the profile of celibate/sexual adjustment. At the height of my inquiry, 25 psychoanalysts, psychiatrists, psychologists, and historians supplied invaluable data, and we were able to check our observations several times in 10 groups of priests in diocesan or religious settings.

## THOSE WHO PROFESS OR PRACTICE CELIBACY

Classical and traditional literature about celibacy is fraught with presuppositions that a celibate regularly achieves the ideal, and this assumption is the starting point of most presentations. But the serious practitioner of celibacy does not take for granted the reality of this assumption. Even in their last years of training for the priesthood, my theological students frequently asked, "How is it possible?" Priests ordained for many years ask the same question, or frankly say, "I don't think celibacy is possible."

Most priests are witness to a stretch for the ideal rather than a firm grasp on it. I have avoided assumptions and sought an accurate portrayal of the state of celibate practice as it exists. I remain convinced that such a representation is more supportive of those who strive for the fulfillment of the ideal than are depictions that avoid the real difficulty in its attainment or that offer simple ascetic schemes for success.

## Achievement

At any one time, 2% of vowed celibate clergy can be said to have achieved celibacy—that is, they have successfully negotiated each step of celibate development at the more or less appropriate stage and are characterologically so firmly established that their state is, for all intents and purposes, irreversible. These truly are the eunuchs of whom Christ spoke in the New Testament (Matthew 19:12). Even more, they are from among that group who have made the decision for celibacy, as Balducelli (1976) describes it, from the beginning, surmounting the crisis of intimacy in favor of celibacy; the crisis of responsibility resolved by community; and the crisis of integrity resolved by permanent commitment (pp. 219–242).

In my experience, this group of men is awesome. They manifest an interior freedom and integration that unite their individuality and their service. Their spirituality is marked by their efforts and achievements.

In this group I witnessed the integrative and transformative power of the celibate reality, which of necessity must transcend corporate and institutional power or status. Celibacy must be personal or it is nothing. Regularly I was struck by the practical effects and manifestations these men demonstrate in the most casual and natural way. Sexual integration rests easily on their shoulders because they have faced their inner sexual structure so thoroughly; gender, orientation, sexual desire have been confronted, penetrated, and absorbed in the loneliness of a spiritual realm and perception of spiritual reality. Most people can only access their spirituality and the reality of transcendence with the aid of direct sexual encounter—love within a sexual relationship.

Celibate men led me to reconsider scripture; through them I gained an appreciation for the origins of celibate love and an understanding of St. Paul. They convinced me that the core of Christian and celibate experience was in St. Paul's exclamation, "There is no longer Jew or Greek, slave or free, male or female; we are all one in Jesus Christ" (Galatians 3:29).

If the celibate/sexual system is to be transformed from within, if a theology of sexuality develops that has credibility and foundation in the true nature of sex, this group and their experience will be crucial factors. These male celibates are not afraid of sex; they are not competitive with married Christians; they do not fear or disdain women; they do not confuse celibacy with power or domination. Celibacy is their deeply personal, hard-won adjustment—they own it: it is their spiritual tie to the Reality most of them call God. These men are rare and a precious spiritual resource (Fiorenza, 1992, pp. 160–236).

## CELIBATE CONSOLIDATION

There is also a group of men, 8%, who, although their course of celibate practice has not been without its missteps and fumblings and, for some, serious reversals in the past, enjoy a present condition so refined and in which the practice of celibacy is so firmly established that the group can be said to have consolidated the practice of celibacy to such a degree that it approaches the ideal.

This group represents those who clearly have the charism of celibacy. It also includes brave, courageous, and devoted men who say that although they feel they lacked the charism, they have embraced— even if at times unenthusiastically—the discipline required by a church they love because of a work they truly feel is their own.

Priests in this group can discuss their battle scars with a certain amount of gratitude for wisdom gained and disaster avoided. Perhaps they are a bit like the band of early Christian followers of Christ who came to the endeavor with mixed motives and unexamined emotion. Some, at one time eager for a place at the right hand in the kingdom, sooner or later came to a realization of the truth: "The Kingdom of God is within you." I heard one priest, firmly consolidated in celibate practice, lament the number of priests "who had never fallen in love." He felt that they had missed a dimension of the human reality that celibate consolidation entails.

The vast majority of these men, as I have experienced and evaluated them, have escaped one of the most common psychological pitfalls of men who practice celibacy but cannot be said either to consolidate or to achieve full integration. That pitfall is a solidification of an adolescent psychosexual pattern of adaptation. Psychic adolescence must be transcended to consolidate or achieve celibacy as a full integrative and transformative force within one's spiritual perception of Reality.

## CELIBATE PRACTICE

In addition to the above-named groups, 40% of priests are, at any one time, practicing celibacy (see Figure 4.1); that is, they are sexually abstinent by intent, and on a daily basis they operate realistically in ways that assure their active involvement in the process of celibacy.

Their practice does not obviate an occasional lapse, but it does exclude any pattern of noncelibate involvement or adjustment.

Celibacy in practice is not a legalistic or transient figment. It is a quest of spiritual relationship and religious reality based on unflinching self-knowledge and radical truth about one's innermost desires (Stewart, 1990).

A person who is technically in the state of grace at the moment cannot be counted among the practicing if he is involved in a pattern of sexual activity that will be repeated when the opportunity presents itself. This group is quite labile. Young priests may be among its ranks for a period of 5 or 6 years and then abandon it to become experimenters—those looking for sexual experience, oftentimes motivated by normal but delayed curiosity. Some return to celibate practice after filling some gaps in their retarded adolescent development. Others progress to a sexual relationship with either a woman or a man, where they can remain for a prolonged period. After a few years a number of priests return to the group of those practicing celibacy. This history can precede consolidation of celibate adjustment later in life or may remain more or less fluid and open to additional periods of noncelibate involvement.

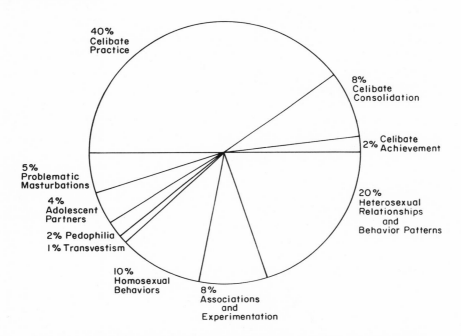

**Figure 4.1  Celibate/Sexual Adjustment** (adapted from Sipe, 1990a).

Confession and absolution do not assure that one has moved from the sexually active to the celibacy-practicing group. That determination is sophisticated, subtle, and again demands radical honesty with oneself. For instance, some priest child abusers will compulsively go to confession after every act of sex with a minor; they may even insist that their sexual partner go to confession. But the reception of the sacrament for these priests is equally as compulsed as is their sexual activity. They must in honesty be numbered among the sexual abusers of minors and not pretend that they are practicing celibacy or are in any way involved in the celibate process. (I wish to make an exception here of masturbation, an activity that technically is a violation of celibacy. However, 80% of men dedicated to celibacy do masturbate on occasion.)

A solid number among the group of sexually abstinent are also actually arrested or limited to the degree that celibacy can transform their lives and integrate their personalities and relationships. They are men whose personality structures have consolidated around a set of characteristics that can only be described as adolescent.

As I mentioned earlier, the celibate/sexual system and the education of priests institutionalize and reward an adolescent level of adjustment. Certainly it is clear from the process of celibacy that if one is to take full advantage of celibacy as a lifestyle and spiritual adjustment, one cannot indulge such a fixation or regression without sacrificing some of the potential of celibacy. Such an adjustment should not be denigrated, but it must be acknowledged for what it is and not elevated beyond its realistic value. It is not the ideal, but it *is*.

Anna Freud's classic description of an adolescent is relevant here. In more than 30 years of teaching and counseling priests, I have used it repeatedly with students and teachers as a checklist and yardstick to measure the individual and institutional adjustments of priests.

> Adolescents are excessively egoistic, regarding themselves as the center of the universe and the sole object of interest, and yet at no time in later life are they capable of so much self-sacrifice and devotion. They form the most passionate love relations, only to break them off as abruptly as they began them. On the one hand, they throw themselves enthusiastically into the life of the community and, on the other, they have an overpowering longing for solitude. They oscillate between blind submission to some self-chosen leader and defiant rebellion against any and every authority. They are selfish and materially minded and at the same time full of lofty idealism. They are ascetic but will suddenly

plunge into instinctual indulgence of the most primitive character. At times their behavior to other people is rough and inconsiderate, yet they themselves are extremely touchy. Their moods veer between light-hearted optimism and the blackest pessimism. Sometimes they will work with indefatigable enthusiasm and at other times they are sluggish and apathetic. (1974, pp. 137–138)

Bishops are aware of this clerical deficiency, which amounts to an adolescent lock. A study of the psychological maturity of American priests published by the Bishops' Committee on Priestly Spirituality states the case clearly:

A large proportion of American priests are underdeveloped psychologically. This does not mean that they are sick, but that their growth has been arrested. Generally they have not worked through the problems of intimacy, and their level of maturity is lower than their chronological age. They do not relate deeply or closely to other people. . . .

As a matter of fact, however, the spiritual life of these priests is generally of a piece with their emotional arrest. Their faith tends to be superficial and not integrated into the rest of their lives. They tend to excuse themselves from the pain of the growing process into full maturity in Christ. The priesthood, the Church and the faith are used as screens and cover-ups for psychological inadequacy; religious ideals remain abstract and unactualized. (National Conference of Catholic Bishops, 1973, p. 3)

What should be acknowledged is that the system holds certain men at a level beneath their native and spiritual potential. The celibate process, like all of life adjustments, confronts men with a series of choices and crises. One inevitable step comes at a time when the priest must buy into the spirit (with all of its attendant lonely spiritual responsibilities) or sell out to the system (with all of its power compensations).

A middle-aged priest confronted his good friend, an auxiliary bishop, for not standing up for certain principles he knew the bishop thought important. When the priest questioned the compromises the bishop was making, it became clear that the bishop was being a good boy in conforming to directives he abhorred on moral grounds so that he could move on to his own diocese someday. "I only lie when I have to," the bishop said.

The priest evaluated the behavior of his friend correctly. He said, "I thought celibacy was in the tradition of martyrdom. It was supposed to give us the courage of our convictions." He added how sad it was to see a grown man have to kowtow and please others, not make waves, to succeed in the system.

J. F. Powers, one of the most significant literary voices, along with Ignazio Silone, to describe the priest and the clerical culture, tends to portray priests from this group of practicing celibates. They truly are the footsoldiers who maintain the system. They are human; they are vulnerable; they are struggling and should be given credit for their efforts. What Powers's portrayals provide more than anything is a mirror for reflection, into which any priest can look and ask himself in Powers's words, "What am I willing to go to the cross for?" or "Is there *anything* I am willing to go to the cross for?" The meaning of celibacy cannot be separated from that question.

## HETEROSEXUAL RELATIONSHIPS AND BEHAVIOR PATTERNS

We estimate that at any one time 20% of priests are involved in a sexual relationship with a woman—marked by a certain stability—or involved in a more or less identifiable pattern of sexual relationships. I should note here that in African, Latin, and South American cultures the "priest's woman" and even married bishops seem to be taken for granted. These are phenomena that merit serious study. At present I have only anecdotal material, but it is highly suggestive because of impeccable and knowledgeable sources in those locales. For instance, one bishop from a South American diocese said that he had difficulty finding a suitable candidate for the episcopate who had not fathered a child.

Eyewitness accounts of married bishops and priests in parts of Africa are too numerous to be ignored and, although reliable, as yet too spotty for drawing general conclusions. Celibacy in these diverse cultures offers the ethnologist the fascinating challenge of comparing different results from the same religious custom and requirement, inculcated in more or less standardized educational curriculum, maintained and united under one universal authority, and espousing one well-defined celibate/sexual standard.

## SEXUAL EXPERIMENTATION

At any one time, 8% of priests are involved in sexual experimentation. Sometimes this is part of the prolonged adolescent-like phase during which, in clandestine ways, priests pursue their sexual curiosity aroused by pastoral work and broader social association. In 1985 I concluded that this activity was mostly heterosexual. In the past 10 years, with an additional 1,200 clerical histories available for review, I now estimate that this experimentation is evenly divided between heterosexual and homosexual outlets.

## HOMOSEXUAL RELATIONSHIPS AND BEHAVIORS

In chapter 7 I will deal at length with this difficult, complex, and substantial reality within the celibate/sexual system. Fifteen percent of priests involve themselves with homosexual relationships or identifiable patterns beyond experimentation. In 1985 I estimated that 23% of Catholic priests in the United States could claim a homosexual orientation. I have consistently tried to identify homosexuality among Catholic clergy just as heterosexuality is—as an element of self-discovery and self-disclosure (Nash, 1990).

Homosexual orientation is not an accusation but an acknowledgment of fact, even if the entity is frequently misjudged. In the past 10 years my data have been examined by those who also had available to them the same additional histories I had. I now estimate that at any one time 30% of Catholic priests have a homosexual orientation. But I find no proportionate increase in sexual behavior; that is, roughly 50% of homosexually oriented priests are celibate just as are the heterosexually oriented.

One must be very cautious not to confuse sexual orientation and the object of sexual desire, as for instance in cases of same-sex child abuse. These are two separate factors among several to be accounted for in understanding the sexual behavior with minors among those who claim celibacy.

## TRANSVESTISM

One percent of priests can be identified as transvestites. By psychiatric definition cross-dressing is a problem only when "arousal and facilitation or attainment of orgasm are responsive to, and dependent upon, wearing clothing, especially underwear, of the other sex" (Money, 1986, p. 272). Indeed, to draw my conclusion, I had a sufficient number of informants report behavior strictly defined as transvestism. For most priests it is of no sexual consequence that the ministry occasionally demands that one wear skirts or flowing robes, which, from a secular point of view, could be thought of as feminine. The silks, satins, brocades, laces, and ermines required in some ceremonies are no more than a uniform to the vast majority of clergy.

A deeper understanding of the clerical transvestite, as in the understanding of the other manifestations of sexual elements, requires an examination of transvestism in its strictest clinical sense. In addition, the church must look at the psychosexual developmental dynamics underlying it and the system that chooses, perpetuates, and values certain forms of dress as emblems of power.

St. Jerome, who died in 420, was one of the most colorful Fathers of the Church. He was a staunch and implacable proponent of clerical celibacy, a scholar who spent a half-century translating the Scriptures. His sexual life found some autobiographical witness, like that of his contemporary, St. Augustine, especially from the record of Jerome's dreams; they provide provocative intimations that are worthy of a psychohistory.

History records a famous incident in which Jerome appeared in the monks' choir wearing a woman's dress. Biographers have called the occurrence a mistake on Jerome's part, saying that he fell into a trap set by monks who were jealous of his popularity with rich Roman women—friendships that were the subject of much gossip. According to biographers, an evil monk substituted a woman's dress for Jerome's habit, and in the dark Jerome put it on, not realizing what it was. Whatever the motives or facts of the incident, it propelled Jerome to leave Rome, never to return. He subsequently spent 4 years in the desert and was known to wear a hair shirt rather than soft garments.

Jerome's life and dream records make more sense if we understand this episode of cross-dressing not simply as a trick of wicked monks but as a manifestation of Jerome's sexual development, which must be reconciled with his brilliance and later sanctity. His asceticism and hair shirt, although not entirely uncommon practices at that time in Christianity, can be seen as a reaction to his having been caught in behavior that was little understood by his contemporary religious observers at that time.

There is a broader systemic problem with ceremonial dress. What impact do the preservation and sanctification of ritual dress have on the celibate/sexual identity and role of power? Certainly some important questions are raised when a male-dominated power system solidifies its ritual identity in robes that lack gender specificity, from historical eras—especially the Roman and the Renaissance. Or even more strikingly, why glorify what might commonly be considered feminine by those who exclude women from the robes and roles of power that the garments represent?

## SEXUAL ABUSE OF MINORS

Chapter 1 has already outlined the scope of this symptom as it has erupted into public consciousness. My estimate of 6% (2% sex activity with prepuberty minors, 4% with adolescents) is being verified over and over again in one diocese and religious community after another. Father Andrew Greeley, a sociologist from Chicago, estimated in 1993, from his own database, that between 2,000 and 4,000 American priests abuse minors (that amounts to between 4 and 8%). One official church representative estimated that 2% of priests are abusers.

In January 1994 a representative from the National Conference of Catholic Bishops said that 400 priests had been identified as abusers; and the costs of treatment, legal fees, and settlements to victims have amounted to $100 million. I consider these figures defensive. Leaders of the victims' movement judge that spokesmen for the bishops do not take into account those other priests who are known — at least by their own bishop or religious superiors — to have abused, nor are the sealed financial settlements that bind the compensated victims to silence counted.

I have confidence in my estimate because one third of my informants were the sexual partners of priests. Prior to 1988 few officials gave credence to the stories of victims. Since the beginning of my observations I have trusted the experience of laywomen and laymen as valid in reading the practice and failures of celibacy.

## THE VALIDITY OF ESTIMATES

How valid are these estimates? Even the reader who is accustomed to think only in terms of the ideal may be open to considering the realism of these figures if he or she recalls the history of clerical celibacy, the complexity of sexual development, and the difficulties of spiritual integration. It is important that those who care about religion seek and face facts.

The average person is not scandalized by the portrayal of clerics by Chaucer in *The Canterbury Tales*. The Monk has an aversion to the quiet and seclusion of his monastery, and he is consumed with his interest in material things, good food, and worldly pleasures.

Chaucer's Friar is frankly evil and cunning—using the confessions he hears as a ruse for financial profit. Another implication is clear—he is sexually familiar with another man's wife. The Pardoner, that special envoy of papal power, is drawn as an unattractive homosexual. The Nun's Priest betrays his vanity and vacuousness in his story of the cock and the fox. The Canon's alchemy and duplicity are exposed by his Yeoman.

All of these characters are believable, and each has his parallel in modern-day ministry. However, just as true to life is the Oxford Cleric—the serious student who aspires to the ministry and church office—and the Parson—the poor and devoted parish priest, of whom Chaucer says,

> This fine example to his flock he gave,
> That first he wrought and afterwards he taught;
> Out of the gospel then that text he caught,
> And this figure he added thereunto—
> That, if gold rust, what shall poor iron do?
> For if the priest be foul, in whom we trust,
> What wonder if a layman yield to lust?
> And shame it is, if priest take thought for keep,
> A shitty shepherd, shepherding clean sheep,
> Well ought a priest example good to give,
> By his own cleanness, how his flock should live
> . . . . . .
> There is nowhere a better priest, I trowe.
> He had no thirst for pomp or reverence,
> Nor made himself a special, spiced conscience,
> But Christ's own love, and His apostles' twelve,
> He taught, but first he followed it himself. (1934, pp. 16–17)

This is the kind of priest the celibate/sexual system intends to produce. The reality, however, more closely reflects Chaucer's panoply of characters and their sexual adjustments.

The publication of my figures in 1990 did result in a firestorm of denials and rejections—the most strident and ardent—before the study was available for review.

The objections have been: "It can't be true; no one can know that." "It is invalid because one third of the informants were in some form of psychotherapy and don't represent all priests." "It doesn't count because the informants do not constitute a random sample." "It's true but you should not print it." "It's invalid because one third of the informants are not priests." It is easy to understand the difficulty of scholars who are well trained and rely on sociological, epidemi-ological, and demographic methods of survey for their understanding and conclusions. The study of sexual/celibate behavior in a culture bound by a celibate promise does not immediately lend itself to any of these methods of investigation. The long, cumbersome data col-lection in which I have indulged is nonetheless accepted by some scholars who are well established in traditional methods of investi-gation and hold responsible positions.

The solidity and modesty of my estimates have been ac-knowledged by enough people even within the establishment to encourage further study and refinement. Dean Hoge, a sociologist experienced in research on ecclesiastical topics, said publicly, "they are the best figures we have at this time" (1990). Author Lisa De Nike recorded Hoge's response in her article "The Challenges of Celibacy":

> Dean Hoge, a sociology professor at Catholic University in Washington, D.C., believes Sipe's research is thorough and hon-est. But he also says that fear of Sipe's findings makes it difficult for church officials to take it seriously.
>
> The quickest way to lose friends is to talk about [Sipe's] work and theories and to question the celibate system...Sipe is an honorable guy trying to do something worthwhile for the church. He's not trying to be sensational. I'd trust his judgment, because he has compiled his research carefully. (1994, p. 22)

Several seasoned religious superiors reviewed all of my esti-mates both during the progress of the study and after its completion and found them on target. More than one bishop has said that my figures are in complete accord with their years of experience. And on May 28, 1993—on camera for the BBC—José Cardinal Sanchez, Prefect of the Vatican Congregation for the Clergy, said in response to a review of my estimates of celibate/sexual adjustment of American priests, "I have no reason to doubt the validity of those figures."

## METHOD

For the present, the description of my method in *A Secret World* (Sipe, 1990a) is sufficient to honor the anonymity of all institutions and the confidentiality of all participants in the study. The data I have collected over more than 30 years, from which I have made the foregoing estimates of celibate/sexual behavior and adjustment of priests in the United States and which lead me to the analysis of the function and structure of the celibate/sexual system of the Catholic Church (see Parts II and III of this book), could not have been gathered by conventional methods. Conventional sociological surveys or self-reporting opinion polls could not have captured the dimensions of sexuality within the system of celibacy. Although Father Victor T. Kotze of Newville, South Africa, who studied clerical stress in a strictly controlled random sample of priests, found a frequency of sexual involvement at over 40.5%, there is no longitudinal observation to delineate the process or the behaviors.

In her 1992 study on intimacy among vowed religious, psychologist Shelia Murphy found that 62% of her male respondents "reported being sexually active, 32 percent said their partners were exclusively male and 58 percent exclusively female... actual behaviors do not necessarily coincide with reported orientation, and vice versa" (p. 63).

Certainly there are many aspects of the forbidden and secret sexual lives of priests that need study if a refined understanding of celibacy and its significance for the future of life are to be supported. But the subject matter and the population do not lend themselves to easy objective observation and analysis. For me, the psychotherapeutic perspective and setting provided the arena and the long-term support for self-disclosure in which memory and development, intention and discovery could be elicited, recorded, analyzed, and validated. In one way I have indulged in guerilla research that has a long history, noble tradition, and productive track record.

Guerilla research includes the use of unconventional methods, or cross-disciplinary skills to address unanswerable questions. It is important that those of us who are genuinely interested in religion and spirituality think creatively about age-old verities and assumptions. Again, we can learn from the process of science.

Dr. Herbert Hauptman, a mathematician, is an excellent example of the use of guerilla research; he solved a problem in chemistry that was considered unsolvable by chemists themselves. Dr. P. A. Griffiths pointed out Hauptman's contribution at a dedication of the mathematics building of the Institute for Advanced Study at Princeton University on April 3, 1993:

> Around 1950 a scientist named Herbert Hauptman, who was trained as a mathematician, became interested in a puzzle regarding the structure of crystals. Chemists had known since early in the century that x-rays passing through crystals are scattered, or diffracted, when they strike atoms within the crystal. . . . This problem had baffled chemists for over forty years.

It was Hauptman's genius to realize that this issue could be formulated purely as a mathematical problem, and one that had a very elegant solution. . . . Dr. Hauptman recalled in a speech a few years ago that prior to 1950, his work was regarded as ridiculous, and he himself as rather foolish. . . . Nonetheless, in 1985 he was awarded the Nobel Prize in Chemistry for his use of classical mathematics to solve a puzzle that had defeated generations of chemists. (1993, p. 596)

In a self-critique of his *Theory of the Novel*, Georg Lukacs includes a meaningful aside: "(at that time it escaped the notice of the younger ones among us that men of talent were arriving at their genuinely sound conclusions in spite of the method rather than by means of it)" (1987, p. 13).

I cite these men as examples of the kind of minds and heroes I have looked to as I pondered the questions about celibacy/sexuality, convinced that there is not yet any one adequate method for studying spiritual realities and the complex ambiguities inherent in them. Most importantly, I point to these models from science and literature knowing that the questions of sexuality facing the church in crisis are considered by many as either already solved or unsolvable—certainly unchangeable. They are neither. But we cannot hope to address our questions with less conflict or creativity than science addresses its thorny problems.

Perception of reality—close observation, and the clear record of that observation—is the bedrock on which progress in the knowledge of how things work—even holy things—is made. Time sorts out what is lasting perception and what is a passing glimpse, a partial perspective, or an illusion. Truth is the goal. Open discourse is a means of clarifying and sharpening perception and sharing data.

Emotional argumentation is a useless indulgence. Resistances and defenses that keep self-knowledge at bay are inevitable but very costly in every way for religion and for the Catholic Church in light of the dimensions of the sexual crisis that faces them.

# PART II
# FUNCTION AND FAILURE

# 5

# SYSTEM:
# FUNCTION/DYSFUNCTION

*No good purpose is served by trying to pretend that only priests who leave [the priesthood] have found celibacy difficult. It is even more unhelpful to pretend that those who stay are all keeping the rules. . . . It is only when we begin to be honest and open about the problems of celibacy for those who do not leave that debate will get anywhere.*

Father Brian O'Sullivan

*The human's elaborately developed cerebral cortex and complex psychology contribute to making him unique in some respects, but, despite these specializations, systems theory assumes that* homo sapiens *is far more like other life forms than different from them.*

Murray Bowen, M.D.

What distinguishes priests from other men is not their individual psychology but the shared choice each makes to enter a system that theoretically rejects all sexual activity for themselves and teaches that any sexual act outside marriage is gravely sinful. How that system functions and how each priest adapts to it form a spectrum of religious witness from frank sanctity to basest hypocrisy; at stake is the operational system that surrounds belief and behavior.

It is impossible to understand the real nature and dimensions of the current sexual crisis in the church without some appreciation of the physiology of the clerical system.

This chapter explores seven elements that are essential to the function of the celibate/sexual system: (1) the balance between the celibate and sexual elements; (2) private and public elements; (3) homosexuality; (4) spiritual and temporal power; (5) the dynamic of guilt and forgiveness; (6) women: idealized and denigrated; (7) secrecy.

## THE CELIBATE DIFFERENCE?

Priests are not the same as other men when it comes to sexuality. One set of experiences extending over a period of several years vividly highlighted the celibate/sexual tension peculiar to men preparing for the priesthood. During the 1970s I was lecturing on human sexual development at an urban Catholic college and simultaneously presenting the identical material to seminarians who were in their final years of preparation before ordination to the priesthood.

Each semester prior to presenting any material, or even the syllabus, I asked each student to give a written response to the question, In your experience, what are the 10 most commonly asked questions about human sexual development? The college students' responses were compiled and divided according to general content in 15 categories from male and female anatomy and physiology (i.e., What size is the average penis? or What is the process of menstruation?) to ethical considerations (i.e., Can love remove evil from intercourse? or What is sexual freedom?).

Over five semesters 262 lay students responded with 253 distinct questions. In 1985, 10 years after I stopped teaching the course to lay students, I administered the same question to 55 sociology students at the same Catholic college. Their responses fell into the same 15 category divisions. The only remarkable change in the distribution of questions was an increase in the number of questions about venereal diseases (herpes and AIDS).

The responses of the 63 theological students were so remarkably distinct from those of the Catholic college men and women that I could not factor them in with those from the lay students. Several seminarians wrote simply, "I can't respond to this." Others responded with almost incoherent ramblings about the "meaning of life"—productions that could be labeled dissociative. Others could list three or four questions (i.e., Isn't the church's teaching clear?). One man responded, "I have no questions. I know it all." Which of course betrayed his overpersonalization of a question that was clearly noninvasive: a solicitation of most frequently *asked* questions. Only two respondents were in any way comparable to the lay students.

Certainly the celibate striving expected of each seminarian had something to do with the remarkable discrepancies between the responses of the two groups. But clearly it was more than a simple reflection of personal differences between men and women who were mostly looking forward to marriage and men who had actively selected a lifestyle that obviated marriage. The system of celibate culture, already operative in the seminary, manifested itself in the collective resistance to facing issues necessary for sexual or celibate maturity.

One afternoon in January 1991 a priest whom I did not know stopped me on the sidewalk of my hometown. He walked with a cane, and I guessed his age to be in the mid-sixties. In a gruff tone he barked, "Did you write that book [*A Secret World*]?" I pleaded guilty. Without altering his tone he said, "Good! Except your numbers are too low." In a more conversational tone he went on to tell me that as a deacon, 3 months before his ordination to the priesthood, he approached the rector of the seminary because he was concerned about sexual feelings and had questions about celibacy. The rector's response was, "Don't worry, after ordination it will all fall into place." The priest, resuming his harsh tone said, "It doesn't!" He walked off; I've never met him again.

The idea that "It will all fall into place" is an eloquent code phrase opening the secret door into the celibate/sexual system and how it works. The system is a brotherhood of guaranteed employment, respectability, prestige, and power. The price is the appearance of celibacy; for all of the benefits accrue automatically as long as the semblance of celibacy is publicly or officially espoused. One can divorce oneself from celibate practice for brief or extended periods of time or resist the celibate process altogether and still maintain all of the benefits of the celibate/sexual system. The secrets that mask the celibate system are transpersonal: they are the covert implementations of power. This is precisely why opinion polls that measure liberal or conservative attitudes about doctrine or morals have little or nothing to do with how an individual practices celibacy—or lives his belief. Power is conferred and maintained unless public exposure threatens scandal. Personal exposure is not even the greatest danger: psychological revelation—how the system works, how it all falls into place—poses a higher degree of threat to institutionalized power and is thus assiduously resisted.

Many women who have had long-term sexual and affectionate relationships with priests are caught up short when the priest is forced into a decision because of public exposure of their relationship. He must give up his love affair or lose the benefits of the system. In the words of one superior to a priest so exposed, "You cannot maintain long-term obligations to the community and to another individual person. [Our religious community] must protect itself against legal liabilities in this time of great sensitivity to sexual misconduct by priests." Thus, 20- and 30-year relationships are brutally ended, at least for the women involved.

## THE PHYSIOLOGY OF THE SYSTEM IN CRISIS

At one time I focused almost exclusively on the personal practice, process, and achievement of celibacy. This was in line with the ascetic and biohistorical tradition. One can study the life of Dorothy Day, Gandhi, Pope John XXIII, or of any celibate ideal and extrapolate the factors that made celibate practice imperative and important to them and then use such a person as a role model or ego ideal. The personal process of celibacy holds great significance for the reality of the religious entity called celibacy. Religious authorities know a great deal about the sexual lives of priests, but until the recent crisis wherein victims have appealed to the media and the court-room—open forums—that knowledge has been locked within *the system*, ferreted out only by undeniable revelations, indictments, and depositions.

One jolt into realizing that celibacy was not merely a personal ideal and achievement came again while I was teaching theologians in their final years of preparation for ordination. Teaching a course on pastoral identity, I was struggling with the challenge to help these men internalize the integrative and transformative factors that could help them become pastors and servants of their people. I used novels of vocation—Ignazio Silone's *Bread and Wine,* Graham Greene's *The Power and the Glory,* Sinclair Lewis's *Elmer Gantry*—to help students access their own experiences and reflect on the essence of the pastoral person. We spent a great deal of time in class discussion.

One day, to focus the internal, personal, and spiritual dimensions of the pastoral reality, I asked the students to discuss how they would be priests—pastors to their people—if they came to an area where there were no parishes, chaplaincies, or institutions set up to welcome them. I was surprised that more than half of the group said they would not be priests if that were the situation. It became more and more apparent that to many a *parish* meant a set of buildings rather than a group of people; that for some a priest was an employee; that celibate striving for many was part of a group and institutional bonding, not an ascetic and personal spiritual commitment.

I am indebted to these men and to a host of priests, religious superiors, and bishops who have helped me understand that beyond personal discipline, celibacy in the Roman Catholic Church is a system, it has a physiology. That system can function well, in balance and meeting its stated goals; or it can be diverted, corrupted, and perverted. The history of celibacy is not merely the sum of the stories of individuals, it is also the story of a transpersonal reality that demonstrates essential factors as it functions.

## CELIBATE / SEXUAL BALANCE

Whenever celibacy progresses beyond individual commitment to become part of a group expectation or requirement, there will be both celibate practice (and perhaps achievement) and celibate failure within the group. Religiously motivated celibacy is an unusual path of living out one's life course. Whenever that process has been recorded the drama of the struggles are remarkable (see Ignatius Loyola, *A Pilgrim's Journey* [1991], or Athanasius, *The Life of Antony and the Letter to Marcellinus* [1980]). We have no basis for thinking that it should be otherwise today for anyone seeking the goal of celibate achievement or striving to approximate the ideal.

One can practice sexual abstinence for a variety of reasons or declare "I am going to be celibate from this point in time," but religious celibacy is a process that takes time, shifting awareness, and progressive integration that transforms relationships. In any group there are bound to be members who are in various stages of development. One can expect the neophyte to have different struggles and be prone to more failures or lapses because of this naiveté and lack of experience than more seasoned practitioners or the elders who will have their own particular stresses with sexual and relational pressures.

The individual phenomenon of celibate commitment epitomized by the apostle Paul or the early anchorites like St. Antony of the Desert (250–355) is easier to understand and analyze than the more complex groupings of early monasteries and communities that bonded together for mutual support and advantage.

A further dimension of systemic organization was added to celibacy when it was solidified into a requirement of religious power and authority. Several forces conspired to consolidate celibacy with power. One of the purest was religious experience that expressed itself in genuine holiness like St. Paul's. His integrative and transformative relationship with Christ found its fulfillment in complete service to others and is expressed in the culmination of his lived convictions: Paul's celibacy was *spiritual* power.

The repeated desire and need to harness spiritual power in service of the group and the recurring need to reform a system prone to divisions and even corruption motivated men to enlist the spiritual power of celibates in service of the system.

Less noble and more practical forces also supported an unmarried clergy. The preservation of church property favored those who had no spouse or heirs. Marriage is a far more complex social and economic state than singlehood. Economic control of the single priest is simpler to regulate than that of a man engaged with the more elaborate network of a family.

More distressing in the development of celibacy as a system was the creation of the myth that women/sex/sin/pleasure are inextricably bound together. This thinking rationalized and distorted the tradition of Jesus' celibacy. The *more perfect* way of imitating Christ was therefore touted as celibate and progressed to a denigration of marriage as imperfect or a necessary evil.

The final element was the need to centralize power and control. The early doctrinal arguments about Christ and nature (Donatists, Arians, Manicheans) split the church into factions. St. Augustine (354–430) intuitively knew the danger of the doctrinal divisions; his personal synthesis unified the power of celibacy and the control of sex with the power of Roman centralization.

Augustine's understanding about sex and celibacy has been decisive theoretically and practically for all of Western Christianity in spite of the continuing debate for and against mandatory celibacy. The universal requirement of celibacy for priests in the Latin rite was legislated only in 1139 at the Second Lateran Council.

Even in the current crisis of the church these elements of power, control, and economics almost obscure the spiritual dimensions of the question of celibacy: is it a reality or a figment?

The point is that within the celibate/sexual system there will always be a dynamic tension between celibate practice and sexual activity. This is inevitably so, not only because of the nature and process of spiritual growth individually and within any system, but also because the system has goals beyond spiritual striving and commitment toward temporal power and control. The economic and power/control dimensions, coupled with the mandatory requirement allied with priestly ordination, produce a complex interaction of sometimes contradictory forces.

When the balance within the system is in favor of celibate practice or development, lapses and even a certain amount of corruption can be tolerated and absorbed. History and experience show that even a small number of exceptionally dedicated and honest celibates can sustain the system for more or less extended periods of time.

But crisis is inevitable when the critical mass of those neither practicing celibacy nor involved in the process of development passes beyond a point of systemic toleration. This is part of what is happening today; it has happened at other times in history. What makes the current crisis unique and dire for Catholicism is that the intellectual justification for celibacy—a distortion that amounts to an assertion that sex and pleasure are the source of all evil—no longer has credibility. This misrepresentation has persistence and force because it has been bastardized into popular religious consciousness from no less an authority than St. Augustine, in spite of the fact that "Augustine," in the words of Margaret Miles, "more than any religious leader, understood and emphasized the dangers for exploitation of sexual relationships. He knew these first hand, as he confidingly admits in his *Confessions*. Sex is, for Augustine, an evidence of the fallen nature of humanity; sex/conception is also the moment of transmission of sin" (personal communication). Augustine's personal integrity and theological elegance were obscured by the lack of a developed discourse on sexuality. Instead, the institutionalized and control formulation became an "Augustinian synthesis" equating sin/sex/pleasure/women. Our understanding of human sexual nature has progressed to the point that it cannot sustain an economic and power system built on blatant falsehood and a misunderstanding of nature.

Effects of the abuse of children and women, even if the behaviors have remained at a relatively stable rate, obviously have reached critical mass, exposing the function and structure of the celibate system as never before.

## PRIVATE AND PUBLIC FUNCTION

Every system has its private elements, functions hidden from public scrutiny. The private elements of function are those shielded from public view by archives, historical or, more importantly, emotional. The Catholic historian Lord Acton said, "What archives revealed is the wickedness of men. . . the one constant result is to show that people are worse than their reputations" (O'Toole, 1992, p. 4). Power depends on keeping certain realities private. The thrust of spirituality propels itself in exactly the opposite direction – toward exposure of truth and complete self-revelation and total accountability. Public power is in part dependent on secrecy and the avoidance of responsibility.

This dynamic between concealment and the exposure of truth is built into the celibate/sexual system. Part of this tension is a necessary facet of individual growth, development, self-discovery, and appropriate self-disclosure. In the broader system it has to do with concealment, avoidance of scandal, and the preservation of control.

The public assumption of celibate practice was so widespread until recently that severely abused – criminally abused – men and women hesitated to confide their experience even to their most trusted friends and family members. "Who would believe me?" is the constant refrain of victims of abuse or partners of priests in sexual liaisons accomplished in private.

The celibate/sexual public/private dialectic, even when exposed to the courtroom or other open forums, does not easily resolve itself before the force of truth. One of the reasons is that a multitude of people can benefit from the public ministry, services, and kindnesses of a priest, whereas one or a handful of women, men, or children can suffer from the secret sexual actions of the same priest.

I have seen this played out in the legal system where a state's attorney refused to pursue well-substantiated allegations against a priest or bishop because of the cleric's power or popularity in the community. I have seen this dynamic in action within the ecclesiastical arena where priests, whose sexual activities were fully known to the bishop or religious superior, rebuffed, denigrated, and even threatened the sexual partners seeking redress.

## EXTERNAL FORCES

The private/public dynamic of the system is being disrupted by two additional factors beyond the exposure of priests' victims and sexual partners – namely, the corps of priests resigning from the active ministry and the proliferation of psychotherapy.

An estimated 20,000 priests in the United States have left the active ministry since 1965, the majority to marry. It is estimated that between 80,000 and 100,000 priests worldwide have abandoned the ministry in that same period. This group has significantly shifted the balance of the private elements of the celibate/sexual system toward the public. In a very real sense, this coterie of men has opened the emotional archives of the system. What was unthinkable and unspeakable about the private functioning of the system becomes not only known and believable but verifiable.

The development of the psychological sciences and the increasing use of psychotherapy by priests as an adjunct to growth, development, and problem solving—and in many ways as a substitute for sacramental confession—have also helped to shift the balance from private to public. Although psychotherapy is bounded by confidentiality much like the sacrament of self-revelation, it demands a self-criticism and challenges a person to empowerment in ways that rebound on the system of secrecy. Psychotherapy is often the springboard from which priests speak up about sexual practices, even their own, previously held captive in the system.

The current sexual crisis finds the church in an interesting double bind with the psychological sciences. Formerly, when the church denied the validity of alcoholism as psychological illness, for instance, it had to assume moral responsibility for transgressions. During that phase it had to deny the existence of a problem with clergy alcoholism. Once it accepted alcoholism as a disease, it could face, to a modest degree, the extent of the problem hidden within the system.

But sexuality is not alcohol. And even sexual addiction cannot be equated entirely with substance abuse and alcohol addiction. Being forced to face the problem of child sexual abuse by priests (whose exposure was in part fostered by people who have had the benefit of psychotherapy and been empowered by it), the hierarchy has been quick to run for cover under the psychiatric umbrella—"these men are sick."

The more the celibate/sexual dynamic is examined under the psychotherapeutic microscope, the less chance there will be to maintain the former homeostasis between the public and private elements of the system. Not only will the extent of the abuse of children be exposed, but all of the sexual activities and the mechanisms by which they are rationalized, denied, and defended will inevitably come to wider and wider public attention.

Psychiatry and psychology are necessary tools in addressing the current sexual trauma in the church. They will not save the celibate/sexual system. A study, *The Psychological Society* by Martin L. Gross (1978) defeated itself by its strident negativity, but it was nonetheless a valuable assessment of some limitations and failures of the psychological revolution of the last century. In spite of all their limitations, psychiatry and psychology will help to shift the balance of the celibate/sexual system toward public disclosure rather than secrecy;

what was sequestered in private will become increasingly open to public scrutiny.

# HOMOSEXUALITY

The reader should be aware that the following brief discussion of the function of homosexuality in the celibate/sexual system cannot be understood in isolation from the consideration of individual patterns of homosexual adjustment as described in chapter 7 and in the sections of chapter 8 that outline the homosexual elements in the celibate structure. Together they do not resolve all of the ambiguities and nuances of homosexual orientation, behavior, and systemic function, but within the total celibate/sexual context, the different perspectives challenge us to consider this phenomenon deeply and honestly and to recognize its reality within religious striving.

Homosexuality exists within the celibate/sexual system in three ways: first and foremost, as an essential factor in its systemic drive and organization; second, by men who have an innate homosexual orientation; third, by some other men who involve themselves in homosexual behaviors.

## Systemic Factors

Men can choose to be and are celibate regardless of their sexual orientation. The celibate impulse, grace, and practice can inhere equally in men who are heterosexual and homosexual. But the system of priestly celibacy is homosocial; the celibate system cannot exist without a sufficient number of men who are comfortable and can be productive within the emotional confines of a same-sex system. Sexual orientation is directed to bonding, not merely reproduction; this is equally true of heterosexual and homosexual men (Boswell, 1994). There is an equality enjoyed by either the homosexual or heterosexual man who makes his choice of celibacy individually and lives it independently of any system of celibacy. When one makes the same choice for celibacy when it is essentially intertwined with a system of law, ideal, gender exclusiveness, economy, prestige, and power, the tables are turned in favor of those who are homosocially compatible, in spite of the inherent personal dynamics of the process of celibate growth.

Homosexually oriented men who may or may not have a strong reproductive drive are compensated within the celibate system by a bonding that is natural to them – the affective support of other men. The heterosexually oriented man not only must compensate for his reproductive drive, should he have one, but also must be capable of tolerating affective support by an exclusively male power system.

There are complex sets of interactions in a male-exclusive system whereby personalities compensate for the deprivation of women's presence and inclusion. In a one-sex culture in which direct sexual gratification is eschewed, wide latitude and even high value are often given to both male and female qualities and roles latent in the members of the system. Although there may be analogies in other male-dominated systems – that is, the military and prisons – the explicit and public ideal of celibacy is lacking in those two systems; in them there is no expectation of or value placed on sexual abstinence.

Homosexual orientation and behavior exist across a broad range of species and probably in all human cultures. We must presume, supported with ever more evidence from biology, anthropology, endocrinology, and psychology, that homosexuality is a natural disposition for some men and that it is part of a rich biosexual diversity that is part of evolutionary reality and exists for the advantage of the species. God created nature as it is.

The celibate system is intended to serve others. This altruistic intent has analogues in nonreproductive segments of other species (Hamilton, 1972, pp. 193–232; Wilson, 1975a, pp. 106–129; 1975b, pp. 38–50; 1978, pp. 149–168). Just because the celibate system is rationalized by highly refined religious motivation – love of humanity – does not mean that it lacks a natural component. Some of the qualities that make celibacy desirable for the community – male bonding, love of beauty and learning, willing self-sacrifice for the group generally in the absence of reproductive preoccupation – are qualities sponsored within the homosocial system.

Certainly one must be most careful not to overgeneralize and even more careful to assiduously avoid stereotypes either positive or negative, at the same time as one honestly distinguishes qualities particular to heterosexual and homosexual orientation. It would be false to assume that fear or hatred of women is intrinsically bound up with male homosexual orientation, any more than hatred or fear of other men is intrinsically bound up with heterosexual orientation. There is much yet to be learned about sexual orientation.

The celibate/sexual system could not persevere, indeed it could not have been initiated with any vigor and naturalness, without a strong homosexual component within its organizational principles. This force is part of the essence of the system. The system fosters nonsexual, celibate/affective relationships by creating a family system in which all men are brothers to one another. Otherwise, within the wider system, priests have a familial relationship to all men and women—that of father—reinforcing the incest taboo.

## Homosexual Orientation

One thing is clear: the celibate/sexual system has always benefited from a large proportion of homosexually oriented men. History is proof. Part of the energies of my research is devoted to examining the psychohistory of priests portrayed in biography, autobiography, and novels from the perspective of their celibate/sexual development; this includes assessing their sexual orientation. Such study is a logical if difficult extension of the use of psychotherapy in the evaluation of behaviors and emotions in celibacy.

There is a solid artistic tradition suggestive that St. John the Evangelist had a homosexual orientation. John Henry Cardinal Newman (1801–90) is an apt study and an exemplary celibate who in my estimation had a homosexual orientation (see Ian Ker, 1988; Newman, 1986, 1990). The Jesuit poet Gerard Manly Hopkins (1844–89) gives evidence that he carried a homosexual orientation with less ease than Newman, even if with religious devotion and celibate success (Ong, 1986). The history and practice of celibacy within the Catholic tradition defy the 1986 Vatican document that declares homosexual orientation a tendency "ordered toward an intrinsic moral evil."

The celibate witness of homosexually oriented men is the strongest argument against the Vatican's position. Historical studies have brought into perspective revered celibate authors of the Middle Ages, such as Alered, Anselm, and Alcuin who expounded on "passionate friendships." Cassian (365–435) dealt frankly with sexual drives, tendencies, and temptations within the homosocial setting of monasteries. Michel Foucault's studies are also helpful in delineating the function of sexuality within the church system. The genetic and endocrinological studies by Dr. Dean Hamer (1993) and Dr. William J. Turner (1992) have linked a predisposition to sexual orientation to a pattern on the X chromosome. Roger Gorski, who in 1977 noted a dimorphism in the size of the hypothalamus (between men and women), continued and developed his work with Swerdloff. Simon LeVay and Dean Hamer (1994) recorded a difference in size of the same gland between homosexual and heterosexual men. Former Jesuit John McNeill (1976) has written convincingly about the biblical and legal tradition that has distorted an understanding of the nature and morality of homosexuality.

Peter Damian (1007–72), an enthusiastic and even ferocious church reformer, insisted on celibacy for all priests and therefore was a vocal proponent not only of the religious discipline but also the system of celibacy. He demonstrated a very problematic sexual development. His mother hated him and rejected him when he was 5. His celibate practice is clear, but his achievement seems clouded by his disdain for women. His orientation also seems homosexual.

Medieval expression, devotion, and practice that glorified men and incorporated the feminine within the celibate expression—for instance, Jesus as mother, the Abbot as mother—can be translated into our understanding of gender and sexuality and must be studied. Sexual language has changed; sexuality has not. It was not absent from the function of the celibate/sexual system from the beginning.

If the Catholic Church were to excise from the list of its honored saints all men who had a homosexual orientation, the roles would be decimated. The list of outcasts would include apostles, martyrs, popes, bishops, and founders of religious orders.

If the church today were to exclude all men of homosexual orientation from its celibate/sexual system, the church as we know it would cease to exist.

## Homosexual Behavior

Some men who are members of the celibate/sexual system involve themselves in homosexual behaviors. This number is neither more nor less remarkable than the men of heterosexual orientation who involve themselves in sexual behavior. In the process of sexual exploration, some heterosexual priests experiment with same-sex behavior, sometimes in response to their social situation, sometimes as part of an adolescent-like test of their sexual identity. Men of homosexual orientation can experiment with heterosexual behavior for the same reasons.

I have not found homosexual men within the celibate/sexual system any more sexually active than heterosexually oriented men in spite of all the cultural disadvantages the former group has to endure. Men of homosexual orientation do not have the advantage their heterosexual brothers enjoy of an acculturation that is positive and progressive—role models who demonstrate and teach progressively what is sexually appropriate, what is sexually responsible, and finally what is sexually mature. For instance, the child is taught that it is not appropriate to undress in public, to touch one's own or another's private body parts indiscriminately; one is coached that it is not responsible to impregnate a woman even if one is engaged in age-appropriate sexual experimentation. Lastly, if heterosexual, one is encouraged to explore relationships until one finds a suitable life companion with whom shared goals of bonding, family building, mutual love, and sex can be fostered and integrated.

All of these stages have more or less solid social support within families, schools, and even from religious mentors. The homosexual male lives in an atmosphere of social, religious, and oftentimes self-rejection. Seminary training and the celibate/sexual system generally tend to hold men in a stage of psychosexual development where sexual differentiation, specification, and identity can remain un-resolved. All of this tends to foster eventual sexual experimentation for men of either homosexual or heterosexual orientation.

If embraced and followed the celibate process leads an individual to profound self-confrontation and eventual self-acceptance. It is this struggle to know oneself at the very deepest level of one's being that offers appropriate, responsible, and mature sexual adjustment regardless of sexual orientation. The celibate/sexual system within which men strive to achieve this goal of self-knowledge in the absence of sexual gratification has an essential homosexual element. That element has proven supportive and beneficial both to heterosexual and homosexual men in their quest; it has also been a stumbling block for others who have used the system as a cover for sexual activity rather than celibacy.

## POWER: INDIVIDUAL AND SYSTEMIC

Power—control—over one's vital functions has long been considered a ground for admiration and a proof of personal superiority. Intellectual, athletic, or artistic prowess sets individuals apart and imparts to them an aura of power over the minds and hearts of others because of their personal accomplishment rooted in superior control, proof of self-discipline, and mastery over self.

But celibacy, like athletic or artistic mastery, is a personal achievement and in itself it is not transferable. One can inspire others by one's own control, can speak or teach others from his own experience, but each person must *do* it for himself.

St. Paul, the lone scriptural testimony to the value of celibacy, apart from the ambiguous reference to eunuchs in the Gospel of

Matthew, presents it as a personal experience—one he wishes others could value and experience as he did. Antony of Egypt is considered the prototype of the celibate. His life, recorded by St. Athanasius (293–373), remained an inspiration and model for centuries for others who wished to follow the ascetic ideal. The magnetism of his example and wisdom, which seemed to encapsulate the gospel directive—"If you would be perfect, go, sell what you possess and give to the poor, and you will have a treasure in Heaven" (Matthew 19:21)—drew thousands of others to consult him during his lifetime. He was a hermit and not a monk, but he is considered the father of monasticism—groups of men who banded together to live celibately and to support one another in their religious practice.

There is some evidence that at least some of the other apostles and earliest disciples of Christ chose to live and minister in a state of nonmarriage. Celibacy was encouraged for Christians who had been widowed. Celibacy persisted during the earliest centuries of Christianity as an individual and nonsystematized practice among priests, laymen, and women. St. John the Evangelist, the only apostle of Jesus not to endure martyrdom, has traditionally been regarded as unmarried regardless of his sexual orientation.

Celibacy has been compared with martyrdom. The power that celibacy demonstrated was personal and spiritual, because like martyrdom it tested to the breaking point the practitioner's motivations, self-knowledge, and devotion to a religious ideal.

Celibate practice was not merely confined to mastery over the sexual drive but over *all* bodily instincts—the regulation of food and the use of all material things. The growth of the celibate movement facilitated a quantum leap in human psychology because it demanded "radical honesty about the self" grounded in monitoring and taking responsibility for the workings of one's own mind and feelings without resorting to blame or credit of external forces (Stewart, 1990, p. 25).

There was a recurrent movement throughout the centuries to harness this core, individual, spiritual power in the service of broader control by the religious organization—even to ensure temporal dominance.

St. Augustine (354–430) solved his personal life questions by a deep spirituality; but his synthesis was used systemically as a unified intellectual and practical justification for making celibacy synonymous with priestly power and control. He was inspired, personally, by Athanasius's life of Antony; his espousal of neoplatonism led him away from the egalitarianism of the Gospel to a philosophical dualism that split body and spirit, male and female; his personal and intellectual struggle with the problem of evil led him to the definition of original sin; wrestling with contemporary heretical groups—Manicheans, Donatists, and Pelagians—led him to defend orthodox power and the centrality of Rome. Priest/celibate/male/power and orthodoxy became a system.

The church appealed repeatedly to the Augustinian synthesis as it struggled with internal corruption—an appeal to spiritual reform—and struggled with threats from external powers and forces, temporal and religious. The universal requirement of celibacy for the priesthood was not legislated until the twelfth century, thus codifying a spiritual achievement into a legal requirement—a feat some scholars judge impossible and even immoral (Vogels, 1993).

The paradigm of the struggle around power and celibacy for the first Christian millennium was epitomized in the 1077 meeting of Pope Gregory VII and Emperor Henry IV at Canossa. Pope Gregory VII, Hildebrand, was trained as a monk and was drafted to aid popes Gregory V, Leo IX, and Alexander II to reform a church infested with sexual and financial corruption. He was a celibate, patently holy man and exerted personal spiritual dynamism; he was elected pope by popular acclamation in 1073. His confrontation with the emperor was over lay investiture—that is, the custom of allowing secular rulers to bestow on church officials the symbols of authority. The pope excommunicated and deposed the emperor to wrest church power from secular hands; the emperor pleaded for reinstatement on bended knees.

Although the reconciliation between church and state was only temporary, it stands as a symbol of how commingled religious power and secular power had become. Less than 100 years later, at the Second Lateran Council in 1139, Rome consolidated sexual control over its priests by imposing celibacy as a requirement for ordination. It is a law that has never been well observed, but it has been an essential part of the functioning of the clerical system since that time (Cantor, 1991).

## GUILT AND FORGIVENESS: A DYNAMIC

Sexual sin has progressively been incorporated into the celibate/sexual system to the point where it—lust—has become the preeminent, uncompromised, and dominant moral concern for clergy and layperson alike. This emphasis is not consistent with Scripture or the earliest concerns of the Christian community. But as the questions of power and control were fought out, more and more attention was given to sex and celibacy; greater and greater power over sin and forgiveness was taken by the priest.

The validity of the aphorism "Control a person's sexuality and you control the person" was not lost on the power system of the church as it struggled for the hearts, minds, and welfare of its priests and people. The practice of personal, private, individual confession of sins to a priest was not a product of early Christianity, where public admission of sinfulness and public reconciliation were incorporated into the liturgical calendar (e.g., on Shrove Tuesday and Holy Thursday), much in the tradition of the Jewish public Day of Atonement (Yom Kippur).

The law requiring confession to a priest for every Christian at least once a year was introduced only at the Fourth Lateran Council (1215).

Confessionals have long been architectural components of every Catholic church. Before Vatican II they usually had separate compartments divided by a grill—one for the penitent to kneel and recite his or her sins, another for the priest to sit, hear, and administer absolution. But they were introduced only in the sixteenth century. Milan's St. Charles Borromeo in 1565 was the first churchman to introduce the metal grill separating the priest and penitent.

Michel Foucault has carefully traced the development of confession and attitudes toward sexuality. He is correct that sex was and remains the "privileged theme of confession." In contrast to pagan culture, "For us, it is in the confession that truth and sex are joined, through the obligatory and exhaustive expression of an individual secret" (1978, p. 61).

Although Friedrich Nietzsche's analysis will be odious to some, it has an undeniable element of validity:

Psychologically considered, "sins" become indispensable in any society organized by priests: they are the real handles of power. The priest *lives* on sins, it is essential for him that people "sin." Supreme principle: "God forgives those who repent"—in plain language: those who submit to the priest. (A. Miller, 1988, p. 114)

One of the surest signs of the crisis in the Catholic Church today is the loss of credibility in its teaching about sexuality and the increasingly infrequent use of the confessional (the sacrament of reconciliation) by most Catholics.

Sexuality has not lost its interest, force, or general concern; it has lost its containment by secrecy. Sex, with its guilt or forgiveness, is no longer under the control of priests. The current crisis underlines the fact that priests do not have the appropriate control over their own sexuality. Sex, even sexual sin, is spoken of openly or in the office of the psychotherapist where understanding, integration, and self-empowerment, not absolution, are sought. The functioning of guilt and forgiveness, which was so laboriously constructed over centuries, is disintegrating beyond all reconstruction.

## WOMEN: THE FUNCTION OF IDEALIZATION AND DENIGRATION

On May 28, 1993, the final event of the 3-day International Conference on Celibacy sponsored by a papal commission was an address to the participants by Pope John Paul II in the Vatican Palace. I approached the site through the Scala Regia and ascended via four or five ever grander, wider, and more magnificent staircases to the hall for the audience. The atmosphere conveyed its message clearly—we were approaching a place of power. And every architectural detail, the placement of each member of the household guard, and each Swiss Guard emphasized in calculated synchronicity with the frescoes and the statuary that this is a place of nonwomen.

The pope addressed us, a group of fewer than 100, in a modestly sized *sala* off the grander *aula* of Clement VIII (1592–1605). His message was: The Latin priesthood is for celibate men only. This rule would remain despite all objections and in firm opposition to any change, no matter what difficulties celibacy has encountered or will encounter.

Each of us had a photograph taken individually with the pope as we passed back into the magnificent Hall of Pope Clement VIII, which was decorated in 1595 with Renaissance splendor. As I waited for the group to reassemble for a group photograph with the pope, I reflected on how out of place women are in this world—in this circle of power. (There were one lay secretary and four nuns in the group.) A cardinal and an archbishop in their red and purple flanked the pope's white presence; a bearded young Franciscan, clothed in full habit, knelt at the pope's feet, the papal left hand on the shoulder and in the hand of the friar. This is a world of men. The frescoes are male centered—power centered—in which women and children are confined to corner panels separated from the action by magnificent pedestals and columns painted in perfect and awesome perspective.

I also had time to reflect on Pope Clement VIII—lawyer, a holy and celibate reformer ordained priest at age 44. He was conscientious, and historians say, "his piety was transparent. He fasted, meditated, said mass, made his confession with exemplary frequency" (Kelly, 1986, p. 275). Although he denounced nepotism when he was a cardinal, as pope he promoted his relatives and "so doted on a fourteen-year-old grand-nephew that he made him a cardinal." He also expanded the Index of Forbidden Books and included a ban on Jewish books. He intensified the Inquisition; during the 12 years of his pontificate more than 30 heretics were burned at the stake (Kelly, 1986, p. 276).

This center of the celibate/sexual power system is a place for boys and men, not a safe place for women or Jews. How and why must women (and Jews) be kept in their place?

## THE PLACE OF WOMEN

Although a substantial number of priests have a healthy attitude toward women, the male celibate/sexual system functions with a deep ambivalence—even hostility and fear—toward them. The basis of this attitude is not scriptural, nor does it have a foundation in earliest Christian experience (see chapter 10). The subjugation of women did not evolve; the place of women was carved out and constructed by the assemblage of the celibate/sexual system (Duby, 1983; Fiorenza, 1992; Furlong, 1987; Miles, 1992; Noble, 1992). As the celibate/sexual system of power was forged during the third century, justified by Augustine's definition of original sin in the fourth and fifth centuries, consolidated in the eleventh and twelfth centuries, and solidified in the sixteenth century, one can trace the progressive and massive idealization of the image of virgin/mother and the denigration of lover, wife, and sexual equal. The system could not endure or function in its current mode if the place of women within systemic functions were altered.

Equality of women is the single most threatening factor to the homeostasis of the system as it now exists and operates. The crisis of priestly sexual abuse of children is only one link in a chain that exposes the sexual activity of priests and bishops who are bound by celibate law and who preach the celibate ideal. Hundreds of women are stepping forth to tell their stories of love affairs; of involvements in which they were used to help a priest quell his anxieties about his sexual orientation, comfort him while he ascended the lonely ecclesiastical ladder, and assist him in his struggle to grow beyond his emotional adolescence.

These are by church definition sinful affairs, no matter how loving or how useful they eventually prove to be in the maturation of priests and their pastoral instincts. Women get used. By their sinfulness women can save priests. But priests can remain within the system and retain their power—now purified—while women retain their identity in the system as evil unless they are virgins, martyrs, or mothers. These are the only roles accounted worthy by nature and God's will.

This idealization of virgin/mother and the denigration of women, however subtle (as the ultimate source of evil and death), are necessary to maintain the celibate/sexual system of power in the church, even if it is rejected by individual priests and churchmen. The place of women in the life of a priest is frequently conditioned by his relationship with his mother. The place of the priest's mother is often enhanced by devotion to the Blessed Virgin Mother Mary. This spiritual emulation tends to fixate the priest in the role of a son who is affiliated with a male-centered idolatry. Women are correct when they contend that this function in the church justifies men's right to dominate all women. The male child for whom mother is the center of the affective universe becomes very special in the real or imagined reciprocity of her love (Daly, 1985; Furlong, 1987).

By revising their view of Christian womanhood, women and some men are challenging the traditional function of power, which has become inextricably interwoven with male celibacy. A celibacy that is dependent on immature sexual identity will be threatened by women and, equally important, will be frightened of them (Stern, 1965). Women's experience of the church and their articulation of it are helping the priest experience his own gender conflicts and have exposed them in bold relief. Questions of sexual identity can be manifest in behaviors involving pornography, transvestism, and exhibitionism, among other things. Priests who cannot enter the celibate process—which involves transcending the system at some point—are prone to sexual paraphilias because of their overweaning sexual curiosity about or fear of women.

Both the idealization of women as virgin/mother and their demotion to a role less than equal to man stultify emotional growth and actually retard celibate development. The appointment of altar girls or even the assignment of women to minor administrative positions within the system does not change the essential function of the power system, nor does it enhance or clarify the true identity of woman as man's equal.

The idealization of women and minor meaningless concessions really amount to rejection. The church espouses the ideal at the same time that it rejects, in Monica Furlong's words, "the living, breathing, subjective people that we are" (1987, p. 1083).

If sexual development, which includes a realistic view of women, does not mature, not only is sexual identity stifled or delayed, but untimely childhood behavior becomes overly attractive, often in an attempt to solve the immaturity.

## Fear of Women

Fear of women is frequently observed in the attitudes of priests and bishops. Fear reinforces fixation at immature levels of psychosexual development. Devotion to the idealized Blessed Virgin often serves to enhance early concepts of other women as dangerous and, therefore, unapproachable, inaccessible, and undesirable.

In some priests, the sexual flame of curiosity is actually fanned by their fear, their attempt to overcome it, and by their sexual inexperience. The *Report of the Commission on Obscenity and Pornography* (1970) applied to priests as well as to the general population when it stated, "Most patrons of adult bookstores and movie houses appear to have had less sexually related experiences in adolescence than the average male, but to be more sexually oriented as an adult" (p. 134).

Since seminary education is part of the celibate/sexual system, it reinforces traditional attitudes toward women, if not actively and explicitly, at least by its inadequate training in the realities of sexuality, celibacy, and the true equal nature of women. Some priests resort to pornography as a source of sexual information.

Many people would question the value of pornography as an educational element in any man's life, let alone that of a dedicated celibate (Dworkin, 1981). Sexually explicit visual representations are an ancient fact and in some cultures an art form, but not in Christian tradition. " 'An erotic art,' Foucault said (in *The History of Sexuality*), 'is the usual way for a civilization to make sense of its knowledge about sex.' He pointed to the existence of such artistic expression in Etruscan, Roman, Arabic, Persian, Indian, Chinese, Japanese, and many other civilizations but not, alas, in the Christian" (Sipe, 1987, p. 89).

Pornography flourishes in a Christian culture that lacks religiously inspired erotic art. Many women have objections to a pornographic portrayal of sex because it violates and exploits the women and men who produce and view it. Homosexually oriented men may also question the implications, effect, and value of the pornographic portrayal of gays. Distorted views of women have an effect on behavior:

When we look closely at the behavior that makes up a man's perversion— when we get an in-depth subjective description of the erotic behavior—we find, regardless of the overt form of the behavior, that he is under pressure from envy and anger toward women. . . . The evidence is found in the fantasies these men have that they are degrading women. (Stoller, 1985, p. 18)"

Having a realistic view of women holds some special significance for the priest whose sexual experience and education are limited, and who is, therefore, unduly influenced by a system that excludes women from all power (Dworkin, 1974). A priest's unresolved fear of women often manifests itself in a harsh and denigrating attitude toward them, which has multiple pastoral and even theological ramifications.

## Word Shifts: Systemic Stability

Pope John Paul II addressed a group of American bishops on July 2, 1993, in the same Vatican *aula* in which he had met our group from the International Conference on Celibacy. His remarks were centered on the preservations of the celibate/sexual system, the preservation of roles and the hierarchial system, which keeps people in their place. The threat of women is clear:

A question closely connected with what we are saying here is that of the role of women in the life of the church, a question which needs to be addressed with a keen sense of its importance. At the same time the question as it affects the church is influenced by the fact that the place and role of women in society at large is undergoing profound transformations. Respect for women's rights is without doubt an essential step towards a more just and mature society, and the church cannot fail to make her own this worthy objective. . . I myself have spoken and written extensively on the subject. However, in some circles there continues to exist a climate of dissatisfaction with the church's position, especially where the distinction between a person's human and civil rights and the rights, duties, ministries and functions which individuals have or enjoy within the church is not clearly understood. A faulty ecclesiology can easily lead to presenting false demands and raising false hopes.

What is certain is that the question cannot be resolved through a compromise with a feminism which polarizes along bitter, ideological lines. It is not simply that some people claim a right for women to be admitted to the ordained priesthood. In its extreme form, it is the Christian faith itself which is in danger of being undermined. (*L'Osservatore Romano*, July 3, 1993)

Pope John Paul II did issue an apostolic letter, *On the Dignity of Women*, in 1988. Certainly it is an example of the church's increasingly positive words on the nature and roles of women. Yet only when the opinions of women are heard and heeded will the church develop a healthier mode of educating and evaluating its priests, and only complete equality will fulfill the Gospel message and reform the intellectual, theological, and practical abuses perpetuated by the celibate/sexual system.

The equality of women is a cause that cannot be turned back, and yet no other shift in awareness has so threatened the celibate authority functioning of the church. Pope John XXIII (1958–63) wrote in *Pacem in Terris* (1963), "Since women are becoming ever more conscious of their human dignity, they will not tolerate being treated as mere material instruments, but demand rights befitting a human person both in domestic and public life."

Pope Paul VI (1963–78) also spoke of the issues of womens' rights:

> For in truth, it must still be regretted that fundamental personal rights are not yet being universally honored. Such is the case of a woman who is denied the right and freedom to choose a husband, to embrace a state of life or to acquire an education or cultural benefits equal to those recognized for men. (Hebblethwaite, 1993, p. 432; see also pp. 638–656)

Although these popes have endorsed the theory of women's equality, the practical implications of such a theory still wait to be unfolded because of the peril they bode to a celibate male hierarchy. Actually, there has been little support for women's equality in the celibate tradition since the time of Augustine. The traditional argument for the exclusion of women from positions of power is posed as theologically unassailable: nature and God's will. Witness St. John Chrysostom writing in about 386:

> Divine law has excluded women from the ministry...but they endeavor to force their way into it. Because they can do nothing of themselves, they seek to accomplish everything through others. They have gained such power that they can appoint to the priesthood and depose from it whomsoever they wish. . . . Everything is topsy-turvy, and the old saw is certainly true—"Servants lead their masters". . . . And would that it were men who do this, rather than those who are not permitted to teach. . . . Yet I have heard someone say that women now assume such liberties as to rebuke the bishops of the Church more sharply than masters do their slaves. (Jurgens, 1955, p. 17)

The male virgin—the celibate—is one *not defiled by woman*. Sexual defilement and the threat to power are inextricably bound to a concept of woman as the weaker sex and as the spoiler.

As the celibate system took shape, power had to be limited by one factor: sex. Women cannot have *power*. The idea that the place of women is subordinate to men runs deep not only in the history and culture of the church, but also in the conscious fiber of many men and women who accept this bias as natural and sanctioned by grace.

Both the justification for a male superiority and the introduction of evil into the cosmic system via sex hinge on the church's view of women.

John Chrysostom spoke eloquently about the priesthood. How does he justify nonmarriage? "It is not good to marry!" Why? "What else is a woman but a foe to friendship, an inescapable punishment, a necessary evil, a natural temptation, a desirable calamity, a domestic danger, a delectable detriment, an evil of nature, painted with fair colours!" (Jurgens, 1955, p. 49).

Pope Innocent VIII (1484–92), a man who fathered several illegitimate children prior to his ordination and subsequently elevated one 13-year-old grandson to the cardinalate—authorized a book in 1486 that became a guide for the Inquisition and a standard text in all Catholic seminaries for two centuries—*Malleus Maleficarum* (*Witches Hammer* [1971 edition]). The book was written by two Dominican priests, Heinrich Kramer and James Sprenger. Both men reflected and perpetuated the negative understanding of the nature of women by the system. Many of the attitudes expressed by these two priests are ground into the unconscious of the celibate system.

Women are seen as essentially wicked: "When a woman thinks alone, she thinks evil. . . .Women are naturally more impressionable. . .they are feebler both in mind and body" (p. 43). Of course it is assumed here that Man is the norm. "Women are intellectually like children. . . .Women also have weak memories; and it is a natural vice in them not to be disciplined, but to follow their own impulses without any sense of what is due" (p. 45). Inferiority is, the celibate authors erroneously claim, supported even linguistically, for they say "*Femina* comes from *Fe* (faith) and *Minus* (less), since she is ever weaker to hold and preserve the faith" (p. 44).

Not just that, but "She is a liar by nature" (p. 46). And now we come to the core of the matter: "She is more carnal than a man, as is clear from her many carnal abominations." Carnal lust "in women is insatiable." But Kramer and Sprenger are very graphic about it, expanding the image by saying, "the mouth of the womb is never satisfied" (pp. 45–46).

There are those men of goodwill who would like to distance themselves from these attitudes and yet who cling to the theological bias that justifies all of them: "And blessed be the Highest Who has so far preserved the male sex from so great a crime [witchcraft]: for since He was willing to be born and suffer for us, therefore He has granted to men this privilege" (p. 47). The logic is that men are the preferred sex because Jesus was a man; he rejected women by his incarnational choice.

These may seem like outlandish and archaic expressions and fallacious rationale for limiting power to celibate men. Yet one can hear them voiced sentiment for sentiment by priests, bishops, and popes. Unfortunately, this negativity toward the person and place of women is unconsciously but effectively fostered as a support of celibate power system.

In spite of the encouraging words of recent popes about the dignity of women, the real attitude toward women can be traced in the comments of other highly placed churchmen. For instance, Cardinal Giaccomo Biffi, archbishop of Bologna, Italy, compared modern women with the figure of Eve, "squalid" and a "collector of death." He clearly exemplifies the dynamic between the idealized and denigrated woman operative in the systemic function:

> The splendor of the Immaculate Madonna allows us to see with biting clarity how great is the misfortune of our era, in which the prevailing image of woman...is one that appears to be the deliberate contradiction of that of the Virgin Mary; a woman who even if externally refined is substantially squalid, who appears to detest virginity and maternity in equal measure; a woman who does not say to God, "Here I am, I am yours" but who cries, hysterically, "I belong to myself"; a woman...who claims the right...to decide the existence or nonexistence of the fruit of her innards. (Biffi, 1989)

The Vatican radio endorsed the message by pointing out that the cardinal's speech "could provide an important opportunity for reflection on the role of woman in society and in the church."

When our group posed for a photograph with the pope in the Hall of Clement VIII, I recalled those words from the *Malleus* which would have been well-known to Clement; they justified in his mind the Inquisition, the violence to women, and the need to keep them in their place:

She is more carnal than a man, as is clear from her many carnal abominations. . . . All witchcraft comes from carnal lust which is in women insatiable. . . . Three general vices appear to have special dominion over wicked women, namely, infidelity, ambition and lust. Therefore, they are more than others inclined towards witchcraft who more than others are given to these vices. . . . Women being insatiable it follows that those among ambitious women are more deeply infected who are more hot to satisfy their filthy lusts. (Kramer & Sprenger, 1971, p. 47)

Clearly, women who seek power—or even equality within the church system—are perceived not only as evil but also as dangerous.

## THE SECRET SYSTEM

The current sexual abuse crisis in Catholicism has shattered the function of secrecy by which the church maintains its power. Accountability and secrecy cannot coexist. The church has never before been called to account for its sexual teaching and practice to the degree that it has at the present time. Nietzsche spoke wisely when he said, "Let us speak of this, you who are wisest, even if it is bad. *Silence is worse; all truths that are kept silent become poisonous*" (A. Miller, 1988, p. 103).

The silence and even dissimilation about priest sexual abuse have proven to be the cancerous sore exposing the systemic infection that has abused women, exalted men, and justified cruelty and war in the name of moral orthodoxy (Cantor, 1991, pp. 403–404). In short, the celibate/sexual function, which of course has positive elements, is the product of an "Augustinian" equation: sex = pleasure = women = evil. This is the dynamic that keeps the system of power on track. If its functioning is too closely examined, it will disintegrate because of its own indefensible foundation.

Truth will not be the victim of exposure; Christianity will not disintegrate or be reviled if secrecy is abandoned. But unauthentic priestly power will—a power based on the myth of the superiority of sexlessness and moral teaching that denigrates sexual nature and ignores sexual reality.

There are important considerations in Nietzsche's observations about the Christian "life-denying moral system." Rightly he connects it with the system of power.

The morality that would un-self man is the morality of decline *par excellence*—the fact, "I am declining," transposed into the imperative, "all of you *ought to decline*"—and not only into the imperative. This only morality that has been taught so far, that of un-selfing, reveals a will to the end; fundamentally, it negates life.

This would still leave open the possibility that not humanity is degenerating but only that parasitical type of man—that of the *priest*—which has used morality to come to *power*. Indeed, this is *my* insight: the teachers, the leaders of humanity, theologians all of them, were also, all of them, decadents: *hence* the revaluation of all values into hostility to life, *hence* morality. (A. Miller, 1988, pp. 124–125)*

Priests assume power within and because of a system that pretends that all of them are sexually virginal, that mandates a sexual morality that claims all activity outside marriage is cause for perpetual damnation, that teaches that masturbation is an intrinsically evil act, and that homosexual orientation is a tendency ordered toward an intrinsic moral evil. Priests are different. The system makes them so in one of two ways. If they believe what the system teaches, they are men who can abandon their own judgment and minister without insight or compassion. If they do not believe what the system teaches, they use their own pastoral judgment that countermands official teaching—a ministry marked by prudence and compassion. But even goodness must be a secret act—one that unwittingly contributes to the preservation of secrecy.

Jim Bowman, journalist and retired priest, writes eloquently of this latter group in his study of 34 Catholic priests to whom he posed 10 questions. Five questions concerned sexuality: birth control, abortion, marriage after divorce, women, and gays; five questions concerned power and authority. He accurately titles the results of his conversations *Bending the Rules: What American Priests Tell American Catholics* (1994).

It is significant that most of Bowman's priests could speak freely only under the protection of anonymity for fear "of being penalized if their views and practices became known." An additional 18 priests refused an interview. The point is clear: even compassion, reason, and good judgment must be kept secret lest they disestablish and threaten the power and control of the system.

---

*Author's Note: I purposely quote Nietzsche from Alice Miller since I think for our purposes Nietzsche's work is best understood in the context of Miller's insights. However, Walter Kaufmann's biography of Nietzsche as well as the assessments of Georg Lukacs and Steven Aschkeim are indispensable to putting his critique of Christianity and Nazism in perspective.

The dichotomy between moral sexual teaching and pastoral application is magnified by the fact that pastoral practice must be hidden from authority. Those who appeal to Jesus' example of his application and defiance of the law as a justification fail to acknowledge that Jesus preached and practiced his ministry in the open, in full sight of religious authorities and with complete accountability for his practical judgments.

Priests or bishops who fail to impose the full rigor of sexual rules need to do so privately, unofficially, and *sub rosa* to avoid censure. For instance, a woman who obtained an abortion at the insistence of the priest who impregnated her was kindly advised by the bishop she consulted to stay away from mass on a particular Sunday because abortion was designated as the required topic for the sermon in all churches of the diocese on that day. This sensitive pastoral care had great meaning to the woman suffering the loss of her child and her lover.

But the reality is more complex. She—the woman—is relegated in the end to the role of sinner and outcast—indebted to the church authority for forgiveness from her secret sins. The priest is welcomed back into the ministerial fold as the prodigal, and promoted within the system; now bound *to* the system by secret covenant and debt.

The question here is not the rightness of compassion but rather secrecy in the service of power and control. The doctrinal/pastoral ambiguity locks judgment, virtue, sin, and guilt into a system of power that blocks all exits short of duplicity or rejection of the officially mandated function. This ironclad mode of functioning is being challenged, not by doctrinal invocation but by revelation of precisely how the celibate/sexual system works. People are talking.

A 25-year-old man who had been sexually abused by a neighbor 15 years earlier gathered five additional victims of the same abuser and sought assistance to confront the perpetrator. In the confrontation, which was supervised by therapists for victims and perpetrator, the latter told how he himself, the survivor at 3 years of age of a car accident in which both of his parents were killed, had been sexually involved with a priest from the time he was 5 until he was 17 years old. The priest abuser, now deceased, eventually was consecrated a bishop. The abuser/abused told his victims, "I never thought there was anything wrong with what I was doing. I knew Father loved me." The ability to function in secrecy allowed the relationship to remain unexamined and unexaminable, and able to replicate itself. Sexual activity publicly condemned can be privately indulged if it is kept secret.

• • •

The current crisis of child sexual abuse cannot be contained and isolated as an issue of a few priests who violate minors. Exposure has begun to reveal how secrecy and power operate across the board within the celibate/sexual system.

"Sex is sinful. Celibacy is superior. The church and the priest hold ultimate moral power in these domains." These assumptions are being challenged vigorously by the real stories being spoken by those who know how the celibate/sexual system functions. The truth of these voices, some only whispers, some spoken in the legal forum or shouted in the media, is the real force that is assailing the secrecy of the celibate/sexual function. Truth, not the legal system or the media, has the power to match the ingrained force of traditional operation.

Sexual abuse of minors by priests is only one factor in the puzzle of the function of the celibate/sexual system, but the discovery of that piece makes the exposure of other pieces inevitable, ensuring the eventual completion of the whole picture. This is a major threat to the way the celibate/sexual system of power operates.

# 6

# PRIESTS AND WOMEN

*For so many years, now, we have baptized so many men to no effect, if there are none here who preserve the vows of chastity they took. . . . Far be it from me to believe that this is so. It would have been better not to have been your bishop than that this should have been the case. But I hope and I believe the opposite. It is part of my sorry situation that I am forced to know all about adulterers, and cannot be informed about the chaste. The virtues in you that give me joy are hidden from me, while what distresses me is only too well-known.*

Augustine of Hippo

*A Catholic can be a member of the Ku Klux Klan and not be liable for excommunication, but anyone can be denied the sacraments for even driving a woman to get an abortion. What this says is that what moves the Catholic Church is an appetite for sexual repression that eclipses all its other priorities.*

Mary Gordon

In his day St. Augustine was concerned with the double standard of morality by which a man could do whatever he pleased in his own household—take a concubine, abuse his wife and slaves—while he held his wife to the strict prohibition against adultery embodied in laws that became "even more oppressive in the Christian era" (P. Brown, 1969, p. 248). Augustine's problem was how to exert some moral authority over the sexual behavior of men. Celibate dedication was seen as a decisive action for taking control of it. Religious authority constructed celibacy first as the ideal and second as the law.

If the dichotomy between marriage (sexual activity) and celibate practice were clean cut, automatic, or irreversible, life might be simple and the Catholic teaching on sexuality plausible. But celibacy, friendships, sexual relationships, and marriage all pose realities that demand personal and social integration and transformation not yet clear in Christian theology.

The "Augustinian" solution was to dichotomize virginity as good (spiritual), and sex as a necessary evil for some (the married) and always dangerous (counterspiritual). Some scholars project Augustine's values backward into biblical times and claim that all of the apostles eschewed sex and marriage after pentecost (Cochini, 1981, 1993). But other scholars are very critical of such a reading of the sources (Hastings, 1983). Such an interpretation of the early Christian experience cannot claim psychological substance, either historically or in present reality. However, for some men religious conversion was also a conversion to celibacy. St. Paul was a married man prior to his conversion to Christ and his captivation by the idea of the *eschaton*—the imminent kingdom of heaven. Even in declaring his personal sexual solution—celibacy—he left others free to marry. "Given my preference, I should like you to be as I am. Still each one has his own gift from God" (1 Corinthians 7:6).

Augustine experienced a 13-year loving, sexually active relationship and joyful fatherhood before his conversion. The division of celibacy and sexuality was more problematic for him than for Paul, who did not share a view of the intrinsic evil of sex and pleasure. Also, Augustine had to surround himself with a group of men as a shelter from excessive sexual temptation. Nonetheless, he did not demand that others adopt celibacy.

Ignatius of Loyola led a sexually active life and most likely fathered a child before his conversion. His religious genius and the resolution of his sexual drive had their psychological complications (Meissner, 1992), but their interactions were intrinsically bound up with the power system and the centrality of religious authority (O'Malley, 1993). For prolonged periods he maintained several colorful friendships with women, notably a wealthy patron, Isabel Roser. But he was delivered from any sexual temptations.

Thomas Merton, the most popular American spiritual writer of the twentieth century, also fathered a daughter prior to his religious conversion and entry into the Trappist order. Even the cloister of one of the strictest religious orders could not defend Merton entirely from his sexual feeling and behavior. He pursued some kind of love affair with a young nurse 20 years his junior more than two decades after he vowed his celibacy. The details of his celibate/sexual struggles are yet to be completely revealed (Mott, 1984).

Alypius, Augustine's friend and fellow bishop, was one of those priests who did not like women overmuch (Greeley, 1983b). He tried sex in his youth and found it to be a negative experience (P. Brown, 1969, p. 174).

Antony of the Desert and Benedict of Nursia (480–547) fled society at age 15 or 20, in search of isolation and a life of the spirit. The protection of the hermitage did not spare them intense internal sexual struggles, causing Benedict to throw himself into a thorn bush for relief, while Antony suffered all of the agonies of sensory deprivation with its concomitant hallucinations and psychological tortures.

These are the heroes of celibate achievement. Each willingly and eagerly entered the process of religious celibacy. Each is a model for the ages because his struggles ring true and engender compassion as well as admiration. These men were not universally considerate or responsible toward women.

Within the ranks of the celibate are men who have admirable, respectful, and healthy friendships with women. But thousands of women are stepping forward to relate their stories of sexual involvement with priests; an increasing number of priests will be exposed in courtrooms and the media. Some are horror stories that reveal a disdain and abuse of women every bit as flagrant and abhorrent as the abuse of minors.

In short, in spite of celibate intent, determination, and practice, the reality of sexuality remains (like Paul's thorn in the flesh). Celibacy always entails a personal struggle, and when the histories of a broad spectrum of priests are examined, we find heroic adjustments and a host of sexual compromises.

There is a double standard in the celibate/sexual system: sex condemned and sex indulged. Not all sexual missteps among priests are in the service of a celibate process and growth. Some heterosexual activity is a frank rejection of the reality of celibate striving; some is blatantly abusive; all of it exists and is maintained under the aegis of the celibate/sexual power system.

## MYTHS ABOUT PRIESTS AND WOMEN

A number of myths concerning priests and women need to be dispelled. The current sexual crisis in the church is exposing these myths for the fallacies that they are. As personal stories are told, the numbers are tallied and the body count is taken; that is, as a more accurate portrait of women's treatment within the celibate/sexual system is delineated, the crisis in the church will expand with ever greater explosive force.

## Myth 1: Priests Are Not
## Involved Sexually with Women

Certainly many priests keep celibacy and do not involve themselves sexually with women. But that is not the whole story. One priest writes, "While celibacy is not necessarily honored all the time, perhaps, it is nonetheless the normal behavior of most American priests" (Greeley, 1983b, p. 5). The *perhaps* and *not necessarily all the time* betray the myth. Some priests in America and around the world do involve themselves with women, and some women are abused by sexual involvement with priests.

A noted sociologist, the late Joseph H. Fichter, S.J., quotes a priest of Paderborn, Germany, Professor Eugen Drewerman, who estimates that one third of German diocesan priests are living with women. I heard similar estimates in Rome from different sources. Fichter says this situation "implies out-of-wedlock partnerships. Some of them are brief love affairs, others are long-term relationships, but no one really knows the number of women living in different degrees of concubinage with priests" (1994, p. 14).

When Ignatius Loyola assigned the first German Jesuit, Peter Canisius (1521–97), back to Germany to spearhead the reform of the Catholic clergy in the wake of Luther's influence there, the young Jesuit found 90% of German priests living in concubinage. Perhaps today's transgressions of celibacy seem a significant improvement against the sixteenth-century practice, but only if one discounts the indignity and abuse of a great number of women.

In a random sample study of stress on Catholic priests in South Africa, Father Victor Kortz found that 43.1% were involved in a friendship or love relationship and that 37.7% had terminated such a relationship within the previous 2 years (Kotze, 1991). In 1994 he asserted that these relationships had all the qualities of sexual affairs (1994, p. 320).

No one has seriously challenged similar estimates of American clergy sexual involvement with women. Regional and national churches can make their own assessments. Whatever the number, women are abused in significant numbers by men who maintain their status and privilege within the celibate system while they relegate their women to the status of a backstreet wife.

Some of these relationships are truly tragic because they are dominated by love—love for each other, love for the people they serve, and love for the living core of Christ's message transmitted in the tradition of the church. Alas, the love for a woman cannot be proclaimed openly but is always compromised to some degree by the ambiguity of public deceit. The priests and their lovers do not deceive each other or themselves; however, their love is not celibate.

Most priests' sexual relationships with women are not this complicated. Many are sequential involvements determined by the priest's opportunism, selfishness, immature exploitiveness, or character deficits, which leave the women traumatized and confused. Priests perpetuate and participate in the cultural distortions, where (in the words of Andrea Dworkin) "men expect to be individual, whereas women are supposed to get used to being interchangeable and replaceable" (personal communication).

## Myth 2: Marriage and Celibacy Are Hardly Distinguishable Experiential Realities

Because serious discourse on celibacy is neglected even in the highest echelons of the church, popular myths and glib comparisons between marriage and celibacy prevail. One example: "It [celibacy] is no more impossible, if we are happy in our work, than fidelity is for a normally heterosexually married man [or woman, for that matter] who is reasonably satisfied in his [or her] marriage, which is to say that there are times when it is only mildly difficult and other times when it is extremely difficult indeed" (Greeley, 1983b, p. 6).

Happiness or satisfaction is not a link uniting or separating marriage and celibacy. Nor should *fidelity* blur the essential distinctions between these ways of loving. Chastity in preparation for marriage is not an identical process to chastity in the service of celibacy. The myth of easy comparison keeps unappreciated and unaccounted for three realities, described here, of the difference between marriage and celibacy.

**Biological Base** The first reality is that celibacy and marriage are founded on two distinct biological bases: one physically bonded and potentially reproductive and linked with sexual affection and mutual support; the other group unbonded, nonreproductive, and invested with a more universalized and nonsexual affection. The distinctions are so clear that some theologians claim that celibacy makes a man unfit for marriage. A celibate is not a man who happens *not* to be married—he is not meant to be married; or in the words of another theologian, Paul Dinter, the celibate is "disabled for the kingdom." These attempts to describe the difference between celibacy and marriage are perhaps unfortunate to the degree that they may be misread as pejorative toward celibacy. Words like *unfit* and *disabled* can be misheard unless one reads them as correctives to the distorted claims for the superiority of celibacy. Also belied are the glib assumptions so frequently pressed on children that "every boy is called to the priesthood and celibacy; those who can't meet this ideal have to settle for marriage as a distant second best."

Better or worse is really not the point. What is important is the fact that some people are biogenetically and psychologically suited for marriage; others are just as strongly suited for celibacy. The grace, or gift, of celibacy has to have some natural base. These predispositions are not interchangeable at will. Not every man is capable of marriage. Not every man is capable of celibacy. This is the nature of biosexual diversity; it is also the reality of different graces or gifts. Marriage and celibacy may be sequential; for example, some widowed in the early church were thought to be suited to celibacy, as was probably the case with St. Paul.

**Celibate Versus Sexual Abstinence**  The second reality is that celibacy is not simply sexual abstinence or sexual restraint. Many adolescents live with long periods of sexual abstinence, but their so-called celibacy is often motivated by fear, lack of opportunity, social inhibition, or awkwardness. Their intent is far from celibate. They are making plans or looking for opportunities to have an active sexual life and eventual marriage.

Married people can also abstain from sexual activity for more or less long periods of time because of ill health, age, external circumstances, or periodic conflict and strain. This is not equal to celibate striving, which is a mode of being and a context for relationships and interaction.

Failure to distinguish the basic differences between celibate abstinence within the celibate state and striving and periodic or even prolonged sexual abstinence within marriage or the single state leads some priests to discount their own sexual activity. Priests, so conditioned, view their own sexual involvements as necessary periodic lapses equivalent to a married man's lapse due to a long period of forced separation. The injustice to the woman, used by both types of men for their sexual comfort, may be equal in some regards, but the internal self-deception is of a different order for the celibate. It violates the nature of what he claims to be.

**Concretization of the Symbol/Sexualization of the Spiritual**  The third reality is that some very fancy rationalizations blur the lines between celibacy and marriage. Oftentimes these mental gymnastics begin with scriptural metaphors and analogies. For instance, using the venerable theological idea of "covenant between God and his people" or "the church as the bride of Christ," some priests identify themselves with Christ in ways that make the symbolism concrete and thereby sexualize the spiritual. For instance, a priest explaining his ordination and first mass announced that the priest's ordination was like the marriage ceremony and his first mass was like the consummation of marriage. This is simply nonsense, theologically and sexually. Mass for Catholics is a banquet. The love feast of breaking bread together is a spiritual, not a sexual, union. Pagan rites involved food and sex.

Because sexuality is not well understood, celibates are easily led astray by the concepts of *nuptial covenant* and *eucharistic nuptial love*. This is clear from numerous examples of priests who, in the process of spiritual direction, become involved sexually with their penitents under the guise of demonstrating the eternal love of God. Some encourage a penitent to lie down—"a proper position in which to receive God's grace." Progressively the priest takes an ever-closer physical position of relaxation and comfort, culminating in physical touch, caressing, kissing, and even masturbation or intercourse. This process has been reported by both female and male victims.

The seduction is often so gradual and so subtle that at first the victim does not realize that the line between the spiritual and the sexual has been crossed. The subterfuge is not apparent at the beginning of the process when the symbolism seems so enlightened and at the same time grounded in ancient theological concepts sanctioned by church authorities who speak about the "eucharistic foundation of sacerdotal celibacy" and the "nuptial covenant" between the priest and his people. Often the priest is the victim of his own self-deception. At first he may not consciously set out to seduce or violate his trust. He gets mixed up in his own symbols, which gradually become concretized. He is blinded by the sexualization of his own spirituality because it seems so natural. Of course, the process of spiritual growth should proceed in exactly the opposite direction, from sexual awareness to spiritual resolution.

The struggle of Graham Greene's whiskey priest in *The Power and the Glory* (1972) belies the myth that blurs the distinction between marriage and celibacy. It is in his failure to love maritally and parentally, not in his success, that he learns the meaning of his vocation, even if he can only grasp at it ambivalently.

In the final episode of the novel, the priest confronts head on the dissonance between his growing love for his fellow prisoners and the discovery of his personal love for his daughter. It is conflict, not resolution. As he awaits execution by firing squad the following day, drinking brandy to make the wait more bearable, the priest attempts a confession. But, while dwelling on the absurdity of his "mortal sin" with Maria, the mother of his child, he seems to be stymied; then the significance of his lapse strikes him.

> As the liquid touched his tongue he remembered his child, coming in out of the glare: the sullen, unhappy, knowledgeable face. He said, "Oh God, help her. Damn me, I deserve it, but let her live forever." This was the love he should have felt for every soul in the world: all the fear and the wish to save concentrated unjustly on the one child. He began to weep; it was as if he had to watch her from the shore drown slowly because he had forgotten how to swim. He thought: "This is what I should feel all the time for everyone," and he tried to turn his brain away. . . . Another failure. (p. 197)

## MYTH 3: THE DIGNITY OF WOMEN HAS BEEN PRESERVED BECAUSE OF THE VENERATION OF THE VIRGIN MOTHER MARY

In practical terms this is not true. It is a cover-up for the denigration of ordinary women. If the history of the church and the calendar of saints are reviewed, virgins, martyrs, and widows are the female heroes. The sexless, the silent, and the dead are models for women. Certainly this fact did not deter all women from breaking the mold. For instance, St. Peter's Basilica in Rome houses a monumental tomb of Matilda of Canossa who in Stickler's *Guide to the Vatican* is described as

> protectress of the Roman Papacy in the eleventh century, an age of conflict between the Papacy and the Empire. She is represented holding the papal tiara and St. Peter's keys in her left hand and the scepter in her right hand. On the sarcophagus which contains the remains of this fiery countess is a representation of Henry IV, Emperor of Germany, in the castle of Canossa on January 28, 1077. He is kneeling at the feet of Gregory VII, who had excommunicated him.

Power in marble is not reproduced in reality. Gratitude to the dead does little to ease the restriction of the living to roles of subservience. The woman as man's helper is a common, acceptable role.

Virginity for the woman is so highly treasured that death in its defense is considered worthy of canonization. Maria Goretti, a 13-year-old girl, was designated a saint in 1950 for enduring death rather than rape. Horrible alternatives—but few loving parents would counsel their adolescent daughters to choose the former even in the prospect of violation (Norris, 1994).

Virginity is usually defined from a male point of view—as unused, uncultivated, and unexplored, which assumes, in the words of Andrea Dworkin, that it "is a state of passive waiting or vulnerability; it precedes and is antithetical to wholeness" (1987, p. 96).

The male assumption about the value of virginity and motherhood reached its apotheosis in the definitions of Otto Weininger in *Sex and Character* (1909), where Woman does not exist in herself, but is conferred being by the Man, by his gracious consideration and his self-compromise by sexual involvement. This formula keeps woman in her place and glorifies both male celibacy and sexuality to the point of divinization. Man cannot lose, woman cannot win. If celibate, priests are justified in their treatment of women, regarding only virgins and mothers as valuable, or if a vowed celibate becomes sexually active he favors a woman and only proves his humanity and her dangerousness, vulnerability, and need.

## Myth 4: Women Are Dangerous

This myth is so deeply ingrained that it too has been canonized since the time of St. Augustine by the whole of Western theology. Priests are taught and teach that women constitute a danger. Women are held up as the greatest threat to priesthood and its celibate power.

Studies conducted by the National Conference of Catholic Bishops have determined that 10% of priests in the United States leave the active priesthood within 5 years of ordination, 25% leave within 25 years of ordination—most of them to marry. An undetermined but substantial number of these groups also leave to pursue honest homosexual relationships. Only glibness and bias could see in this phenomenon proof of the danger of women. The celibate/sexual system of the church is its own worst enemy. Mature Christian men—whether priest or lay—reject as untrue and ridiculous the myth that women pose a threat to life, nature, men, or culture. Equality of women does pose a distinct threat to the preservation of male dominance and bias, just as all truth poses a threat to ignorance, prejudice, and evil.

## MYTH 5: CELIBACY BEING A SUPERIOR STATE, WOMEN CAN BE USED TO FOSTER AND SUPPORT IT

Even saints who opted for celibacy after they sowed their wild oats—Ignatius and a myriad of others—leave no bold traces of gratitude to their former partners or a sense of the injustice done by their use of women. They lamented *their* sins, but they have left no history or model for reparation to the women involved in their development. Even St. Augustine, who psychologically owed so much of his greatness to the love of a devoted partner for 13 years, merely records his own anguish at the separation (as tearing his own flesh) and protects her with anonymity. He who could pay tribute of acknowledgment to heretics by volumes, who could preserve scores of letters, relegated this undoubtedly worthy woman to benign neglect. That is the kindest interpretation. Margaret Miles in *Desire and Delight* (1992) has begun a penetrating investigation into the nature of this important relationship.

Many priests use women to prove their masculinity, to comfort their loneliness, and to relieve their sexual needs. Some priests have a group of women, each of whom thinks she is the one special friend who really understands him and his problems. One such situation was exposed when one woman filed a paternity suit only to have four other women come forward; each thought she was in a unique and exclusive relationship with the priest. They filed a class action suit against him.

Some priests have sequential relationships; this pattern can exist for years or even over the whole duration of their priesthood. Other priests have affairs that endure for 1 to 5 years, from which they emerge in their own estimation better priests and frequently make the claim, "I am so much more understanding of married people now." Some are unmitigated exploitations without even the internal pretense of love or care. If repentant, the priest is forgiven, with great compassion for his *human* failing.

What about the woman? The unspoken explanation within the system persists that: (1) she is to blame for the priest's dalliance; (2) she should be grateful and silent for the privilege of such selection or closeness; (3) it is part of the special grace and gift of a woman to be able to save a priest by her love. At times this last rationale is underlined by calling God *She* and emphasizing the gracious love of the mother—God.

None of these myth-saving tactics compensates for the reality that women are abused in the service of perpetuating a celibate power system. Scores of bishops and religious superiors empathize with and support the priest in his lapse or sin. Most of the time there is little or no real feeling for the woman.

A nun alleged that she was raped by a priest. No one who knew the principals doubted the truth of the facts as she recounted them. The bishop supported the priest completely, threatened the nun and her community, legally and figuratively beating them into silence.

In some of his novels Father Andrew Greeley records how deeply this myth is embedded in the unconscious of the celibate/sexual system. In his fiction, a woman very often saves a priest—sometimes by direct action, more often by becoming a sacrificial victim, and sometimes by acting as an ideal worth living for.

Ellen Foley, one of the characters in Greeley's first best-seller, *The Cardinal Sins*, acts directly to save her friend Cardinal Patrick Donohue when a confederation of Mafiosi and right-wing religious zealots conspires to blackmail him (1982a, pp. 470–483).

At other times, Greeley's heroines save priests through sacrifice, and sometimes this sacrifice is direct. In *Virgin and Martyr*, for example, Father Ed, leader of a group of leftist American missionaries, decides that his group needs a martyr (and also a bit of ready cash). So he sells Sister Catherine Collins to a group of deviant right-wing police:

> Ed kissed her. I love you, Cathy. I will miss you. This is for the best. I know it's for the best. It will purify you and it will purify the Movement. At last we will have our heroine, our martyr.
> Even then, knowing that he had betrayed her, she could not hate him. (1985, p. 463)

Sometimes the sacrifice makes little sense to an outsider, as in *Angels of September*, in which a grammar school girl is made to model nude for a deranged priest who is painting the torments of hell. But in the minds of priest and victim alike, the model is expiating a collective (or at least a shared) guilt brought on by a fire that had killed a number of children. In all of these instances, the girl/woman redeems the priest by offering herself as a sacrifice.

These are not, of course, the only ways in which Greeley's women save lives; they can also do so by inspiring love and hope in a priest. In her essay, "The Dance of Creation and Incarnation; God, Woman, and Sex in the Novels of Andrew Greeley," Professor Ingrid Shafer notes that "Maria Manfrady of *Ascent into Hell* . . . saves the Irish priest Hugh Donlon from the psychological equivalent of Dante's frozen hell" (1989, p. 260); and we can extrapolate Professor Shafer's category of salvation of a priest through inspiration to the heroine of *Thy Brother's Wife* (Greeley, 1982b).

In his autobiography, Greeley himself says of his priests that "their responses were made with honesty, integrity, and sincerity, and in each case they were made under the influence of God as mediated by a woman" (1987, pp. 494–495).

## MYTH 6: ABORTION AND WOMAN'S DUTY

Abortion is the one issue in which a male power system would like to stand on moral high ground, pronouncing and defending principles presumably without any regard for personal pressure or bias—unmarried and male, objective commentators on questions of life and death, good and evil, especially in sexual matters.

In reality, the questions surrounding abortion, which involve population, poverty, and not least women's rights, are far deeper and more complex than most priests are willing to discuss.

As the fourth oldest of a family of 10 children, I can well remember the difficult pregnancies my mother endured with my 6 younger siblings. I was about 12 and on my way to serve Thursday evening devotions at our parish church one hot summer evening when my mother whispered to me, "Would you ask the priest to come to the house some time and give me the blessing for expectant mothers?" The young curate was immediately responsive and offered to walk home with me after the service. We entered the house through the front door, a ceremonial aperture in our home, one reserved for rare special visitors. I watched as the priest read from his Ritual with the thin white travel stole around his neck. I watched my mother, ordinarily a slim woman, now confined to a living room chair, her legs swollen beyond recognizable shape, cold wet towels covering her undistinguishable ankles, two electric fans blowing on her. (She was preeclamptic several times and once eclamptic.)

Palpably, she derived a kind of consolation I could not fathom from the priest's parting words, "Remember, Mrs. Sipe, the church teaches that women who die in childbirth go straight to Heaven." She seemed quite peaceful; I was struck dumb with terror because a friend of my mother's, who was the mother of a classmate, had recently died in childbirth.

There was never any question of abortion in my mind or in our home, but somehow I knew even then that something was out of kilter—something I could not define, but rebelled at. The solutions so dramatically portrayed in the novel (and later the movie) *The Cardinal*, always ended the same way: the woman had to be sacrificed on the altar of moral righteousness. The woman gives her life to save the baby (the precious son, most likely).

I was equally puzzled when I learned as a junior in high school that a priest criticized my parents for practicing the rhythm method of birth control. I know now that as a boy I was disturbed by the power factor and the myth of woman's duty to be the victim. Her only choice was to sacrifice herself in order to save.

Precisely because it espouses this myth, abortions of children fathered by priests is one of the most lethal time bombs ticking within the American Catholic Church.

In a loosely affiliated group of approximately 50 women, each has had an abortion at the insistence, with the help, or at the urging of the priest whose child she carried. Although none has yet come to attention through civil litigation, it is only a matter of time before the nature and scope of this issue becomes public record. Some women have received financial settlements that require their silence; most will not speak openly because they want to protect themselves, their family, or the priest they loved and whom they thought loved them. Most of these women are aware of the humiliation and accusations that public exposure and confrontation would cost them. A few women had abortions without telling their priest-lover of the pregnancy. But many of these women track the careers of their mostly former friends. It is especially galling to some women to witness the promotion and advancement of the priest abortionist within the church power structure, while the women struggle to work out the pain of loss, abandonment, and the confusion of the scarlet *A* emblazoned on their memory and soul.

Many of the stories are similar. A woman falls in love with a priest who says he loves her.

*Phase One: The Beginning*—He presents himself as a man who needs help and understanding. Often he speaks of his desire to leave the priesthood or of his conflict over his vocation.

*Phase Two: The Courtship*—None of these victims is a casual encounter like Greene's whiskey priest, whose daughter is conceived in a drunken blur with an unloved partner. Some women have stacks of love letters clearly showing the priest as the pursuer. "My precious darling. . .I have an insatiable need to be loved—so please tell me how you would love me and how you would want me to love you in return. I'm starving." Or in a later letter the same priest wrote, "Yes, my darling, I can't wait to give you my hands—to do with them as you please—and to have my mouth caress every part of your body in an ecstacy of love that neither of us will likely soon forget. You'll probably think I'm the horniest guy you've ever known." And so forth. This priest could close his letters to this same woman, "Devotedly in Christ." Some priests tend to play at love.

*Phase Three: The Relationship*—Courting pays off. Both parties seem to be settled in a working arrangement, with serious talks about the future, how to negotiate leaving the priesthood, livelihoods, living circumstances, and so on. To all intents and purposes it seems like a real relationship, especially to the woman who has been given every reason to count on marriage and who thinks that the difficulties experienced are simply because of the complications in coping with the transition from the celibate system to marriage. Only in retrospect do most women realize how uneven the relationship was all along. Most feel they had to give more to the relationship because the priests had to give so much to their ministry. Later it becomes clear how much the priests were taking from both.

*Phase Four: The Shock*—Pregnancy is usually unplanned by both parties. Contraceptive failure or miscalculation of fertility are the most common conscious reasons. Of course, women are often accused of entrapment, conscious or not, as if women are eager to suffer the complications of an unplanned pregnancy just to force the man into commitment. Bishops and religious superiors who do not listen to the woman are prone to accept the priest's rationalization as he returns to the fold. Most commonly, the pregnancy comes as a genuine surprise to both parties. Only under this pressure does the real quality of the relationship reveal itself.

*Phase Five: Poor Me*—The woman finds herself isolated in the pregnancy. If she suffers from morning sickness, the priest feels himself even more oppressed. Empathy is available not for the woman but rather for the priest who is now threatened with exposure and loss of his status and job. The demands on the relationship are to comfort the priest, who wails, "How could this happen to me?" The psychic scenario fits so neatly into his assumptions: punishment for his sins, and it's the woman's fault. Now he realizes how precious his priesthood is. The center of concern manifests itself: it is not the woman, nor the unborn—it is the priest.

*Phase Six: You Have to Do Something*—The burden to do something is on the woman. It is her fault. No matter how persistent the priest was in beginning the sexual relationship, he now has little to do with the problem. Pregnancy is a woman's concern. How could she endanger his priesthood this way? At this juncture, the woman is often socially isolated because of the secret nature of the relationship, as well as physically abandoned by the person on whom she counted. And she is threatened with exposure as an unmarried pregnant woman (or occasionally still married). Frightened, sometimes by a first pregnancy, and physically ill, she is vulnerable. These priests insist on an abortion. Some pay for it. Some arrange for it in a locale removed from their assignment to ensure anonymity. Some take the woman to the clinic, less to comfort than to make sure she goes through with it. A few make her secure her own transportation.

*Phase Seven: Goodbye, Baby*—No matter how the priest insists that "this is the only way for us to continue the relationship," the event marks the end of the playing, the pretense, and thus the relationship. The woman is only an added responsibility and to the priest a reminder of the betrayal he has experienced at her hands. Even if it takes months or a year, promises of undying love turn out to be the night after the prom. Whatever the words, it amounts to the simple, loaded sentiment, "Goodbye, baby."

*Phase Eight: Reconciliation with the System*—Some priests continue within the system, moving from relationship to relationship hoping for better luck next time. Others return to the system of power, pardoned and devout. It becomes clearer to some now that alliance with the system must be preserved at all costs. Still others merely become more deceptive, exploitative, and careful. If the experience leads to repentance, the bishop or religious superior rarely understands the situation from the woman's point of view. She is the sinner, the priest the ingenue, led astray by the wiles of a scheming woman. If she approaches church authority for some kind of compensation, it only proves her motivation to be greedy as well as impure.

As I have analyzed these cases I realize how few men in the church understand the woman's experience of love, loss, and betrayal. The myth of the woman's duty to sacrifice herself and her life for another becomes patently and painfully clear. It is as if a higher law is invoked. It is the priest who must be saved. He is the valuable fetus, and the mother must sacrifice her life (or a part of it at least) to save the celibate/sexual system or at least that part of it ensconced in this particular priest.

## MYTH 7: SPIRITUAL FRIENDSHIPS WITH WOMEN ARE COMMON AMONG CELIBATES AND EASY TO MAINTAIN

Robert McAllister (1986), a psychiatrist with broad experience with priests and religious, wisely points out that celibates cannot expect to attain the kind and quality of intimacy available in marriage and the family. The demands and gratification of celibacy are distinct from marriage.

A priest of no lesser mind and heart than Pierre Teilhard de Chardin (1881–1955) devised the term the *third way*. The first way is marriage; the second, religious life; and the third, a spiritual bond and relationship between a man and a woman that would consist of deep intimacy without physical involvement. Both would remain chaste, but they would develop "the unfathomable spiritual powers that still lie dormant under the mutual attraction of the sexes." Physical expression would be sublimated (King & Gilbert, 1993, p. 295). Under pressure from the Vatican, the Superior General of the Jesuits condemned this teaching.

In 1934 Teilhard wrote an essay, "The Evolution of Chastity," in which he said he had puzzled over the feminine from the time he was 30 years old. He had friendships that were secure and open enough to permit discussion of the place of friendship within celibate practice. Of his 28-year friendship with Lucile Swan, one witness comments, "a biographer wrote that one year before his death as Teilhard read *The Feminine*, the final chapter of his spiritual auto-biography, *The Heart of Matter*, he wept, 'at the memory of all the re-proachful "Beatrices" he knew he hurt unwittingly' " (King & Gilbert, 1993, p. 297).

St. Francis of Assisi (1181–1226), one of the most accessible saintly images (Erikson, 1970) because of his humaneness and love of animals and nature, was before his conversion, in the words of his first biographer, Fra Celano, "The first instigator of every evil, and behind none in foolishness." His magnetism and later religious fervor attracted many followers, among them St. Clare (1182–1226) who at 17, "ran away from her family of wealthy and nobel Assisiani and became a disciple of St. Francis and later head of the Franciscan order for women, the Poor Clares." The commentator goes on to say, "Whatever the later Church mythology, gratifying rumors were never lacking that there was more to her relationship with Francis than practical piety" (Facaros & Pauls, 1989, p. 408).

St. Ignatius Loyola's life and the history of the early Society of Jesus provide ample proof of how complex intimate friendships are for the practicing celibate. In his study *The Psychology of a Saint: Ignatius of Loyola*, William W. Meissner, a Jesuit priest and psychoanalyst, writes a brilliant description of the development of Ignatius's friendships with women, from early enthusiastic naiveté to seasoned and reverent reserve and distance (1992, pp. 238–271). Ignatius's experiences with women and the problems with the personal devotion he inspired in them, culminated in a 1546 memorandum he sent to Pope Paul III. It read in part:

> For although we are not worthy to loose the shoestrings of blessed
> St. Francis and St. Dominic. . . . Yet we observe how their orders

are much burdened and troubled by the constant complaints of their houses of nuns—indeed, we see this daily at the Roman curia. Therefore we have formed the opinion that in the future our Society might be involved in such disputes and scandals, if we were to undertake the spiritual direction of women and accept their obedience. Even with regard to these women whose direction we have undertaken at the special command of His Holiness, we hope soon to gain the favour of being freed from them again. (Meissner, 1992, p. 270)

We have no reservations about the celibate practice of Teilhard, Francis, or Ignatius in spite of unsubstantiated and frivolous rumors about each. What each does demonstrate is the difficulty of maintaining clear celibate lines in close friendships. Such friendships demand on the part of both parties firm, celibate, or chaste commitments; intelligence; openness; absolute honesty about the internal state of desire; and the strength and flexibility of ego to adapt to changing circumstances within the constraints of celibate demands. Such relationships are not impossible, but those who think such relationships are easy do not know the lonely necessities of celibate practice or the force of unconscious demands and the discipline that self-knowledge requires.

Those who facilely claim that women who have an intimate priest-friend make better lovers to their husbands miss the possible implications of unconscious homosexual gratification for the priest—only one of the dangers of the perpetuation of the myth that intimate friendships between a practicing celibate and a woman are easy or common.

• • •

Each of the seven myths about priests and women is fueled and sustained by an adolescent mind-set inherent in the celibate/sexual system of power: Men (boys) are superior to women; women (girls) have the duty and responsibility to sacrifice and take care of men (boys); women (mother figures, actually) are in charge and to blame, whereas men's needs and work are more important and demanding. Sexual activity is publicly denied but can be privately indulged in and experimented with because of a man's humanity.

These attitudes coexist with bouts of extreme (or mild) asceticism and self-denial and the articulation of high and refined ideals. Unresolved ambivalences can impel the priest between indulgence and sacrifice, dedicated service and self-gratification, sexual abandon and deep remorse, all easily available to him and sanctioned within the system that reveres the woman as mother, virgin, martyr and reserves the right to preach and minister to the shadow side of each image — blameworthy whore and destroyer.

## CODE OF SEXUAL ETHICS FOR PRIESTS

Until very recently it never occurred to anyone that priests would need a professional code of ethics. They are, after all, representatives of moral righteousness, the teachers of right and wrong — what else is needed? Do what you preach. Common sense alone would seem to rule out sexual contact in any professional setting. Psychology shows that such has not been the case over the past 50 years, when sexuality has become a more open topic for discussion and study even as various therapies have identified sexual fantasies and traumas as elements requiring understanding for the resolution of psychic confusion. Perhaps the nadir of common sense in this regard was reached in 1970 when a national convention of psychologists included five presentations on the value of sex between client and therapist.

The possibility and danger of sexual violation within a helping and healing setting are not recent concerns. The Hippocratic Oath contains an explicit prohibition against sexual relations with patients: "I will attend for the benefit of the sick, remaining free of all intentional injustice, of all mischief, and in particular of sexual relations with both female and male persons." Even though most of the early psychoanalysts were physicians and bound by that oath, and even though Freud's firm conviction that "analysis can only take place in an atmosphere of strict deprivation," many of the early analysts overstepped professional boundaries with their patients.

A 1989 review of exploitation among the helping professions revealed among psychologists "that 5.5 percent of the males and 0.6 percent of females admitted having engaged in sexual intercourse with their patients. Ten percent of males and 1 percent of females admitted to erotic practices" (Gabbard, 1989, pp. 17–18). A survey of psychiatrists revealed "6.4 percent overall prevalence of therapist-patient sexual contact" (p. 10), and 1.6 percent of psychiatrist respondents "indicated that they had been sexually involved with their own therapist or analyst" (p. 9).

Comparable surveys of clergy have not yet been conducted, but Dr. Williams Holme, a theology professor, comments,

> The clergy as sexual boundary violators are also unique. Their position as clergy goes with a community in which they are the

VIPs. It is also a religious community in which the clergy are the symbol bearers of the tradition of faith, specifically, of God. . . . The authority and power implicit in the role of the clergy may elicit sexual responses from some members of the community. The same is true with others in positions of authority whose power and prestige attract. But there is more attraction on the part of some of the clergy precisely because this power and authority has the added dimension of transcendence. (Gabbard, 1989, pp. 181–182)

This observation, although it has merit, places the burden of transference on the church member—woman or man. There is a superior obligation on the clergyman to know his deepest motivations in embracing the ministry and its power at the same time that he takes full responsibility for his countertransference. For the celibate, this requires a growing dedication to the celibate process and radical honesty. Both tasks exceed the limits of adolescent adjustment.

Priests profess celibacy but are rarely taught what is morally appropriate, responsible, or mature for the noncelibate or for himself. Current theology does not aid him in teaching others. Too often sexual exploitations by a priest are seen as understandable human slips or regrettable but easily forgivable sins. They are instead grave violations of professional ethics.

*Professionally, it should be clear that sexual contact is never appropriate as part of any pastoral care or ministry. Sexual contact is not only sexual intercourse but includes fondling or any sexual touching, sexual innuendo, kissing, and nudity.*

In 1992 the American Psychiatric Association revised its 1986 code of ethics to rule that sexual involvement with a patient even after the termination of treatment is never permissible. This is consistent with the idea that the physician's commitment to the patient is both sacred and perpetually unbreachable. In her 1992 review of boundary violations among professionals, Marilyn Peterson outlines the demands on the clergy (1992, pp. 15–16) and the power issues involved in abuse by any professional (pp. 34–104).

All clergy and especially priests who claim complete and perpetual chastity can aspire to no less a professional standard than physicians. Celibacy requires a level of maturity that can sustain a professional stance in all ministry and a degree of spirituality that can ensure sexually appropriate, responsible, and honest relationships with all women, men, and children.

# 7

# PRIESTS AND MEN

*What happiness, what security, what joy to have someone to whom you dare to speak on terms of equality as to another self; one to whom you need have no fear to confess your failings; one to whom you can unblushingly make known what progress you have made in the spiritual life; one to whom you can entrust all the secrets of your heart and before whom you can place all your plans! . . . A friend is the medicine of life.*

Aelred of Rievaulx (1110–67)

*Presumably this experience [of sexuality] is much the same for heterosexuals and homosexuals. The search for love, for that person who in her or his gift of self returns us to our own, truest self, usually constitutes the central drama of our lives. How perplexing that the force compelling us toward our most intimate meaningful encounter seems so opaque to rational inquiry, so fraught with moral ambiguity.*

Paul Baumann

The homosexual crisis of the church's doctrinal and behavioral integrity will be revealed more from within the system than from the outside. Priests themselves will bring it to resolution or perpetuate duplicity and abuse.

A notice posted on the main bulletin board of The North American College in Rome—the premier seminary for outstanding candidates for the priesthood selected from dioceses in the United States—reads, *Overt Homosexuality Will Not Be Tolerated In This Seminary.* The linguistic ambiguity cannot be missed; nor the unintentional humor. Is covert homosexuality tolerable? Is homosexual behavior outside the seminary acceptable? What is unmistakable is that homosexuality is a confusing subject in Catholic teaching. It is a

131

perplexing problem in moral doctrine and practice at the very heart of the celibate/sexual system. There are consistent reports that 20% of seminarians experience homosexual contact during the years of their training.

A 1980 study of 50 gay priests by a Roman Catholic priest was startling, and it remains so (Wagner, 1980). Only 4% of that group were sexually abstinent; the other 90-plus % had abandoned the celibate process. The priests in the study ranged in age from 27 to 58. They averaged 226.8 sexual partners each. "Of some note is the fact that nine respondents (18 percent) in this sample had no more than ten partners total, while eleven (22 percent) reported five hundred or more. Kinsey found that 39.2 percent of his sample had no more than ten partners, while 8.4 percent reported having more than five hundred" (pp. 26–27). Sixty percent of the group reported feeling free of guilt; only 26% reported feeling guilty (p. 94). Eighty-six percent of this group considered themselves happy or somewhat happy; only 14% regarded themselves somewhat unhappy or unhappy (p. 98).

This study remains important in several ways. First, however unrepresentative, it records in detail the kind and amount of sexual activity in a group claiming celibate identity; this remains a pioneering excursion into unchartered territory.

Second, it demonstrates that there is no correlation between practicing celibacy or being sexually active and considering oneself *happy*, as some surveys seem to imply. For instance, a *Los Angeles Times* survey of 2,087 priests published February 20, 1994, found that "87 percent of priests...were happy and would renew their vows." Nearly half of the priests (44%) said birth control is seldom or never a sin; and 21% said they "frequently offered advice that conflicts with church teaching; and 58 percent of priests...said Catholics can disagree with some church teachings and still be faithful" (see also Kaufman, 1991). Priest-sociologist Andrew Greeley has written repeatedly that celibates are just as happy, mature, and capable of intimacy as men of comparable age. His statements say nothing about sexual behavior or celibate practice. These are examples that emphasize the importance of clarifying distinctions between celibate practice and the celibate culture.

Third, the study shows the vast number of sexual contacts that can be shielded under the cover of systemic secrecy.

Fourth, but foremost, one must remember that although this study allows an important glimpse into part of the celibate/sexual system, it does not represent the sexual behavior of the vast majority of those priests who have a homosexual orientation. But it does reflect many contradictions and problems that need to be addressed within the celibate/sexual system and in the sexual teaching of the church.

Homosexuality is a reality in human nature, in the function and structure of the church, and in the lives of some Christian men, priests, and bishops. It is also that reality, even if frequently misunderstood, that has the potential for the greatest crisis for ecclesiastical integrity.

There is no area of sexuality more misunderstood, distorted, maligned, and actually feared than the homosexualities. The use of the plural is not accidental. Since we do not have a sophisticated moral and behavioral vocabulary with regard to homosexual development, orientation, and behavior—as we do with heterosexuality—the use of the plural is necessary to avoid glibness and to pursue accurate definition and delineation.

For instance, the man who loves his wife and is devoted to his daughters prides himself that he is heterosexual in orientation and behavior. But he would hardly put himself in the same category as the man who stands by the school yard eager to engage little girls in sexual activity or as the man who lurks in dark corners looking to overpower some woman with his sexual passion. He would insist that one be identified as a pedophile and the other as a rapist. He would not be satisfied that all such men be described as heterosexual in orientation and behavior, but would demand more accurate definition and more precise categories. Heterosexual orientation or behavior is not necessarily a *good* in and of itself.

Generally speaking, the only distinction made about homosexuality is between orientation and behavior. Both are assumed to be, and are often labeled, *bad* or *defective*, although orientation can be tolerated by some moralists more readily than behavior. There is little understanding of the place of the homosexualities in nature or in the developmental process, in spite of Freud's pioneering explorations in his *Three Essays on the Theory of Sexuality* (1905/1953). He distinguished three types of people having "contrary sexual feelings": "absolute" (obligatory), "amphigenic" (bisexual), and "contingent" (situational). He also dealt with the questions of innate predisposition versus acquired character of the sexual instinct, and degeneracy.

Three shifts in awareness are needed to understand the homosexual facets of reality.

First, one must abandon the simplistic assumption that the distinction between homosexual orientation and behavior is sufficient to define the reality accurately, any more than merely distinguishing between heterosexual orientation and behavior tells the whole story.

Second, one must develop an equal neutrality about the concepts *homosexual* and *heterosexual*. *Homosexual* is no more bad than *heterosexual* is good, just as the idea of food tells us nothing about its being good or bad, since it can be applied to pheasant under glass in the most expensive restaurant as well as to a carcass in the middle of the jungle.

Third, homosexual and heterosexual are not oppositional concepts, at least developmentally, as if being heterosexual or behaving heterosexually obviated or protected one against homosexual feelings or behaving homosexually. Psychic bisexuality remains a reasonable assumption. To put it in a homespun way: We all have a father and a mother. It would be foolish to think that we inherited qualities only from the parent of our same sex. Boys are like their mothers and girls are like their fathers, just as much as being like the parent of the same sex.

Kinsey's work first made me aware of the need to expand my own understanding of the homosexualities. A passage that jarred me at first was from his *Sexual Behavior in the Human Female* (Kinsey, Pomeroy, Martin, & Gebhard, 1953): "Heterosexual coitus is extolled in most cultures, but forbidden to Buddhist and Catholic priests. Homosexual activity is condemned in some cultures, tacitly accepted in others, honored as a religious rite in others, and allowed to Buddhist priests" (p. 320).

When I consulted Buddhists about Kinsey's statement, I quickly became aware that their frame of reference regarding the homosexual-heterosexual spectrum was distinct from the Western Judeo-Christian tradition of discontinuity and opposition. The Eastern view, as I understand it, sees sex as one, and homosexuality is part of a developmental phase or variation. One Buddhist monk said he was sure that homosexual activity was common, but it would be seen as a failure of growth and detachment and would be "smiled upon," much the same way one indulges a child involved in some naughtiness that must pass if he is to be promoted or grow up.

A visitor to a Tibetan monastery received a different response to his inquiry:

> Celibacy is an important element in Tibetan Buddhist monasticism. It is taught as a value from the earliest years and is one of the four musts in terms of monastic vows. The four initial vows are: not to steal, not to kill, not to have sexual relations, not to lie. The breaking of any one of these four is cause for immediate expulsion. As far as celibacy is concerned, any violation with another is a serious matter. I asked Kalsang about homosexuality. He said it is

not a problem with Tibetans. If any incident between males did happen, it would mean the end of one's monastic life. (Kelly, 1986, p. 37)

These are not far removed from the attitudes held by seminary officials. Both expulsion and tolerance are recorded. Limited homosexual experience in a candidate's background is tolerated. Coitus, is also tolerated, but considered inimical to completion of the course of studies. As one seminary professor put it, "Once they get a taste of that," it is very tough to keep the discipline"—meaning, of course, celibacy. The shame and guilt of an isolated homosexual encounter, plus the structure of the seminary schedule, are presumed to be positively motivational rather than a deterrent to celibacy.

Here again we see the split between the official teaching (homosexuality is bad) and the practical application (homosexual experience can be tolerated, at least in one's past). Also, the system of secrecy is foreshadowed here. This attitude of pastoral tolerance is in contrast to certain fundamentalist Christian ministries (i.e., the Assembly of God, and the Baptists), where homosexual behavior is an automatic and irreversible disqualification for ministry.

Data from a total of 20,000 men and women led Kinsey and colleagues (1953) to say:

> The data indicate that the factors leading to homosexual behavior are: 1) the basic physiologic capacity of every mammal to respond to any sufficient stimulus; 2) the accident which leads an individual into his or her first sexual experience with a person of the same sex; 3) the conditioning effects of such experience; and 4) the indirect but powerful conditioning which the opinions of other persons and the social codes may have on an individual's decision to accept or reject this type of sexual contact. . . . In actuality, sexual contacts between individuals of the same sex are known to occur in practically every species of mammal which has been extensively studied. (pp. 447–448)

## HOMOSEXUALITIES AND THE CLERGY

"People who mediate between different levels—between mankind and the gods in the case of priests, or between youth and adulthood in the case of initiates—are often made sexually ambiguous and, therefore, sacred. Indeed, part of their sacred quality results from this sexual ambiguity" (Hoffman, 1985, p. 32).

The problems of understanding the homosexualities are complex and not limited solely to questions of behavior or even orientation. Developmental, situational, and stress factors influence both ideation and behavior—sometimes in the service of growth as well as of regression. The Roman Catholic clergy is an exclusive, one-sex institution; that fact alone makes it a productive well of information about sexual functioning and orientation.

In a 1976 statement, the Vatican attitude toward homosexuality was quite compassionate if not entirely enlightened. Although it reasserted that homosexuality and sexual behavior outside marriage were sinful in principle, it urged prudence and understanding in dealing with individuals and acknowledged that homosexuals were suffering from "discrimination which is unjust except for some reservations—unjust because homosexuals often have a richer personality than those who discriminate against them." This relatively liberal and tolerant pastoral attitude is in stark contrast to the October 1986 *Letter to the Bishops of the Catholic Church on the Pastoral Care of Homosexual Persons,* also from the Vatican. Here, there is little pastoral encouragement for latitude or understanding of circumstances or individual conscience. All homosexual acts are described as "intrinsically disordered" and under no circumstance are to be approved. Although homosexual orientation in itself is not called sinful, a strong condemnatory stance is taken in these words: "It is a more or less strong tendency ordered toward an intrinsic moral evil; and thus the inclination itself must be seen as an objective disorder. . . . Therefore special concern and pastoral attention should be directed toward those who have this condition, lest they be led to believe that living out this orientation in homosexual activity is a morally acceptable notion. It is not." These sentiments were reiterated by Pope John Paul II in February 1994, when he chided the European Parliament for giving "judicial approval to homosexual practice." Their move, he claimed, would "legitimize a moral disorder" and give institutional approval to "deviant behavior, not in conformity with the law of God."

This shift in pastoral regulation coincides with an increase in the homosexualities being revealed among the clergy. Generally, 30% of U.S. priests (estimates established from all sources) are either involved in homosexual relationships, have a conflict about periodic sexual activity, feel compelled toward homosexual involvements, identify themselves as homosexual, or at least have serious questions about their sexual orientation or differentiation. Approximately half of these men act out sexually with others.

The reporting of homosexual behaviors has increased significantly, and the reliable estimates of percentage almost doubled from 1960 to 1994. Sexually active homosexual clergy tend to give higher estimates of homosexually oriented or active clergy in their areas. This phenomenon may be partly due to projection but also in part to their greater awareness of and sensitivity to the cues to the secret lifestyle and to multiple shared sexual contacts, both verbal and physical.

Is homosexual orientation and behavior on an increase in the priesthood? Some shifts are real, but some are merely apparent:

1. It is increasingly acceptable today to speak directly and openly about sexual matters—even the homosexualities. Men talk to each other—not merely in the privacy of the confessional or the consulting office—about their sexual fantasies, problems, and behaviors. This makes certain questions seem more prevalent, when they merely were not voiced previously.
2. Proportionately more men leave the clerical state to marry than to avail themselves of a homosexual partner. This gives an appearance of an increase of numbers of homosexually oriented active priests, when in fact it is not. It is merely an adjustment in the proportion of sexual orientations.
3. The feminist movement and the gay liberation movement have made people conscious of the homosocial organization of clerical life (seminary, parish, religious house); that is, men are central and necessary to the organization, whereas women are adjunctive and dispensable. Also, the hierarchical structuring of the church is monosexual; that is, power is reserved to one sex. These are realities that have existed for centuries, but we have only recently gained an awareness of them and an ability to name them. This is an important shift, but it makes the reality only more apparent.
4. The gay liberation movement between 1970 and the early 1980s encouraged open expression of sexual affection. This movement gained acceptance among a certain proportion of the clergy. Overt sexual activity has increased in one segment of the clergy, in spite of their profession of celibacy.
5. The open expression of the homosexualities in the clergy community, the greater tolerance of individual behaviors, the freedom of movement that makes various lifestyles possible, and the increasing need to recruit more priests, which has altered admission standards to seminaries and religious houses, have all increased

the appeal of the priesthood to some who openly identify themselves as gay; some of this group do not wish to live celibately (Nash, 1990; Wagner, 1980).

## PSYCHOLOGICAL DENIAL OF THE HOMOSOCIAL STRUCTURE

Although the Vatican has spoken more voluminously about heterosexual behavior than about the homosexualities, it is in this latter area that celibates have a great deal to teach about sexual development and homosexual reality. There is, however, an aura of psychological denial that surrounds questions of homosexualities and the clergy. Although the official pronouncements from Rome are consistent in condemning homosexual behavior, the pastoral practice has generally become more tolerant with regard to laypersons (Bowman, 1994). Vatican directives are addressed essentially to the pastoral care of the laity by bishops and priests. However, since *any* sexual activity for celibates is a violation of the perfect chastity ordained by canon law, the shift to stricter pastoral application of Vatican teaching has only theoretically to do with laypersons.

In the papal documents there is no acknowledgment of a clerical problem with homosexuality. This is partially because all sexual activity among celibates tends to exist in the secret forum. An average cleric can proceed through seminary training, even 12 years of it, without observing "the slightest sexual impropriety." He may be aware of his own sexual struggles (especially masturbation) and may confide to a priest in the secrecy of confession one or the other of his own transgressions or preoccupations that he may think are unique to him.

Formerly, the pattern of seminary life scheduling was such that every segment of the day was regulated and most activities monitored. Thus, little chance was left for the serious and observant student to get into sexual trouble. The summers and vacation periods, when many diocesan seminarians returned to their homes, were periods when both heterosexual and homosexual experimentation, or at least temptation, presented themselves.

A group of priests who gathered to celebrate the twenty-fifth anniversary of their entrance into their religious order were sharing stories about their novitiate experience. One of the men confided that the novice master had a 2-year sexual relationship with him. The news came as a shock to most of his 30 classmates, who considered the master the epitome of all of the virtues for which their religious order stood. But two other members of the group then confided that the superior was also sexually involved with them during the same period. Each one thought he was the only one so involved.

Frequently, sexual involvement between a faculty member and a student takes on the aura of a spiritual relationship because it is surrounded and immersed in a spiritual setting and religious rhetoric.

The question becomes whether homosexual behavior between the faculty and students increased or whether the inner reality just became apparent. The answer is that both occurred. There is no doubt that the reporting of homosexual behavior doubled between 1960 and 1994. However, it must be remembered that the clergy population itself did not remain stable in those years. More significantly, the homosocial organization of the seminary, which was designed to keep women at bay and thereby secure celibacy, revealed part of its essence as homosexual only under the pressure of the dissolution of its protective facade.

Priests are men who are set aside and given the prestige of being special. Their very existence will in some way bless their families; they have a spiritual perspective and are assured an honored place in society and financial security. They enjoy the economic advantages of not being responsible for child care and will bless the community by their ceremonial significance, moral instructions, and visionary leadership. In all of these ways they are more similar to the American Indian *berdaches* than to students in other professional schools. A look at Williams's *The Spirit and the Flesh* (1986) clarifies the role of the *berdache* in the Indian culture:

> They are set apart as a kind of order of priests or teachers...[who] devote themselves to the instruction of the young by the narration of legends and moral tales...spending the whole time in rehearsing the tribal history in a sing-song monotone to all who choose to listen. (p. 55)

## THE MALE MATRIX

In spite of increased sexual behavior there, the seminary is not homosexual in the sense of being a gay subculture. However, it is homosexual in the real sense that it lacks masculine and feminine definition that can come only from a system wherein men and women are tied together in an interdependent system of reciprocity.

Especially since the Council of Trent, the seminary has been an extension of the hierarchical system of the church. It participates in the church's structure and its essence: only male figures have power, and the ultimate justification for this power structure is that God is sexed. The Ideal for whom one gives one's life is Jesus Christ, masculine and divine. As minister, one is to see Christ in every person. A virginal mother is provided as an inspiring and loving support. All other women are disregarded as love objects, valued only in subservient roles. Spiritual functions are not complementary (male and female), but are infused by one saving Spirit of God, also masculine.

Do seminaries attract men who are inclined to the homosexualities, or does the homosocial organization of the clerical world foster and develop consciousness of and involvement in the homosexualities? Both questions merit an affirmative response.

I have scores of reports from priests about affectionate or sexual approaches or responses from teachers or elders during their training. One priest related a situation that occurred while he was in the philosophy phase of his training, equivalent to the last 2 years of college. There had been a series of student departures in the middle of the term, disruptive enough for the authorities to call in a consultant to ascertain the cause. Some of the students who left were disgruntled and had muttered and mumbled about a bunch of what they called "queers and fairies" around. It was the repercussion from these mumblings and nonspecific accusations that impelled the investigation. The consultants were told nothing except that an unusually large number of the most promising candidates had left the program precipitously.

After interviewing a number of students and teachers, the consultants saw clearly that the concern of those who left was sexual, but an aura of denial surrounded any causal explanation within the organization itself. Secrecy prevailed even in the face of consultants whose aid had been solicited and paid for. The authorities were looking for a culprit among the student body who was driving their students away! The priest reported that one of the most popular professors, whom many seminarians sought out as a confessor, had a practice of embracing, kissing, and even fellating certain penitents. The confessor's conscious intent was to "show God's love, mercy, and acceptance." The isolation of the confessional itself, the intimacy of the confessional sharing, and the unconscious affective strivings of the men were more than some of the students could tolerate.

The underlying assumptions that reinforce denial of the homosexualities in the priesthood are deeply ingrained in the clerical organization structure. After all, celibacy is taken up in the service of religion — "on account of the kingdom" — and it has to have religious and theological justification for its existence and continuance. Maintenance of the male matrix is central to the theological justification of celibacy (and all of the sexual teaching of the Catholic Church). The traditions of male exclusiveness and superiority are deep and central to the Old Testament even if personal celibacy is not.

## THE SYSTEM OF SECRECY

The line between affectionate and frankly sexual interaction from priest to seminarian is not always clear. Reports of hugs and kisses in the public and open forum seem to be in the same category as the exuberant embraces after an athletic contest. Basically, they are generally absorbed easily and pose no threat to celibate practice if other elements in the seminarian's or priest's life are balanced or not sensitized by some particular developmental stage or internal crisis. Hidden, exclusive exchanges that threaten to break the defensive denial have to be preserved and shielded by the system of secrecy, are defended as *acts* rather than *relationships*, and form the core of problematic homosexualities in priestly training.

Each of three elements is essential to the preservation of the problematic system.

First, denial literally keeps any sexual problem out of consciousness. It doesn't exist, or it is not important. This defensive stance keeps at bay the abuse implications of sexual incidents.

Second, a system of secrecy encapsulates any breakthrough into either conscious awareness or behavioral expression. Certainly the system of secrecy is partially in the service of confidentiality, necessary for the individual's growth; but it is also in the service of not giving scandal, thus institutionally sealing the system into a mode of operation that perpetuates the very problems it is designed to eradicate. There is no other single element so destructive to sexual responsibility among clergy as the system of secrecy, which both shields behavior and reinforces denial.

The third element is the definition of any sexual problem as an *act* isolated from its developmental and relationship implications. This element is reinforced by equating incidents with sin. The sin is submitted to the sacrament of confession. It then is forgiven or forgotten, with minimal awareness of the relationship of the behavior to the person and his responsibility. Some priests can continue the same sexual behavior for years, several times each year. Most times they will confess to their regular confessor, but these special acts are often confided to an anonymous priest. The reality of the sexual behavior simply does not break into consciousness, because when one system of secrecy threatens self-exposure, a subsystem is added.

## DEVELOPMENTAL QUESTIONS
## AND VARIATIONS

Homosexual identity, then, evolves out of a clustering of self-images which are linked together by the individual's idiosyncratic understanding of what characterized someone as a homosexual. . . . There is no such thing as a single homosexual identity. Rather, its nature may vary from person to person, from situation to situation, and from period to period. (Cass, 1985, p. 105)

The illusion that the homosexualities constitute a simplicity is exposed with the slightest serious examination of the subject area. Even the most commonly named factors in the formation of gender identity—possible prenatal hormonal factors, biological predisposition, intrapsychic dynamics, parental sex assignment, environmental conditioning and imprinting—defy reductionism.

Kinsey et al. (1948) put it this way:

Males do not represent two discrete populations, heterosexual and homosexual. The world is not to be divided into sheep and goats. Not all things are black nor all things white. It is a fundamental of taxonomy that nature rarely deals with discrete categories. Only the human mind invents categories and tries to force facts into separated pigeon-holes. The living world is a continuum in each and every one of its aspects. The sooner we learn this concerning human sexual behavior, the sooner we shall reach a sound understanding of the realities of sex. (p. 639)

In evaluating Richard Ginder's *Sex and Sin in the Catholic Church*, reviewer Father John L. Thomas says:

Finally [the book] assumes that homosexuality is a condition that pertains to the very essence of the individual and consequently designates a distinctive kind of *being*. But there is no such thing as a homosexual *being*.

What exist are male and female beings who may experience same-sex desires or engage in same-sex activities. But neither desires nor acts constitute *being*. They are dynamic, learnable and unlearnable, mutable in quality and persistence, and always in a state of change and becoming. It is a serious mistake to ignore all the evidence that men and women are amazingly sexually malleable creatures. (1975, p. 11)

The developing body ego is also important in forming sexual identity, which includes a host of sensations, their quality and quantity, and specifically the sensations that come from the genitals. These define the physical and psychic dimensions of the self.

## PRENATAL AND EARLY INFLUENCES

Animal studies have demonstrated that demasculinization of mating behavior is governed by the right hypothalamus. This is accomplished prenatally by using brain implants of steroidal sex hormone (Nordeen & Yahr, 1982). John Money (1984), along with many others, points out the obvious profound implications for adult sexual development of this and other prenatal experiments: "If someone is prenatally programmed so that conformity to either male or female stereotype is difficult, then learning experiences may lead them to develop either a role of trans-sexual gender identity or one of [obligatory] homosexual gender identity" (p. 24).

Bisexuality is also an important area for exploration by the celibate clergy. A career that is dominated exclusively by male power and receives the masculine address "Father," while enjoying the refinement of female nurturance and vestment, makes sense for one who is endowed with both a homosexual and heterosexual psychic disposition. Many researchers assume that the human animal is endowed basically with a bisexual constitution. Biochemical studies are important to determine sexual programming and disposition.

## INFANTILE SEXUALITY AND IDENTITY

Infants experience sexual excitement; from birth, boys have erections, and girls lubricate. They discover their own bodies, including their genitals. At about 18 months of age, the toddler usually increases his masturbatory activity. Children commonly experiment in some sort of sexual play with each other and expose themselves. The reactions of parents to all of these activities have lasting effects on the child's body image and sense of self. Excessive parental shame, accompanied by revulsion and rejection, enforces a sense of embarrassment and self-consciousness in the child. A parent's sense of self and each parent's image of his or her partner and of the complementary sex in general are transmitted and cued to the child and incorporated into his or her own sense of self and gender identity – all within the first 5 years of life. Obviously, gender identity can influence sexual object choice later on.

## THE NEGATIVE OEDIPAL

Freud's oedipal theory is too well-known to belabor here. It is generally accepted that the resolution of the early relationships with father and mother must be accomplished for one to broaden social interaction, leave home for school, form a conscience, and progress to maturity. For a boy, the impulse to love the mother and reject the father must give way to the need to become like the father and find a love object of his own.

But every child goes through a positive and a negative oedipal. For the boy, the mother becomes the love object, the father the object of fear and rejection. Alternately, however, the father also becomes the loved one, and the mother becomes the feared and rejected one. Both experiences can lead to development or regression.

## A NECESSARY HOMOSEXUAL PHASE OF DEVELOPMENT

Another stage of development is relevant here: the surge of sexual strivings that recur between 11 and 13 years of age. In fact, an upsurge of all infantile sexuality occurs at this time. In the face of the challenges of approaching adolescence, boys turn to each other and to adult males – often idealized teachers, sports figures, coaches, or ministers – for masculine reinforcement. An adolescent male's fear of women will lead him to denigrate as ridiculous or "yucky" anything associated with women or girls.

In 1905 Freud recorded this phenomenon in his *Three Essays on the Theory of Sexuality*:

> One of the tasks implicit in object-choice is that it should find its way to the opposite sex. This, as we know, is not accomplished without a certain amount of fumbling. Often enough the first impulses after puberty go astray, though without any permanent harm resulting. Dessoir [1894] has justly remarked upon the regularity with which adolescent boys and girls form sentimental friendships with others of their own sex. No doubt the strongest force working against a permanent inversion of the sexual object is the attraction which the opposing sexual characters exercise upon one another. (1905/1953, p. 229)

Both the negative oedipal stage and this stage of puberty can broadly be called homosexual in that they constitute a turning toward the object of the same sex and away from the complementary sex through devaluation or denigration. It is necessary to pass through these stages on the way to adult heterosexual adjustment. This is why I call it the *necessary homosexual phase of development*.

This latter phase is particularly important for understanding celibate practice and development in the church function and structure. Much of the homosocial organization of clerical culture is fixed at this stage. It is the culture's natural protection. The power structure of the Roman Catholic hierarchy can be seen psychically only in the context of encapsulating, solidifying, and protecting this stage of development; in this sense, it can rightfully and *only* be called homosexual. If it moved to any other level of psychosexual development, it could not maintain itself in its present structure. These steps of psychosexual development are common to all boys in some variation or other to bring them to adolescence, when psychosexual identity and object choice are usually solidified.

One priest is highly representative. He does not know whether he is homosexual or just underdeveloped. He feels that many of the clergy with whom he deals are similarly underdeveloped in their sexual identity. Like so many others in this category, he tends to be sensitive, productive, and conscientious. Some in this group are highly disciplined and have well-developed spiritual lives and consciences. Some also support their celibate resolve and disciplined lifestyle with psychotherapy. Needless to say, with its idealism and sense of sacrifice, this group forms an important core of dedicated religious servants.

The institutional church was intuitively perceptive in soliciting candidates for the celibate priesthood at an early age. Ensuring a better fit into the ecclesiastical organizational and structural reality, it recruited candidates while they were in their necessary homosexual phase of development, when male idealization is high and sexual activity more childlike than adult.

## Pseudohomosexuality

An interesting subgroup of priests is marked by their fear of being homosexual. These men are conscientious and would identify themselves as gay if they could only resolve their internal conflict. But they cannot. They might have had no adult homosexual experience and are relying on their memories of childhood or adolescent sexual play with friends or family. Some have experimented with both sexes briefly in adult life. They are not caught in preadolescent development. They are more like the college student who fearfully asks, "Am I normal?" They wish to be priests, hold celibacy as an ideal, but also want to be like everybody else.

One example of a 36-year-old priest demonstrates the point. He joined the seminary when he was 13 and found the atmosphere supportive and warm, in contrast with his home, where his mother had died 2 years earlier and his father was becoming more and more aggressively and frequently alcoholic. He fit well into the seminary program. The athletic program met his needs, and he became first in his year academically. He was sent to Rome for his theological studies, and it was in his first year there that he experienced his first real questioning of celibacy and his vocation. After a brief depressive episode, he regained his enthusiasm for his studies and life.

When he obtained his graduate degree, he was assigned to the chancery office staff and over the next 8 years became increasingly involved in the administrative decisions of the diocese. Then a policy dispute over a financial crisis abruptly ended the personal and political support necessary for him to keep his job. He was suddenly dismissed by the bishop, a man whom he admired and in whom he had found a father (mother) figure and, he thought, a genuine friend.

For the first time since he had taken his vow of celibacy 12 years earlier, he began to masturbate. His new assignment in a remote parish afforded him time to escape—as he put it—to a large city some distance from his home for several days every few months. There he began to experiment sexually, awkwardly asking bartenders where the action was. These adolescent-like ventures brought him both his first heterosexual and his first homosexual contacts (mutual masturbation). His native sensitivity and training combined to make him "Holden Caulfield-like," as he would say of his approach to sexuality. He could not tolerate the pain of his conflicted conscience and curtailed his experimentation after four or five episodes. He did not feel he could leave the priesthood; similarly, he did not wish to continue to pursue either heterosexual or homosexual liaisons or activity.

After a second parish assignment, which brought him professional success, he was reassigned to an administrative position that again recognized and utilized his talents. At 47, he was practicing celibacy but still feared he was homosexual, although most of his fantasy and ideation was heterosexual.

Some feel we are seeing basic *bisexuality* in this man and in this group. A pertinent observation by Money is:

If one travels the manifest path of bisexuality, then, by the age of sexual maturity, one will almost certainly label oneself as homosexual. The explanation of this error is historical. Homosexuality has been considered as a sin on a par with heresy and treason. Sinners are still labeled for their vices and not their virtues. Thus, bisexuals are still singled out, not for their heterosexual but their homosexual actions. (1984)

I am convinced, however, that Lionel Ovesey (1969) describes more accurately the situation we see frequently among priest celibates:

The great majority of so-called homosexual anxieties are motivated by strivings for dependency and power. These anxieties...stem from pseudohomosexual fantasies that are misinterpreted by the patient as being evidences of frank homosexuality. In reality, the sexual component, if present at all, is very much in abeyance. More often it appears to be entirely absent. (p. 31)

The uncertainty of this group persists in the face of little or no sexual experience. Their fear seems to be the salient element. It is difficult to say whether they are truly bisexual and would become oriented to both sexes no matter what the circumstances or environment or if they are simply a subgroup fostered and held in place by the celibate organization and structure.

## DEFENSIVE HOMOSEXUALITY

Many men fear the idea that they may be homosexual. Others are so homophobic that they cannot tolerate the idea of being close to or friendly with a homosexual person. But there are also a few men who can accept more easily the idea of being homosexual than the idea of being heterosexual; they find the latter threatening and fearsome. There are, as Fenichel (1953) pointed out, "reactive forms of homosexuality also, namely, identification with the same sex, for the purpose of denying fear of the other sex" (p. 310).

The first person who helped me understand this entity was a 30-year-old priest who was productive in his parish and as a part-time high school teacher. He had had only a few homosexual encounters, with no pattern of sexual activity, and did not feel compelled to act on any of his sexual impulses. He was well regulated in his lifestyle and desired to be celibate; he could not see himself being anything but a priest. He was comfortable about identifying himself as a homosexual, in private, but did not openly claim being gay.

His trouble began when one of the women teachers at the school took a particular liking to him. When she declared her feelings and made a move to hug and kiss him—a response he had no awareness of inviting or provoking—he went into a panic. He experienced new acute and vehement physiological response; it made him think he was going to die. It was a genuine heterosexual panic. Freud's observation in 1927 about the threat of castration and various reactions to it is appropriate here:

> Probably no male human being is spared the fright of castration at the sight of a female genital. Why some people become homosexual as a consequence of that impression, while others fend it off by creating a fetish, and the great majority surmount it, we are frankly not able to explain. It is possible that, among all the factors at work, we do not yet know those which are decisive for the rare pathological results. (1927/1961a, p. 154)

Priests with this dynamic form one subgroup within the celibate band. This phenomenon does not need sexual activity to keep it in force. Some researchers miscalculate the number of homosexual priests by including this group in their tallies.

In a paradoxical way, defensive homosexuality keeps some priests bound to their vocation and celibacy. They cannot rationalize or split sexual behavior from their consciousness; they feel guilt about any sexual activity in which they may become involved. The idea of homosexuality does not interfere with their life choice. As one priest put it, "The church demands celibacy of homosexuals anyway. If I'm homosexual and I have to be celibate, I might as well be a priest and be useful." Therefore, to maintain equilibrium, these men reason that prayer, humility, and reasonable vigilance of their lifestyle will keep them safe and save their souls. The idea of being heterosexual, with the possibility of a legitimate sexual relationship with an available woman, threatens their equilibrium since it would destabilize their whole life.

## REGRESSIVE HOMOSEXUALITY

There are types of regression that serve growth, development, and social stability. Play remains one of these situations throughout life. Men hunt and fish together, have their beer and bowling nights to refresh themselves, and return invigorated to their families and work. This is a homosocial regression generally accepted in society. The men do not do anything overtly homosexual, but their orientation for this brief period is "men only." Only men count, understand each other, and bond together, and they exclude women. Behavior and humor here are very much like a prepubertal boys' club.

Freud had a close friend to whom he confided, "The company of the friend, which a special—perhaps feminine—side demands...no one can replace for me...[and] I do not share your contempt for friendship between men, probably because I am to a high degree party to it. In my life, as you well know, woman has never replaced the comrade, the friend." Freud wrote this self-appraisal when his intimacy with Wilhelm Fliess had declined, and he could afford to be clear-sighted. In 1910, looking back on the whole fateful attachment, Freud bluntly told several of his closest disciples that his attachment to Fliess had contained a homosexual element (Gay, 1988, p. 86).

What happens when men live a homosocial existence? To where do they regress? After the male bonding and the intense feelings of friendship, they have no wife and family to ease the sexual tension increased by male competition and exchange.

Under tension and pressure or perhaps under the weight of depressive feelings, some priests regress to a homosexual stage of development—to the prepubertal sexual as well as social exchange. This kind of situation can lead outside the clerical circle into the anonymous and tenuous world of furtive sexual encounters in bars, restrooms, baths, massage parlors, or through hitchhiking. Many priests make a complete psychic split between their sexual behavior and their professional clerical life; this can also be true of those who involve themselves in heterosexual behavior. The maturity, judgment, and values lived and expressed in their professional life are entirely abandoned in their play world, where they operate wholly apart from those values.

A responsible 42-year-old priest reported that over the previous 7 years he had periodically looked for homosexual partners in bars and peep shows, usually after spending time with his good priest friends.

Another priest went to a hotel for a massage twice a month. Although the masseur never touched the priest's genitals, the priest always ejaculated during the massage; it was important to him to have the touch of a male, and he avoided a masseuse. Although it is more common for the regressive behavior to be split from the clerical life, priests report sexual approaches from fellow priests within the clerical setting.

Alcohol can be a factor in this regression. Two priest informants took an annual vacation together at a posh beach resort some distance from their homes. Longtime friends, they enjoyed many common interests. At least one night of each vacation, they would drink to the point of drunkenness, come back to their hotel, and masturbate each other—something they did not do at any other time of the year during their association. They never spoke of it with each other. One of the parties in no way considered himself homosexual; the other man felt he had homosexual tendencies. He wanted to be more involved with his friend but was afraid of being rejected if he broached the subject in any other circumstance.

There can be a compulsive quality to sexual regression. Men reporting this dimension to their homosexual activity describe the inner force that drives them to seek sexual involvement regardless of (or possibly because of) the danger or possibility of damage. Typical is the priest who reported returning compulsively to the restroom of a highway interchange, seeking a sexual contact when he knew intellectually that the police were keeping that exact spot under surveillance. Another priest repeatedly picked up sexual partners from among the young men who paraded on the local meat rack of his city, in spite of having read in the local newspaper that multiple arrests for sexual solicitation had been made there.

## SITUATIONAL HOMOSEXUALITY

Doctor Lewis Hill, former medical director of Sheppard and Enoch Pratt Hospital in Towson, Maryland, used to tell his resident psychiatrists, "Man is a loving animal, and he is going to love whatever he is near." The sexual histories of farm boys frequently record passing involvements with animals. Sucking calves respond equally to their mother's teat, a finger, or a little boy's penis. This is usually a situational phenomenon dependent on sexual development, social isolation, loneliness, and positive loving feelings for a friend.

What happens to the average man when he is isolated for long periods of time with restricted affective (social) outlets and limited positive sexual development? One of the early psychological studies NASA commissioned was to project the effect on astronauts of prolonged periods in space. One set of factors to be taken into account would be the positive affect that would or could mutually develop when the astronauts were dependent on one another, and no other loving objects were near. The logical question then became whether after a long time in sexual isolation homosexual feelings would be aroused. Kinsey and colleagues noted the frequency of homosexual contact "among ranchmen, cattlemen, prospectors, lumbermen and farming groups in general" (1948, p. 457). All of these virile and active groups tend to face the perils of nature practically and approach sex the same way.

However, although priests are faced with homosocial isolation for long periods of their life, they are not allowed to accept sex in the same free way that some of the above groups might. One would expect but does not always find great restraint of sexual activity among clergy as compared with other groups of men. The homosocial situation does stimulate feelings. Although only 30% of clergy report homosexual behavior or identity, 40% report having homosexual ideation at some point during their training or later.

At times the situation rather than the core sexual orientation of the priest dictates his sexual choice. A longtime friendship and isolation in a learning or living circumstance can lead to a sexual exchange between friends. Subsequent history and development can reveal an essentially heterosexual orientation.

## INNATE HOMOSEXUALITY

Innate homosexuality is a state and not necessarily a behavior. It is determined either by genetic endowment or by environmental factors so compelling that the affective orientation toward one's own sex as the primary relational object is irreversible by any known psychological or physical means. In this sense it is determined by nature. More and more biochemical research is examining the genetic influence on development.

In its essence, innate homosexuality has nothing to do with behavior or sin. There is nothing immoral about it as a state—a declaration that can, incidentally, be equally valid about heterosexuality. Of course, it is not the norm in any culture but is rather a variation of nature and development.

As Nash and Hayes (1965) point out, "Awareness of a homosexual orientation does not imply identity; identity does not imply acceptance; acceptance does not imply commitment" (p. 35). A person who aspires to celibacy will sooner or later have to come to grips with the question of his sexual identity, even in spite of limited or no sexual experience. In fact, sexual activity can be indulged in with less thought than sexual restraint. The latter forces one to rely on inner resources moored in one's past and lying deep in one's unconscious, as well as on conscious relatedness to transcendent love objects that can encompass a world.

Since sexual activity of any stripe is forbidden to the celibate, the protected and homosocial environment of the priesthood can be a haven of peace as well as an arena for productive and loving service. Some who have professed celibacy and practiced it for prolonged periods of time have difficulty identifying themselves as gay in spite of tremendous inner honesty and self-awareness. Those who do not act out may not be sure of their sexual identity but use their sexual ambiguity to advantage in the understanding of and ministry to a wide range of persons, both male and female.

There are, of course, those who are aware of their innate orientation and have, from time to time, acted on their sexual attractions, either before their pursuit of celibacy or even after taking a vow. Of special concern here is *addictive* sexual behavior. Addiction is troublesome whether the sexual object is male or female, adult or child. In the celibate, it violates a trust of office if the priest has gained entree to and the confidence of another person precisely because he is a priest and presumed celibate. However, even in the cases of anonymous sex, addiction violates self-trust at the deepest level of one's ego. One literally cannot trust oneself.

Sexual addiction among the clergy abuses both the tortured addict and his victims. The system of secrecy surrounding the sexual behavior only compounds the problem and interferes with breaking the cycle of addiction. The behavior is frequently not mentioned in any confessional. At times, confession is part of a cycle of denial; at other times, behavior is psychically split off from the rest of one's conscious functioning. Even when this behavior is submitted to sacramental confession, it is mostly treated as an act, separated, or not acknowledged as a pattern of addiction. The sin is forgiven, but the state remains.

A priest reported that while he was on temporary assignment at a parish, another priest came to his room, begged to be held, and offered to fellate him. When the first priest declined, the second told him that at times he could not control himself and that he would get into his car and cruise the streets of the city looking for a sexual contact. This behavior had put him in some bizarre and dangerous situations, but he could not stop himself, nor could he predict when the impulse would seize him. Addiction can be controlled but not cured.

The death of a parent, especially a mother, has been reported a number of times as the trigger for either accepting one's innate orientation or for acting on the impulses one had either suspected or known.

A 40-year-old priest who accepted his homosexual orientation and who had a brief sexual encounter in the army prior to entering the seminary had no sexual contact with any other person until the death of his mother. He experienced then a resurgence of his sexual drive and sought out sexual contact with a parishioner whom he knew to be actively homosexual. As he described it, there was a real *compulsion* to his behavior. When his mourning for his mother was completed, he was able to absorb compulsion more easily and he returned to celibate practice.

## GAY PRIESTS

There is a group among priests who identify themselves as gay. Their sexual attraction, fantasy, emotional and social preference, and their self-identification or awareness are all congruent. They may or may not practice celibacy, but if they do choose sexual activity, it is invariably homosexual. This can change over time, since all of these factors are interactive and open to development and alteration (Klein, Sepekoff, & Wolf, 1985).

One priest was assigned to be the superior of the candidates entering his religious community. Situated geographically in an isolated area and separated even from other members of the larger community, he formed strong and affective bonds with his subjects. As the years passed, he developed noticeably feminine characteristics that had not been observed previously, although he was 50 years old.

It became clear that his sexual awareness had been intensified by his isolation and emotional stimulation by successive groups of young men who passed exclusively under his tutelage. He became comfortable with what he termed his *mother* role and demonstrated a tenderness and warmth that had been lacking earlier in his life. This was not unattractive, but it was noticeable to those who had known him in his thirties, when he had given the impression of macho stoicism. He admitted to one period of sexual crisis that had threatened his celibate practice, but he was generally observant and developed no pattern of sexual activity with others, although his fantasies were consistently homoerotic. His self-evaluation and honesty led him to identify himself as gay.

Among this group are the most observant of religious celibates, self-aware and self-restrained, dedicated to their ideals, and selfless in their service to others. They genuinely love humanity and are honest in their internal and external lives. Also represented in this group are part of what one psychiatrist called the "silent current within the ministerial mainstream." They are men who have more or less long-term sexual relationships (from 3 to 20 years) sometimes with other priests.

The wife of a choir director became concerned when she found out that her husband had a long-term sexual liaison with their priest. Prior to that point, she had not been aware of her husband's bi-sexuality or the priest's homosexuality. After her initial shock, she remained tolerant of the friendship and chose not to acknowledge any future sexual activity between the priest and her husband.

Other sexual friendships begin in the seminary and continue through periodic contact over the years. It is not common for priests living in the same small groups or parish house to have a sexual liaison with each other. More common is the situation where two men living in a house suspect each other of being gay while each knows that he, himself, is. They socialize well and have many friends in common, but they are never sexual with each other and rarely discuss their activity with the other.

Most commonly, some distance is necessary for both priests to remain guilt-free in their ministerial work as well as their relationship. Frequently, homosexual activity among gay priests is ego syntonic; often they experience no guilt at all. Many never submit their activity to sacramental confession or do so only in the very beginning of a relationship. Their partners tend to be appropriate in terms of age, mutual consent, and circumstance. They do not come to the attention of civil authorities. Because the activity is not disruptive to their work or the group immediately around them, these men do not command attention.

When sexual activity is completely split off from priests' lives, their religious goals and ideals, it is rationalized as natural and even necessary for their service to the church. They frame their homosexual activity in much the same mold that they do masturbation — necessary and inconsequential. They do not see it as a threat to their vocations as priests.

Celibacy in religious tradition is meant, among other goals, to be a lived example of how to regulate the sexual drive in accord with Christian principles. In the estimation of the general public, celibacy is not merely a legal state of nonmarriage, but a way of life in con-formity with church teaching. It is legitimate to ask not only what is the church's teaching on sexuality, but how is it lived by church teachers and leaders.

Especially in the area of the homosexualities, the time has passed when simple denunciation and condemnation can be sat-isfactory. Labeling, homosexuality a "sin" or "essentially disor-dered" does not aid understanding or responsible sexual practice or abstinence.

One cannot assume that station and power are the keys to sexual orthodoxy in practice or that they will ensure consistency between word and behavior. Bishops, religious superiors, and cardinals have been known to have sexually active lives, some of them gay. In fact, there is ample evidence from a wide range of religious denominations that clergymen can publicly and vehemently denounce sin in others while quietly and repeatedly indulging in it themselves.

Some people assume that guilt is an adequate controller or regulator of behavior. It is not. The ego with the total of its integrative capacities and object relatedness is the agency that determines behavior (Hartmann, 1964). Too little attention is paid to this reality in the education and formation of men who would be celibate.

There is another subgroup among the gay population of priests: the growing and articulate group generally allied with gay rights and who talk freely — in surroundings they deem to be nonjudgmental — about their sympathies and behaviors. They find their support more outside the clergy population than within it. But they also are vocal and often seek out clergy for understanding and support. This group does not split their behavior and their celibate ideal. They frankly disregard celibacy as not possible or desirable for them. The dichotomy in their lives is more between who knows and who does not know their orientation or sexual preference (Nash, 1990).

There are also priests championing the case of justice for homosexuals who believe in celibacy where appropriate. John J. McNeill (1976) is a pioneer in facing squarely some of the theological questions posed by the reality of the homosexualities and the church's teaching. Some of this group have declared their innate homosexual orientation, and others are heterosexual or nondisclosed; they have banded together to support each other in their celibate strivings.

## ACQUIRED IMMUNE DEFICIENCY SYNDROME (AIDS)

According to the conservative estimates of one church official, 350 Catholic priests test HIV positive. It is known in Rome that at least one bishop is seropositive. By 1994 several dozen priests had died of AIDS. Four priests from a diocese of fewer than 100 died of AIDS between 1990 and 1993. Many dioceses and religious orders require candidates to be tested for AIDS as part of routine entrance into the seminary. Altogether, it is obvious that clergy are emerging as a clear subgroup of the homosexual population that has so far contracted AIDS.

Health officials who deal with sexually transmitted diseases have long been aware of the frequency of homosexuality among Catholic priests. In the words of one such official, "I and most of the public health directors I've talked to about this subject estimate that in our communities at least a third of Catholic priests under forty-five are homosexuals, and most are sexually active. They almost always engage in anonymous encounters, the highest risk sex of all, and when they want help they don't come to clinics. I've met with priests in some of the strangest places." (Leishman, 1987, p. 48)

The Task Force on Gay/Lesbian Issues in San Francisco estimates the homosexual population among the Roman Catholic clergy at 30%.

The pattern of anonymous sexual contacts so common among the celibate community is part of high-risk behavior for infection. Several priests who have openly acknowledged their HIV-positive status have admitted that they contracted the disease through same-sex contact.

One priest who died is an example. By preference he sought out black sexual partners and contracted syphilis once and anal gonorrhea twice. Although he considered himself homosexual from his early years, he was not active sexually while at the seminary. Two years after his ordination and the subsequent death of his father, he felt himself overwhelmed with loneliness and isolation in his remote rural parish. He planned vacations to large urban areas specifically to experience sex and found himself feeling accepted and safe with black men. His period of promiscuity lasted about 3 years.

AIDS is a worldwide problem with medical dimensions akin to the effects of cancer and social dimensions akin to the impact of world hunger. That AIDS is a disease that can be transmitted sexually thrusts it into the moral arena. The danger here is that glib moralizing and homespun theologies will replace reason—for example, teaching that AIDS is God's curse for sexual sin. Intolerable fears can be fostered in the name of religion. Worse still is the real possibility that AIDS will be used as an excuse to hate. The temptation for others to abandon an AIDS patient or for the priest patient to isolate himself because of shame or fear should not be indulged. Likewise, cover-ups in the name of avoiding scandal only increase problems and encourage irresponsibility rather than accountability.

• • •

The whole range of homosexualities is difficult for both individual clergy and the church as a whole to address. When homosexual orientation and behavior are approached from an exclusively moralistic point of view (good/bad, or thou shalt/thou shalt not) and when the objective reality is ignored (it exists, people *do* behave thus-and-so) in the face of the subjective experience of some of its members and ministers (this is how I feel, think, have lived), the result is that the church's influence and power are curtailed, thereby limiting its ability to teach, to heal, and to save persons from unnecessary suffering and injustice. In short, to be a moral leader, the church must deal with the realities of nature (Sipe, 1987, pp. 86ff).

There has always been a substantial number of homosexually oriented men who have given themselves to the service of the church. Some of course do not either practice or even care to achieve celibacy. But others find the practice of celibacy possible and rewarding within the homosocial organization of the church. Some achieve celibacy. A growing number of homosexually oriented and/or sexually active men among the clergy are gaining a voice and visibility that must be reckoned with.

# PART III
# THE STRUCTURE OF CRISIS

# 8

# THE STRUCTURE BENEATH
# THE CRISIS

*The mind's road to God always begins in the sexual appetite.*

St. Bonaventure

*All honor to the ascetic ideal insofar as it is honest.*

Friedrich Nietzsche

Celibacy—the choice of nonmarriage, nonreproduction, and at times nonsexual activity—has always been the condition for a certain number of men within the human race. According to the 1990 census, 10.5% of white males in the United States, age 40 to 44, have never been married. This number does not simply correlate with one sexual orientation.

This group is paradigmatic of the sexual diversity of nature. Some men have utilized the predisposition to celibacy in the service of art, science, philosophy, politics, or religion. Numbered among the group are da Vinci (1452–1519), Michelangelo (1475–1564), Descartes (1596–1650), Pascal (1623–62), Spinoza (1632–77), Leibniz (1646–1716), Newton (1642–1727), Kant (1724–1804), Swinburne (1837–1909), and Hammarskjöld (1905–61). A multitude of others embrace celibacy in the service of family or the accumulation of wealth.

Our effort here is restricted to understanding that group that identifies itself as celibate for religious motives or publicly pledges complete sexual abstinence in the pursuit of its cause or the system of power that claims its allegiance. First, we must remember that religious celibacy, in essence, is not dependent on a system; it is a personal commitment and achievement in which the

161

person may or may not align himself with others. For instance, Antony of the Desert and even Benedict in his earliest strivings were both hermits, isolated from any system of mutual support, yet dedicated to the lonely search for religious meaning. Gandhi and Dorothy Day are also examples of religious celibacy pursued outside any ecclesiastical system.

As I studied celibacy as it was practiced, posed, or achieved by hundreds of priests, I became aware that there was an essential hurdle that these Catholic priests had to negotiate to progress through celibate integration. They could be attracted and supported in the early stages of the discipline by a group and sustained by motivations of gross self-interest, but there inevitably came a point at which they had to internalize and claim celibacy for themselves, regardless of any external influence, rejection, or support, if celibacy was to have spiritual dynamism and integral force. Celibates generally confront this phase somewhere between their thirteenth and fifteenth year of practice. Historically, individual witness and spiritual power are the elements that institutions have meant to harness in the service of systemic power. Men committed to celibacy consolidated attempts at mutual support into the process of monasticism or religious communities. Institutionalization evolves into control, economic advantage, societal and political power, as well as mutual support. The history of Catholic Christianity demonstrates a recurring pattern of reaching for celibate practice to purify itself of corruption, reorganize its resources, and mobilize its authority.

The irony is this: for celibacy to be authentic in terms of individual integrity it must transcend institutional boundaries, restrictions, and supports. It must become truly personal and interior. A core element of these men has always been present within the system, but there is no evidence that at any time in history this faction ever dominated the celibate/sexual system. This is witness to the spiritual force of the entity; it can carry the imperfections of the mass. Celibacy, like charity, can cover a multitude of sins.

Celibacy, the reality, is a biological, social, and religious treasure to be fostered by those who possess its disposition, whether by nature or grace, for the growth of life on this planet. Gandhi said, "A nation that does not possess such men is poorer for the want."

Celibacy, as the practice of nonmarriage and sexual self-denial in the service of the community, is not the problem or the crisis in the church today. It never has been. The crisis is the claim to celibate privilege and authority not based on reality and religious service but dependent on law, ideal, and control in the service of economic, social, and political or sexual domination. Power perverted in the name of religion is the problem.

The current crisis involves the exposure of the structure that underlies a power system using celibacy for the domination and control of others. The current evolution of scientific, religious, and social awareness offers us the opportunity to reevaluate a structure that was laid down in the fourth century—a necessary and adequate framework given the knowledge available then. But its inadequacy today does not render it merely a curious or interesting vestige of antiquity but a dangerous social orientation with implications far beyond the bounds of one religious community.

The structure underlying the celibate/sexual system has seven interlocking and mutually reinforcing elements that influence its function and form both the contour and the character of its power. These elements are blame, the superior group, power, subjugation, nature and God's will, sexual inconsistency, and necessary violence.

## BLAME

*The first factor is the insistence on generic blame for perceived ills or evils.* Although this factor could focus on one race or one gender—and historically has centered on both Jews and women—it is the blame of the woman that is the essential element in reinforcing the celibate system.

Identifying women as evil is not unique to Judaism or Christianity. Lévi-Strauss (1988) quotes the account of primal evil from the ancient Greek writer Hesiod (*Works and Days*):

> For the race of men was living upon the earth free from evils, troublesome toil, and painful disease, which bring death to men. But the woman, removing the great lid of the jar with her hands, scattered them, and brought about baneful sorrows for men. (p. 2)

Christian theology refined the blame of woman to a high art form and established it as the bedrock justification for celibacy, power, and male control. Some theologians claim that the curses Yahweh hurled first at the serpent and then at the woman clearly show where the onus rests—with the woman—and if the punishment is to fit the crime, then the curse of the pain of childbearing would indicate that the sin somehow involved sexual pleasure.

> To the woman he said: "I will multiply your pains in childbearing; you shall give birth to your children in pain. Your yearning shall be for your husband, yet he will lord it over you." (Genesis 3:16)

It is not hard to see how body, pleasure, sex, sin, and death became connected by some readings of this mythopoetic rendering of creation. The Hebrews, however, did not interpret the first sin as sexual but rather as a transgression of pride and disobedience. The early Christians also did not primarily, exclusively, or universally regard sex as the primal sin. Reproduction was too natural to be the source of sin and death. Reproduction had been explicitly commanded ("increase and multiply and fill the earth"), and progeny was too essential to a people of God, a people who were especially chosen and designated the *elect*—ideas that both the Hebrews and the early Christians could apply to themselves.

Augustine most likely coined the term *original sin* for the crime of Eve. It was surely Augustine who stamped the first sin as sexually disordered and rendered even a legitimate marriage only the good usage of an evil thing. That judgment has pretty well penetrated all of church teaching on human sexuality even to the present day, even when it is explicitly denied. Christian marriage is frequently compared with the bond of Christ and His Church, but there is often a caveat. Virginity is better; even Christian marriage is dangerous.

Once philosophical dualism, whether in the form of neoplatonism or stoicism, had penetrated Christian thought, Augustine's reasoning was secured for posterity. Body became inimical to spirit (soul); flesh was the enemy to be dominated, controlled, and eventually discarded in the service of real (celibate) love and real (unearthly) life.

Augustine believed that in their original created state, Adam and Eve were in perfect control of all of the inclinations of their bodies, especially their sexual desires. According to Augustine, in the ideal state, children are conceived without any pleasure or at least only with a pleasure ruled and ordered by the will. Paradise and the tree of life protected Adam and Eve from death; but all of this eternity was lost. Loss of rational control, ignorance, and concupiscence, which shows in sexual excitement, are the lasting results for all humanity.

The equation of woman, pleasure, and sin with sex undergirds the celibate structure. All discourse on grace, free will, predestination, and salvation revolves around the sexual nature of humans as defined from this vantage. Historian Jean Delumeau (1990) quotes a Jesuit, Antoine Vieira, who shows how forcefully this idea of blame was incorporated into the system, even in the seventeenth century.

> Of all the miseries that overcome us, all bodily hardships, spiritual vices, all these woes of today and of eternity, these grievous consequences of original sin, what is the primary cause? A woman, a

wife; and not an adulteress, but a lawful and innocent one, sprung from the hands of God Himself. . . . All the sorrows, diseases, private and public disasters, plagues, famines, wars, the rises and falls of nations, some appearing as others disappear forever, all these catastrophes can only have their prime source in the disobedience of woman, who was given to man by God Himself. (p. 433)

# THE SUPERIOR GROUP

*The second element involves the proclamation of one superior group.* This superior group within the celibate/sexual framework is male and virginal. The notion that maleness makes a being superior is carried from the ancients through Thomas Aquinas and into popular ethos in ways too numerous to sort out; it is an idea that is now part of the social atmosphere, having practical ramifications in every area of life. The rationale for this supposed superiority is not always exact or clear, perhaps reinforcing the need to multiply causes: the male is stronger, more noble and trustworthy, has more genius, possesses a penis, and is more emotionally stable.

Male superiority is only reinforced by the idea of the wickedness of woman, with her proneness to evil, which is demonstrated over and over again by her tendency to heresy—that is, thinking for herself: "When a woman thinks alone she thinks evil." She is prone to witchcraft, "which comes from carnal lust, which in women is insatiable." Such witness is given in the official guide for all Catholic seminaries used for the 200 years beginning 1484. The ultimate theological rationale for male superiority is that Jesus Christ, the Son of God, chose to be male.

History has traditionally been written from the male point of view, but the idea that half of the human race can represent the whole is now a well-recognized fallacy. There is a growing awareness that male superiority is a myth created, in part, to support control and establish dominance. The celibate system not only assumes male superiority but reinforces it with the proclamation of the superiority of virginity. Many of the early church fathers wrote about the value of virginity for both men and women.

The development of celibacy was part of the ascetic movement, already strong in the second century (Brown, 1988). But the origins of celibacy were not within the priesthood. Early celibate practice did not align itself with power but was an independent and mostly nonecclesial expression of the Gospel. It was an effort to imitate

Christ, not to exert power; the ascetics fled wealth, power, sex, and society.

With Augustine and Jerome, the die was cast. Nonmarriage was declared a higher state, and the evolution of male virginity as superior has resulted not only in the subjugation of women but also in the denigration of marriage. St. Bernadine of Sierra (1380–1444) said, "Out of a thousand marriages, I believe 999 belong to the devil." In a sermon reflecting on the wedding at Cana, French priest Pierre de la Font said,

> The apostles rightly found it too difficult and onerous to have to keep a woman by one's side. . . a woman replete with defects and disorders; to live with this domestic enemy of one's rest; hence it was more tolerable to resist the natural inclinations that lead to marriage than to make oneself constantly suffer the mad and out-landish behavior of a woman. (1679 edition, cited by Delumeau, 1990, p. 432)

There can be little discourse with a priest like Symon de Rennes who was convinced that marriage holds "great dangers and impedi-ments for salvation. . . [because]. . . most marriages are inspired by the devil, who also presides over them" (Delumeau, 1990, p. 433).

Some priests even compared marriage with hell. Curi L. Requis (1766) said, "ye know better than I, my dear parishioners, [a bad marriage is both] a glimpse and a first step into hell" (Delumeau, 1990, p. 434). N. Girard, another priest, preaching around 1753, did not make marriage sound very attractive, although he was more sym-pathetic to women:

> Married women, behold your hardship; know that a married woman enters into a kind of slavery, she leaves behind her joy and well being; she cannot do anything of any importance without her husband's consent; even her work is not her own, and her livelihood is established by law, and it is criminal to stray from it. For all that, however, nearly all young maids willingly submit themselves to an evidently heavy yoke, and their virginity, which is an inestimable treasure, their freedom and their belongings. . . their life and their health, in risking vexatious pregnancy and dangerous childbirth. But what am I saying, to have a husband? All too often, it is to have a scoundrel, a blasphemer, a lecher, drunkard, or brute. (Delumeau, 1990, p. 435)

The most complete synthesis of the proclamation of male (over female), celibate (over married), and Christian (over Jews) superiority was articulated [1903] by Otto Weininger in *Sex and Character* (1909). In retrospect, this work is neither original nor revolutionary. It is merely a summary and rearticulation in philosophical and schematic form of the church's teaching about sex, celibacy, and women. There is almost a complete reiteration of the evaluation of sex and women from the *Malleus Maleficarum*.

# POWER

*The third element reserves power for the designated* pure *group.*

> The order of bishops is the successor to the college of the apostles in their role as teachers and pastors, and in it the apostolic college is perpetuated. Together with their head, the Supreme Pontiff, and never apart from him, they have supreme and full authority over the universal church, but this power cannot be exercised without the agreement of the Roman Pontiff. (Vatican II, 1965)

The trend within the Catholic Church toward male domination, authoritarian centralization, and celibacy was sporadic but insistent, certainly from the fourth century of Christianity to the present day. It was not marked or dominant in the earliest Christian communities (Wright, 1992). What Gerda Lerner records about the twelfth-century religious movements was similar to

> a pattern already noted in the history of early Christianity: as long as movements were small, loosely structured, and persecuted, women were welcomed as members, given access to organizational leadership and shared authority with men. When the movement became successful, it became more tightly structured, more hierarchical, and more male dominated. Women were then relegated to auxiliary roles and to invisibility. (1993, p. 74)

The restriction of roles of authority to males who professed nonmarriage and perfect and perpetual chastity ensured absolute control by men. Control and power clearly became primary concerns since no exception could be made to the requirement of gender, whereas there could be great tolerance for violations of celibate behavior and even some exceptions to the requirement for nonmarriage in lower levels of ministry (deacon, priest). Even then, restrictions were imposed on sexual activity: deacons cannot remarry after the death of a spouse; sometimes married priests must be celibate within the marriage relationships.

Pope John Paul II has frequently and formally reiterated the fact that he "does not wish to leave any doubts in the mind of anyone regarding the church's firm will to maintain the law that demands perpetual and freely chosen celibacy for present and future candidates for priestly ordination in the Latin rite" (Pastores Dabo Vobis #29, 1992). The theological rationale presented to justify this position is increasingly under attack from within the ranks of the church. Catholic theologians claim that there is no essential theological justification for a men-only authority structure or a celibate-only priesthood. If these questions were simply religious, they would have been settled long ago. But the realities of power, undergirded by a long-standing genetic/social and evolutionary struggle, must be taken into account. Any resolution would be more satisfactory if issues could be discussed within a spiritual framework.

Free speculation about the origins, effects, and interaction of sex and celibacy within religious expression is one small but significant area in which the experience of the natural sciences can be applied to the current crisis in the church. Lumsden and Wilson claim that experience "teaches that the strongest theory is created when the real world is visualized within the matrix of possible worlds" (1981, p. 2). The force of the power group within religion only emphasizes the need to explore its structure. Think of what would result if maleness and celibacy were required of every major business executive. Certainly it would open up some opportunities for the nonreproductively determined and the altruistically motivated. But such a requirement would certainly eliminate a great number of men from competition, and it would encourage some unscrupulous and power-driven men to take advantage of the opportunities offered.

## SUBJUGATION

*The fourth element is the restriction or subjugation of the inferior group at the pleasure or for the use of the group in power.* Many men and women within the Catholic Church will object to the bold and unnuanced wording of this dynamic, but there is no other way to phrase this reality accurately. The sexual abuse by clergy of children especially, but also of women and men, demonstrates without a doubt that such an attitude of subjugation to those in power is operative. Female (and some male) historians and theologians are recording with epic force this dynamic across the spectrum of society. Some women have found relief from oppression and mystical ways of survival within church tradition, clinging to gospel values. Nonetheless the celibate/sexual structure of the church has neither led the way nor fostered the equality promised in the gospel (Daly, 1985; Davis & Farge, 1993; Delumeau, 1990; Duby, 1983; Dworkin, 1987; Eisler, 1987; Fraisse & Perrot, 1993; Klapisch-Zuber, 1992; Lerner, 1986, 1993; Noble, 1992; Pantel, 1992; Ruether, 1983, Thébaud, 1994).

The sexual abuse of children and women could not exist systemically if this dynamic were not operative on a daily basis and in the practical operation of the celibate/sexual structure. The response of the hierarchy to public and private revelations and accusations of sexual abuse generally exposes and documents this element clearly in the courtrooms and lawyers' offices of this country. Anyone willing to listen to victims' stories will conclude that they are hearing history in process.

The official church, the celibate/sexual structure in action, sits, like Pilot washing his hands. The claim is made that sexual abuse is the aberration of a deviant few. It is not. Sexual abuse of children, impregnation, abortion, seduction of minors, sexual involvement with adults by those who claim celibate status and privilege are manifestations of the deviation and distortion of spiritual service to a system of power that tolerates subjugation and restriction of the nonselect group at the pleasure of the select.

This is probably the hardest reality to accept among those who care deeply about the church and who are aware of the good it accomplished throughout history. But none of that can obscure or mitigate the overwhelming evidence that the elements of subjugation and restriction exist and are a structural support of the celibate/sexual system of the church.

African theologian Bernadette Mbuy Beya (1994) underlines the systemic nature of this element in the celibate/sexual structure of the church when she points out how the church in Africa, so vocal about and committed to the struggle for justice and freedom, is "silent or even show(s) complicity when it comes to the question of women." She goes on to list the types of abuse African women commonly suffer in which the church participates, "although perhaps it never does so quite so overtly as the rest of society" (p. 592).

It is the covert participation in socially sanctioned abuse that is exposed, worldwide, in the current crisis of the church. Mbuy Beya is explicit about the abuse African women suffer:

> This violence may be physical, psychological, or moral. We have noted ten types of physical violence which affect women's health, which we classify as follows: beatings and wounds, rape, venereal diseases, premarital pregnancy, abortion, multiple pregnancies, physical remodeling and embellishments, sexual mutilation, purification rites, and prostitution. We have defined psychological and mental violence as acts against a woman which deprive her of her thought and will or alter her behavior. They range from insults to the complete negation of woman's personality. (p. 591)

Clergy anywhere cannot distance themselves from this pattern of violence and abuse by a simple, sanitized disclaimer that retains the essence of the systemic element. In practical reality, a system that can tolerate the exploitation of women and children will never be able to lead a fight against the destruction of the environment effectively. This is because the forces that exploit one vital resource can and will violate the other.

## NATURE AND GOD'S WILL

*The fifth element is the belief that the restriction of one group by the other is justified by an appeal to nature or God's will.* In 1946, as a freshman in high school, I was taught that the basic genetic superiority of men over women was demonstrated by the genius of men in science, law, politics, literature, art, and religion and by the lack of genius among women in those same areas. This was nature. It was a static, stable, and immutable condition established in creation. The destiny of gender was firmly rooted in nature. It was also God's will that each person fulfill his or her destiny. Women were given the task to bear children, and to take care of them and men, and to sacrifice themselves lovingly in these services. Men were destined to protect, rule, guide, and generally think for women and children.

This understanding of nature and God's will, whatever its deeper evolutionary roots, is a clear construct of the celibate/sexual system. David Noble (1992) records its development in science. Recent church statements about the restriction of women from priestly ordination deny that the decision has anything to do with the inferiority of women; it is solely determined by God's will. One opines that the episcopal statements have more to do with political correctness than with conviction.

As the structure of the celibate/sexual system developed and ossified, celibate law and power were rationalized by doctrine, and the differences between men and women became hierarchic questions. The influence of the *Malleus Maleficarum* cannot be overestimated — not merely because it was an officially sanctioned teaching, but because it compiled the judgment of the ages, from pagan authors through the early fathers of the church and the Middle Ages to the Renaissance.

Certainly the document is critical of negligent and sinful clerics — the corruption of the best becomes the worst — but the judgment of sinful churchmen is of a different order than the criticism of women.

Harking back to the serpent of Eden, woman holds her own when it comes to evil.

> All wickedness is but little to the wickedness of women. The many lusts of men lead them into one sin, but the one lust of women leads them into all sins; . . . . Women are naturally more impressionable [than men]. . . . They have slippery tongues. . . . They are feebler both in mind and body. . . . Women are intellectually like children. . . . She is more carnal than men. . . . Women also have weak memories; and it is a natural vice in them not to be disciplined, but to follow their own impulses without any sense of what is due. (Kramer & Sprenger, 1971, pp. 44–45)

There is another quality pointed out in the *Malleus Maleficarum* and central to Weininger's evaluation of woman, "She is a liar by nature" (1909, pp. 268–300). He elevates that accusation to an existential level: "Woman's incapacity for truth—which I hold to be consequent on her lack of free will with regard to the truth, in accordance with Kant's 'indeterminism'—conditions her falsity" (p. 268).

Weininger's view of sex and character (the title of his 1903 treatise on gender), male and female psychology, and cultic purity was far more influential in the Catholic worlds of Italy, Austria, and Germany than were Freud's theories during the first half of the twentieth century. It was Weininger's answer to the feminists, and it was embraced because it was part of a Catholic understanding of the sexes. "However degraded a man may be, he is immeasurably above the most superior woman, so much so that comparison and classification of the two are impossible; but even so, no one has any right to denounce or defame woman, however inferior she must be considered" (p. 252). It is the "ontological untruthfulness of woman" (p. 264) that makes her so passive, so impressionable, so lacking in self-direction and needing man's guidance since women's standard of morality "comes from without" (p. 269), a gift of man to her. Even woman's mysticism is dismissed as superstition; in religion as in other areas of life, "she never has done anything of any importance" (p. 277).

Weininger poses the question of the meaning of male and female in the universe and comes to the conclusion, "Women have no existence and no essence; they are not, they are nothing. . . . Woman has no share in ontological reality, no relation to the thing-in-itself, which, in the deepest interpretation, is the absolute, is God" (p. 286). Man of course is capable of all things, genius is in his nature, he is capable of immortality. Woman is "anxious" *to be.*

Weininger also glorifies Jesus Christ who, by His celibacy, freed Himself from woman (and the feminine in himself) and, to Weininger, that other loathsome and despicable quality, Jewishness. He ennobles any man who eschews sex because it is dehumanizing:

> Coitus is immoral because there is no man who does not use woman at such times as a means to an end; for whom pleasure does not, in his own as well as her being, during that time represent the value of mankind. (p. 336)

If man listens to woman he will be sexual and abusive.

> If he is going to treat her as she wishes, he must have intercourse with her, for she desires it; he must beat her, for she likes to be hurt; he must hypnotise her, since she wishes to be hypnotised; he must prove to her by his attentions how little he thinks of himself, for she likes compliments, and has no desire to be respected for herself. (p. 337)

The only solution is celibacy: "The rejection of sexuality is merely the death of the physical life, to put in its place the full development of the spiritual life" (p. 346).

Although Weininger's verbalization would be consciously rejected, the essence of his message and logic is alive and well within the celibate/sexual structure of power. One only has to analyze the operation of that system in Rome, in any diocese, or in official documents that deal with issues of gender or celibacy to validate the appeal to nature and God's will for the place of men and women in the order of things.

## SEXUAL INCONSISTENCY

*The sixth element is that behavior condemned and found intolerable in the general population or among the subservient is tolerated or encouraged in a group of the select.* A review of the history of the celibate/sexual system and an examination of how it functions reveal clearly that people pledged to the power system enjoy a latitude of understanding, forgiveness, and tolerance of behavior—from masturbation to abortion—which is condemned vigorously in the general populace.

It is also very clear that this structural element has essentially nothing to do with sexual orientation; there have been times in the history of the celibate system when promiscuity of all kinds, concubinage, and fathering illegitimate children were commonplace in the priesthood—among bishops, cardinals, and popes. Today it is popular to cry gay wolf and to claim that homosexuals with their "lavender rectories" are overrunning and ruining the priesthood. Such accusations and attacks are glib, superficial, and ironically rooted in the very power system from which these critiques are offered.

It is not essential whether sexual activity is heterosexual or homosexual, but rather that it exists and is tolerated within the system of power, based on celibacy, at the same time that the same behavior is condemned among laypersons. What comes into focus here are the official absolutistic pronouncements on sexual norms concomitant with patterns of extreme tolerance for behavior within the system. In Rome I was told that the early Jesuits had begun to develop a more reasoned sexual norm; for instance, they taught that there could be "poverty of matter" in sexual matters (still a common pastoral response toward adolescent masturbation). The Vatican commanded them to cease and desist from that teaching, reinforcing the norm that insists that every sexual transgression must be a mortal sin.

## SEX AND POWER

A most chilling example represents this element of the celibate/sexual structure. A weeping young priest—struggling to absorb an experience that threatened his idealism, shook his self-confidence, and jolted him into an awareness he was trying hard to deny—tells the story. Having completed graduate school, this priest was flattered when his bishop asked him to accompany him to a high-level meeting attended by a large number of the hierarchy. During the priest's time there, a bishop from another diocese approached him and propositioned him sexually. The young priest declined, to which the bishop remarked, "You know, Father, if you want to progress in this organization, you are going to need friends."

There are women who can relate to similar abuse by clergy—women who have been sexually involved with priests and bishops. Most find it difficult to speak about their experience since they fear the retort, "You were a consenting adult." After the Anita Hill/Clarence Thomas hearings on television, I asked a black woman friend of mine, who had worked a long time for church officials and held an important administrative secretarial post, whether she believed Miss Hill's story. She looked at me for a long time, deciding I suppose, how much to confide in spite of our longtime acquaintance. In measured tones she said, "If you are a black, working woman you *have* been sexually harassed." With a nod of her head, she indicated which authority had approached her.

A sexual approach by a churchman is part of a power play whether the abused is male or female, but the full force of the dynamic is most clearly demonstrated by what knowledgeable insiders call the *network*.

## The Network

Some priests allege that there is a churchwide network of sexually active clergy who are bound together by their mutual knowledge of sexual activity either with others—both male and female—or with each other. The bishop cited earlier seemed to be inviting the young priest into that company. It is known among historians of the American church that a now-deceased cardinal, although homosexually active himself, held an Italian archbishop who was an apostolic delegate very much under his control because of knowledge of the latter's ongoing affair with a woman.

Another priest who was repeatedly invited into the network, but resisted becoming a part of it, recorded his experiences for his bishop. His first sexual experience was with a fellow seminarian during his college years. The seminarian told him of priests with whom he had sexual experiences and especially one who encouraged sexual friendships. That seminarian, a priest for 25 years and now a pastor, is still sexually active. The priest about whom the seminarian spoke not only made sexual advances before and after our informant's ordination but also assured the young man that he was "on new moral ground," with the clear implication that the church recognized sexual friendships among the clergy in practice, if not in theory. When the young priest resisted involvement, the same older priest told him that he would find out how difficult it is to be celibate and he would have to learn for himself that he "could not possibly maintain a totally celibate life."

When our priest sought out advice from a confessor whom he admired and trusted, that confessor revealed that he himself had a relationship with a priest in Italy, at the Vatican, and went on to extol the sexual aspects of that friendship. Disillusioned, the young man sought the assistance and intervention of a seminary rector who did, in fact, intercede at the chancery office only to inform the young man that the bishop's staff was well aware of the activity. In fact, the young priest was to find out later that some men on the bishop's staff were themselves sexually connected to the network.

Although this man was sustained by several long-term celibate friendships during his parish ministry, he was assigned with pastors who regularly invited young boys to spend the night in the rectory.

He witnessed priests who won promotions based on sexual involvement and was offered pornography and endured sexual advances from a number of highly placed fellow clergy.

During his years of active ministry, he observed the network operating in other dioceses. One bishop was notorious for inviting a group of priests to his recreation retreat. At bedtime there was always one bed less than the number of priests, and one priest was selected to share the bishop's, an arrangement not every priest so selected found comfortable. One cannot say whether such antics are motivated by naiveté, adolescent denial of sexual reality, or exploitation, but they do strain good judgment.

Over a period of 34 years I have had the privilege to review the stories of groups of priests from the same diocese or religious order — priests who sometimes do not know each other and were never involved with each other. It is astounding how the same names repeatedly come up in their stories; the interlocking mesh that casts its net widely and into high places becomes undeniable. This situation could not exist without a tolerance for behavioral inconsistency aligned with power.

## Those Who Fight the System

Another man, a religious priest who is actively involved in the process of celibacy, was profoundly affected by an older priest's betrayal and has been motivated to fight the system that fosters betrayal and abuse. He is convinced, "underlying the crisis of celibacy, one finds a far greater crisis — the crisis of Christian theology about sexuality." Here is his story.

> My intention in telling my story is to move beyond the usual dichotomies of perpetrator and victim, priest and parishioner, adult and adolescent, defendant and plaintiff. I know that the realities elude polarizing and demonizing and resist simplistic analysis.
>
> When I was in my teens, a parish priest whom I admired and in whom I had confided my adolescent struggles with sex took me away on a holiday and sexually abused me throughout our 10 days together. Although it was not my first sexual experience, it was my first with an adult, and what he asked me to do was new to me. It became obvious that I was not his only sexual partner when I contracted a venereal disease from him.
>
> No one considers my pastor an evil man. He is an outstanding and beloved pastor. He claims that I was by far the youngest person he ever had sex with, and I believe him. But

the doublethink in his life at the time he abused me was extraordinary. As we traveled, he would by day discourse on theological and ecclesiastical matters, share clerical gossip, and celebrate mass for the two of us in mountain meadows. He remains a fierce defender of the traditional model of the priesthood with all of its burdens and its privileges. He venerated the Roman Catholic Church and its hierarchical structures. But by night he expected me to service his sexual needs. When I told him after our holiday that I was considering the priesthood, he warned me that because I was attractive I had to be careful of priests who might prey upon me sexually.

The abundance of allegations of sexual abuse by priests and religious—allegations that have touched my own community—finally unlocked what happened to me half a lifetime ago. It happened so slowly, beginning with a question one night as I went to sleep: did my experience have anything to do with what we have been hearing so much about? It took a year before I could finally tell the whole story from start to finish, a year before the emotions held since those nights emerged from deep storage. The intricacy of what has emerged stuns me, touching issues of power and authority, status and role, ministry and service. The Christian tradition has consistently dealt seriously with sexual matters, and although the focus has often been too narrow or too intense, the underlying truth is that sexuality is a universal and powerful human experience. Both inescapable and potent, sex encompasses the gamut of human behaviors from the worst to the most sublime. In my own case, this priest's inability to use appropriately the energies of his own sexuality led to a profound subversion of his pastoral responsibility.

Could it have been different? Although the responsibility was his, he was somehow able to rationalize a sexual involvement with a teenaged parishioner. Although I know his behavior was evil, it is difficult for me to think of him as an evil man. At that time in his life, he was sexually active, though until our trip together it was with people closer to his own age. His seminary training provided no help in discerning a charism of celibacy or in developing a healthy discipline. The rhetoric and models of spiritual perfection available to him made it easy enough to concede spiritual defeat and find solace wherever possible.

The inability of the church, whether among the hierarchy or the laity, to discuss anyone's sexuality in an open and reflective manner made a professed celibate's struggle to integrate sexual attractions into productive ministry very difficult. Perhaps at some key moment the priest was taught or discovered that a secret sexual life was an acceptable compromise. Perhaps he never met the right priestly mentor who could hear his struggles with compassion and call him to fidelity, or never felt he could trust ones he knew. Perhaps he never thought much about it and simply followed an instinctual path of self-fulfillment. The very success of his ministry gave him the status within the system which allowed him to choose his own way sexually. I know how the system works. I am now part of it, but I refuse to live a double life. I refuse to abuse another. (Didascalos, 1994, pp. 855–856, reprinted with permission)

## NECESSARY VIOLENCE

*The final element is that violence is accepted as necessary or inevitable in the establishment or the retention of the system.* Most reluctantly, one has to accept that this principle of *violence accepted* is part of the celibate/sexual power structure. Celibacy, as inspired by the Gospel and the example of Jesus Christ, seems unconditionally and irreversibly nonviolent, even to the point of "turning the other cheek." The Crusades, the Inquisition, the tolerance and even profit from slavery, the doctrine that states that "error has no rights" only repudiated at the Second Vatican Council (1962–65), the Vatican's belated rejection in 1993 of the idea that the Jews were responsible for the death of Christ are only a few examples of traces of the tolerance for violence in the service of the celibate/sexual system and its power. We must remember that the yellow star of David, as a required piece of identification, was not a Nazi invention, but a medieval demand imposed by Catholics.

There is a direct connection with the consolidation of celibate law (1139) requiring its observance by all priests in the Latin rite and the tolerance of violence. In the *Origins of the Crusading Ideal* (1935, translated 1977), Carl Erdmann claims that Pope Gregory VII (1073–85) was also the greatest betrayer of the Christian ethic of peace:

"The pope harmonized warlike practices with the ethical ideal of the church and gave his wars the spiritual character of crusade. He regretted bloodshed but found it justified at any time for his ecclesiastical aims and for the rights of the papacy. . . . More than anyone before him, he overcame the inhibitions that had once restrained the church from being warlike in preaching and warlike in action. . . . He was as much a warrior as a priest and politician." The result in Pope Urban II's First Crusade of 1095 was the most corrupting amalgam of all, a church-centered imperialism: "Urban II's idea of crusade did not arise from a concern for the Holy

Sepulcher and pilgrimages. His original and primary basis was the idea of an ecclesiastical-knightly war upon heathens." (Cantor, 1991, pp. 403–404)

With these eleventh- and twelfth-century developments, the celibate/sexual system had completely lost its gospel meaning of peace and poverty, which had been so energizing in the desert with St. Antony and his followers. It had mutated far beyond any recognizable form from the vision and practice of Cassian and Benedict. It had distorted itself out of any shape envisioned by Augustine. Francis of Assisi and Dominic renewed the Gospel vision among small groups within a larger structure that was no longer free, no longer in the image of Christ, and burdened with a power and a mission even contrary to the Gospel. The celibate/sexual system became hardly distinguishable from secular power structures.

Freud makes a gentle comparison between the Catholic Church and the army in his *Group Psychology and the Analysis of the Ego* (1920/1955a):

> In a Church (and we may with advantage take the Catholic Church as a type) as well as in an army, however different the two may be in other respects, the same illusion holds good of there being a head—in the Catholic Church Christ, in an army its Commander-in-Chief—who loves all the individuals in the group with an equal love. . . . A democratic strain runs through the Church, for the very reason that before Christ everyone is equal, and that everyone has an equal share in His love. It is not without a deep reason that the similarity between the Christian community and a family is invoked, and that believers call themselves brothers in Christ, that is, brothers through the love which Christ has for them. There is no doubt that the tie which unites each individual with Christ is also the cause of the tie which unites them with one another. The like holds good of an army. (Vol. 18, pp. 93–94)

Freud goes on to point out how contrary feelings arise toward those outside the group—ruthless and hostile impulses toward other people make their appearance

> toward people who do not belong to the community of believers, who do not love him, and whom he does not love, stand outside this tie. Therefore a religion, even if it calls itself the religion of love, must be hard and unloving to those who do not belong to it. Fundamentally indeed, every religion is in this same way a religion of love for all those whom it embraces; while cruelty and

intolerance towards those who do not belong to it are natural to every religion. (p. 98)

Freud does not consider the result of the violation of the democratic core within the system, but Peter Gay, exploring nineteenth-century aggression, comes close to the inherent ambivalence in the celibate power system when he explains, "I am tacitly presupposing a measure of collaboration, and of clashes, between sexuality and aggression. The two are instinctual allies and adversaries. Pure specimens of aggression are as rare as pure specimens of love" (1993, p. 7).

This observation is as valid psychically for the anchorites of the desert as for Victorian bourgeoisie. Individual celibate striving must wrestle with the interaction of sex and aggression on the deepest levels of the psyche. Transformation of these forces into productive love is gradual but inevitably marked by radical self-knowledge, self-confrontation, and self-honesty. Since no desire is unacknowledged, the true celibate emerges with a sense of universal identification: in the word of the ancients, with *humility*. In psychoanalytic terms, where the id was, there is ego.

• • •

The failure of the celibate/sexual structure to capture the spiritual force of celibate integrity in the service of power is apparent from history. Its current operation is patently revealed in both its production of sexual victims and their treatment when they speak of their abuse.

Tolstoy struggled with the violent aspects of the ecclesial system in his 1894 classic *The Kingdom of God Is Within You* (1984). The expression, dissemination, and service of spiritual power remain the eternal tasks of religion. Sex and aggression cannot merely be dismissed or discounted by pronouncement or law. Internal resolution, not power or domination, is the achievement and the goal.

The most frightening aspect of analyzing the structure of the celibate/sexual power system is to realize how it was determined by banal sexual impulses in which women are the object of domination. Power and the glorification of the man are necessary goals. Christ is reduced to an idealized symbol, used as a justification for control.

When I substitute *Jew* or *homosexual* for *woman* in the schema, I am struck with how everything fits with Nazi theory and practice. Although Alfred Rosenberg sets *The Myth of the Twentieth Century* (1982) in conscious opposition to what he called the Roman-Jewish antimyth, which repressed the true mythos of men and race, his production resonates with tones and timber reminiscent of the structure of the celibate/sexual power system. Klaus Theweleit analyzes Nazi fascism in his *Male Fantasies* (1987, 1989). Numerous parallels with the celibate/sexual power system make it chillingly familiar and force us to acknowledge that they both, system and power, spring from the same human impulses. I cannot forget that the people and forces that generated Nazism and the Holocaust were all products of one Christian culture and the celibate/sexual power system.

This brief analysis of structure gives some clues to the relationship between celibacy/sexuality and power. To avert future destruction and abuse, we must analyze the system further and harness its positive elements at the same time that we eliminate fearlessly that which leads to oppression, domination, and misuse of spiritual energy in the service of death.

# 9
# PRIESTS WHO SUFFER;
# PRIESTS WHO SUCCEED

*While involved in sexual relationships, Augustine says, he felt unfree, driven, compulsive. When a religious resolution occurred in his life, its first and decisive result was that it was a solution to his problems with sex: renunciation of all sexual activity, accompanied, he reports, by feelings of relief and freedom. Augustine's conversion was to celibacy.*

Margaret R. Miles

*The desert fathers knew that one of the fundamental characteristics of fallen humanity is that we think we can keep things going by hiding and pretending. They saw that Christ hides nothing, and promises that all will be made known: they took him at his word and got on with making it all known.*

Columba Stewart

There are multiple valid models of the church (Dulles, 1974). The model I am exploring is one described graphically by the German theologian, Romano Guardini, when he reflected, "The church is the cross on which Christ is crucified daily."

There are many priests who suffer for, with, and at the hands of the church because of their dedicated sacrifice for their people and their exemplary representation of the Christian experience and community. Pastors who agonize because the mass of the people they see are burdened by the church's teaching on sexuality are among the crucified. They also see their people crucified. People trying to love and care for their children and families are stretched beyond every psychological, physical, spiritual, and economic bond that constrains them.

Similarly, some theologians agonize—those who know that the church's teaching on sexuality does not make sense philosophically,

181

theologically, biogenetically, or to the masses of people who would like to follow the Gospel (Moore, 1992). They know that the official teaching of the church has not changed the basis of its logic since the mid-eighteenth century when a priest could say,

> Impurity encompasses all other sins. . . . This vice . . . is not only a sin like the rest, [it] is the epitome of all sins; it is sin itself. . . . A sin is more weighty according to the extent to which it outrages and injures God. Now, the sin of lust is all the greater because the thing preferred to God is more vile, and contemptible. For such is the voluptuary: he prefers the pleasures of the flesh, a moment of desire, to God and a blissful eternity. . . . impurity profanes the entire faith of a Christian . . . . Those who have just a smattering of our holy books will note that God has always punished the sin of impurity more severely than all others. (Delumeau, 1990, p. 439)

Such teaching, which could be matched by hundreds of modern statements on marriage and sex, are grossly inadequate and in error. The teaching does not support life. It is destructive to the lives of young people who need to learn to love and relate; it is a burden to the lives of married people who need to foster growth in a future generation; it adds to the pain and struggles of the mismatched; it disregards men and women of homosexual orientation who are called to love and life equally with the married; it is destructive to celibates as well.

Priests and theologians who seek a more solid basis for sexual teaching are persecuted or silenced if they discuss sexuality in any terms except the official teaching. The danger? Of course, the real danger is that truth will disestablish the outmoded and destructive power base of the celibate/sexual system, within which a fraudulent celibacy is more tolerable and preferable to a celibacy or sexuality, authentic in its spiritual essence and freed from the restrictions of gender and the demands of legislation. In spite of oppression, there is a movement toward awareness, change, and integration.

## SUFFERING SERVANTS

Although bishops must be very cautions in their public statements, there is no doubt that some of them grasp the magnitude of the current crisis and its implications. Archbishop Rembert Weakland hinted at such awareness in his 1993 Easter message:

> We have a problem in our church today with pedophilia and we must face it. It is not enough to say that we have less pedophilia than other groups in society.

What we have is real and impedes our ministry as a church. We have to ask the tough questions about how to deal with it, how to uncover it in our seminary admission processes, how to create the correct atmosphere for good psychosexual development of our candidates, and *many other related issues*. (Weakland, 1993)

Another American bishop, interviewed by Jim Bowman, is bold in his vision:

We hurt the priesthood by limiting it to male celibates. That's a very small segment of humanity from which to draw for the exalted position of being a priest. I would like to see the day when priests are the best people.

I would like to see single, married men and women at the altar because of their qualifications—their piety, dedication, knowledge, skill, and the rest. I know so many nuns who would be extraordinary priests, far more than some young fellows who are ordained—nuns with twenty-five years experience, with well-rounded spiritual life, articulate. (1994, p. 192)

Some priests endure a triple burden of pain. First, they are capable of true empathy for the agony of the abused. They really do understand what it means to be taken advantage of by the trusted. Second, without excuses or blame, they understand something about the pain and pressures of their abusing brother priests. These priests assume full responsibility for themselves. They balance a delicate Gospel-like challenge with steady dedication to life and truth. Third, they care about people and life. They experience the abuse of poverty and hunger, overpopulation, crime, waste of all life as a personal burden.

The refinement of practiced celibacy leads a person to the depths of human ambiguity, desire, pain, passion, and delight. These men reach a kind of awareness of universality that makes real the shibboleth, *there but for the grace of God, go I*. Their personal integration does not ease their own pain or their capacity to feel for others; in fact, their transformation makes peace possible even amid exquisite awareness of the realities of death and life.

These men are rare; they are a treasure for the individuals and institutions they serve. Men from this group, more than any other source, gave me insight so necessary for any analysis of the celibate/sexual structure of the church—namely, to achieve celibacy, one must at some point, integrate sexual energies beyond any institutional alliance. Power and control over oneself are the issue. Institutional power, and certainly domination of others, are not only extraneous, but sometimes a hindrance, and always a danger to the Gospel reality of celibate love.

## STRUGGLING SERVANTS

Another group of priests suffer with the church in crisis. They are conscientious ministers struggling for integration. They become confused, confounded, and saddened by the sins of priests and the public uproar about priest sexual abuse. They feel assailed and attacked for something they did not do. Although they have a growing empathy for victims and victimizers, they, like many in the general public, are mystified by the loss of image and confidence. Once proud to wear the Roman collar in public, they now avoid it when they can. Once comfortable in social ministry, they feel inhibited and awkward around youngsters and women, fearing to give a false impression of overfamiliarity. Many of this group are self-aware and know temptation. They can be counted on to face the current challenge, and to help victims and their brother priests wherever possible.

Also, there is a new breed of young priests on the American and world scene. They can be caricatured easily by their Pontiff-three Roman collars (widest possible), spit-polished black shoes, french cuffs and gold links. Their real characteristics are more internal, represented by a rigid adherence to doctrine, complete devotion to authority, and imposition of the letter of the law based on a confidence that they have answers. This group is epitomized by the Opus Dei, an organization that has a special relationship to the pope and the Vatican. It is a formidable group, motivated by explicit religious ideals, and insistent on personal and organizational discipline. The long-range influence and effect on the celibate/sexual power system are yet to be determined. These men are deeply affected by anything that seems to impinge on or tarnish the image of ecclesial authority. Their suffering in the current church crisis is with and for the church as an institution.

## SUFFERING OF EXPERIENCE

Priests who are conscientious in their ministry and ambivalent about celibacy also suffer with the sexual crisis of the church. They have pursued a noncelibate path within priesthood, but their relationships have been, for the most part, appropriate and responsible in the sense that their partner has been knowledgeable, informed, and consenting. The relationships have not been seductions through ministry. These priests suffer for their partner; they suffer because of the impossible bind within which they and their lover exist; and they are acutely aware of the dilemmas, constraints, pain, and joy that sexuality can bring to human life.

## SECRETLY REFORMED

Priests who acknowledge to themselves their own sexual sins and past transgressions, some of which are similar to those exposed in head-lines and courtrooms, use the crisis of the church to reinforce their resolve to become celibate and compassionate. Fear of future exposure dominates some, whereas others use fear to motivate growth. Others take the occasion to resolve their adolescent naiveté. They experience some of the relief and freedom Augustine says accompanied his renunciation of all sexual activity because they have faced the human condition and the difficulty of sexual integration.

## EXPOSED IN RECOVERY

The public sensitivity to sexual abuse of minors has exposed the sexual involvement of hundreds of priests. The exposure of this minority has opened the way, for the general public as well as concerned church people, to ask questions openly about celibacy, sexuality, and the church's teaching, which have been areas of restricted concern and contained by secrecy for centuries.

Priests who have been exposed by their victims are often given the chance to reform their activities with the help of church-supported psychiatric centers. Some of these priests respond well to the revelation of their true celibate/sexual adjustment and, like alcoholics in recovery, can lead the way to help others and in the prevention of abuse by other priests. Priests who have suffered public exposure call attention and give credence to adult men and women who have also been abused by priests who pose celibacy.

## IMAGE AND ECONOMY

Certainly priests who care primarily about the image of the church and priesthood and its material possessions suffer to maintain and repair what they experience as assaults from lawyers and the press. If this suffering is accompanied by religious dedication to truth and profound compassion for suffering victims and abusers, it can be in full conformity with Gospel values. Deprived of truth and compassion, these pains are not different from the anxieties and pressures of any corporate executive for the interests of himself and his organization.

• • •

A crisis is a kind of passion. Pain is widespread, personal, and unavoidable. The crux is how to use suffering in confronting and solving the real structural and functional problems that caused the crisis in the first place. Suffering in the service of resolution is meaningful. Some priests are utilizing the current crisis to reevaluate their celibate/sexual awareness, to integrate their own desires and ministry, and to transform their energies to service and reform.

The greatest danger is that the crisis will not be met in terms of the early Christian experience and biological reality, but as it has been recycled in the past—in terms of power politics. And that is a great danger indeed, for as Jean Delumeau points out, "It is true that from the point of view of power politics, the dramatization of sin and its consequences reinforced clerical authority" (1990, p. 3).

I am convinced that the confrontation of celibacy/sexuality in biological terms will produce a deeper awareness of life and the means to control it productively, and a return to the Gospel experience will reinforce a more realistic and balanced view of love as central to every theological and human exploration. Both will resolve control by guilt and foster more rational self-determination and the preservation of life.

# 10
# THE CHRISTIAN EXPERIENCE

*If you wish to discipline the flesh and make it a thousand times more subject,
then place on it the bridle of love. Whoever has accepted this sweet burden of the
bridle of love will attain more and come much further than all the penitential
practices and mortifications that all the people of the world acting together could
ever carry out.*

Meister Eckhart

*The being who is the object of his own reflection, in consequence of that very
doubling back upon himself, becomes in a flash able to raise himself to a new
sphere. In reality, another world is born. Abstraction, logic, reasoned choice and
inventions, mathematics, art, calculation of space and time, anxieties and dreams
of love—all these activities of inner life are nothing else than the effervescence of
the newly formed center as it explodes onto itself.*

Pierre Teilhard de Chardin

The Christian experience is based on consciousness and love.
Mysticism is not an illusion but a vision of the totality of existence
based on an acute perception of reality. This is one reason why modern science, especially physics, and traditional mysticism grope for
expression amid some of the same problems of language (Anonymous, *The Cloud of Unknowing*, 1946; Capra, 1991; Lederman, 1993).

The current sexual crisis of the church is dire precisely because
there is no way out of it except by confronting the biological base of
Christian experience and doctrine. Any adequate response to the
sexual crisis will involve a shift of perception as profound as the
Copernican shift demanded in the sixteenth century. There is
something basically awry in our understanding of human sexual
nature; it cannot be fixed by minor calibrations or resorting to old

187

formulas. We must confront the dilemmas Augustine faced with as much directness, courage, and honesty—God, creation, sin, church, grace, and human nature—in short, the origin, nature, and destiny of life.

## RESPECT FOR THE BIOLOGICAL BASE

Sex is not a new problem for religion and Christianity. Part of the problem is intimately intertwined with its Judaic seed and the Roman and Hellenistic soil in which it grew up. God and the church got "sexed." Father Walter Ong (1989) expresses the situation elegantly:

> Since sex is a biological phenomenon, the masculine-feminine dialectic is basically biological, however complexly related to much, or indeed virtually everything else, in human life. *Catholic doctrine has a biological base in the sense that the female-male relationship forms the human ground in which redemption, freedom, and love take root.* A residual Manichaeism—from which Christians have still not entirely liberated themselves—would downgrade the material universe and make a biological foundation for anything human distasteful. But the foundation is there nevertheless, and should not be dismaying to those who truly believe that the Word became flesh. (pp. 171–172)

My understanding of the current crisis of sexuality in our time is based on the assumption that the mind and heart of Jesus Christ (His consciousness and love) represented an evolutionary leap that culture has not been able to absorb. Jesus did not speak of Adam's sin, Eve's culpability, or sexuality. He represented an integration of all existence and an impulse toward life and truth.

I was led to an awareness of this universal value of life from interviewing committed and achieved celibates. They did not disdain the body or life, but they had been chastened by a radical knowledge of their own desires and the meaning of existence beyond themselves. Their experience, like that of Jesus Christ, largely escaped institutionalization, where fear and distrust of sexuality and the body in general accompanied a glorification of ideal and the ideation. Historian Delumeau describes the process:

> The distrust of sexuality involved several converging ethical values and attitudes: the Judaic concern with ritual purity, the rejection of the body by neoplatonic pessimism, and the mistrust of worldly attachments common to Stoicism and the Book of Wisdom. These

three ancient traditions thus also involve the discourse of the *contemptus mundi*, which in fact had adopted, accumulated, and propagated them. (1990, p. 446)

There is great danger in contempt for this world inspired by dualism. Disdain for life was not universal within the monastic movement or even among all of the ascetics, but dualistic contempt for the material inevitably corrodes the individual sense of self. Mistrust of biology violates creation and the place of human life within the whole of material nature. The body, sex, and matter are not an accidental part of existence. Matter and sexuality are not necessary evils. Just as physical laws and reality are disregarded in the insistence of a literal biblical and a pre-Copernican understanding of the sun rising or orbiting the earth, so a dualistic explanation of sexuality violates natural science. Evolutionary biology, archaeology, pale-ontology, genetics, and astrophysics all point toward a unitary, monistic, and materialistic philosophy necessary to undergird a theology of sexuality. Father Pierre Teilhard de Chardin confronted the dilemma at its origin in 1922:

It is a doubly serious difficulty for us to retain the former representation of original sin, and this difficulty can be summed up as follows: The more we scientifically revive the Past, the less we find any place for Adam or the earthly paradise. (1969, p. 62)

Although Pope John Paul II spoke positively, welcoming the interaction of religion and science — to purify religion of superstition and magic, and science of idolatry and false absolutes — the process is not a simple or easy marriage. It is a bit like a shotgun wedding, more determined by inexorable reality than by approval or ceremony. If science is to purify religion of its sexual superstitions and errors, we will have to examine the concepts of God, our appeal to God's will, our interpretation of Scripture, our understanding of natural law, and our uses of power.

The roots of sexual distortion and misunderstanding run deep. Many people feel threatened by questioning these roots, as if dissolution and rootlessness would result. In the face of threat, some are tempted to reinforce the very roots that should be pruned. Examination does not pose a threat to God/meaning/existence/love. It may require the removal of auxiliary individual and cultural supports we have constructed to keep us secure while we search for better and more complete answers. Fidelity to religious tradition does not merely entail preserving the past, but also requires the ability to grow beyond the past, learn from it, revise the present, and shape the future in light of past lessons and mistakes. Such is the message and life of Jesus.

Sex and religion have a notorious ability to retain their infantile and primitive force—aided and fostered, albeit sometimes unwittingly, by Church, state (law), and medicine. Denial, rationalization, splitting, and reaction formation can be institutionalized beyond individual mental mechanisms that defend against integration of reality into awareness and behavior. Our task is to confront at the deepest personal level possible our own persistence and style in avoiding the real issues that confront us in these two areas of our understanding and behavior: sex and religion—that is, *our* sexuality and *our* religion.

One must, if motivated by any true religious spirit, be extremely tolerant and careful not to judge another's religious experience. But the same spirit of religious honesty (desire for Truth) will motivate one to be most exacting about one's own religious and sexual experience and conviction. There is no justification for sloppy or negligent attention in the rigorous examination of one's religious or sexual integration.

Peter Medawar (1990, pp. 144–177), Roger Penrose (1991), Daniel Dennett (1991), John Eccles (1989) and others point out the challenge from the vantage of science. Christopher Mooney in his working notes for *Theology and Evolution* (unpublished) commented on this perspective:

> Today most biologists, neuroscientists and philosophers would opt for a monist rather than a dualist approach to the mind-body problem. That is to say, human self-consciousness represents the total state of the brain at any given moment, not the functioning of a non-physical "mind" interacting with the brain but distinct from it. In this view it is the *total state* of the brain, not the functioning of any particular set of neurons, that constitutes human self-consciousness. The incredible complexity of this "total state" places it as of now beyond description in purely neurological terms, though humans use the language of reason and intentions to speak of it quite clearly.
>
> Such self-consciousness is obviously causal, with the brain controlling bodily movements as well as environment. The precise direction of such control, moreover, is in any given instance undetermined and unpredictable, something that corresponds to the common human experience of inner freedom.

To meet the current crisis, the church must make a profound shift in its understanding of human sexuality. The shift has to be thoroughgoing—as profound as any that has challenged the church in its 2,000-year existence. The natural sciences now challenge irrevocably and incontrovertibly former understandings of human sexuality and love. There is no turning back. There can be no avoidance or denial of the profound effect that new knowledge in the natural and social sciences has brought to the human condition.

## THE EARLY CHRISTIAN EXPERIENCE

I can turn to a written source even earlier than the gospels for a deeper understanding of the celibate/sexual reality and conflict. Paul, like me, never saw Jesus in the flesh. He was smitten by the story and words of Jesus. They transformed his life. I spent many years thinking that Paul was a misogynist, that he extolled celibacy as the price of male glorification, domination, and the avoidance of female inferiority and contamination. I was wrong.

My eyes were originally opened not by studying St. Paul but by listening to men who took celibacy seriously. Over and over I observed men, many of whom were clearly defined as achieved celibates. They shared one striking characteristic: an expanding awareness of universal interrelatedness. This quality that I found on the hoof, so to speak, led me back to St. Paul and his ecstatic declaration, "There are no more distinctions between Jew and Greek, slave and free, male and female, but all are one in Christ Jesus" (Galatians 3:28). This was not merely a doctrinal definition of baptism. This declaration has the force of personal experience—conviction born of insight and transformation.

How could I reconcile Paul's denunciation of women, his explicit putting them in their place as for instance in I Timothy 3:1–13 and Titus 1:6–9, passages that declare only males could be considered ministers: "I am not giving permission for a woman to teach or to tell a man what to do. A woman ought not to speak, because Adam was formed first and Eve afterward, and it was not Adam who was led astray but the woman who was led astray and fell into sin" (I Timothy 2:12–14).

Paul had explicitly repudiated the distinction of creation primacy in I Corinthians 11:7–12: "both come from God." The prohibitions for women to speak in I Corinthians 14:34–35—"Women are to remain quiet at meetings" and "they must keep in the background"; if they have questions, "they should ask their husbands at home"—run counter to Paul's doctrine and his experience of the Gospel community (Wright, 1992). Father Jerome Murphy O'Connor of the Ecole Biblique says it "has long been recognized that these verses are an intrusion, which appeal to a non-Pauline argument based on the Law, and which contradict Paul's position on women praying and prophesying in public (I Corinthians 11:5). These verses were inserted after Paul's death in order to borrow his authority for a view which he would have energetically refused" (1992, p. 311). O'Connor and his fellow Scripture scholars likewise reject as unauthentic the household codes that subjugate women. They believe these were not written by Paul but by his disciples (Colossians 3:18; Ephesians 5:22).

Paul embraced and articulated equality by referring to women as *coworkers* not distinct from males (Philippians 4:3). He calls a woman *an apostle* (Philippians 4:7). It is clear that St. Paul believed that women who labored for the Gospel deserved to be leaders in the community "because their gifts had been achieved in service." These women were collaborators—coapostles in Paul's estimation, not merely patrons, like Phoebe, Romans who supported the church with their contributions of money and by acting as hosts to the apostles.

The history of the people of God is not dissociated from evolutionary struggles, where sometimes culture and custom triumph over spiritual reality. The early church, the early Christian community, and culture were not ready or able to absorb the celibate/sexual experience of either St. Paul or Jesus Christ. The evolutionary leap that Jesus represented—one that established religion and tradition could not absorb—was correctly perceived and experienced by St. Paul and a myriad of other Christians, married, single, and celibate. Even so, some of Paul's disciples could not translate his experience into ecclesial reality (Fiorenza, 1992)

## CONCLUSION

In personal terms, celibacy either involves one in an integrative and transformative process, or it becomes a sham—or worse, a religious perversion. The analysis of sincere celibate men and women demonstrates a living process, not merely incorporation into a culture or state, as theological literature tends to categorize celibacy and marriage.

Jovinian, a fourth-century monk, claimed that marriage and celibacy were equally valid modes of imitating Christ and of achieving Christian love. Augustine and Jerome riled against him and espoused the theory of a state of perfection that excluded marriage and sex (Miles, 1990, p. 99). The condemnation of Jovinian in regard to sexuality, marriage, and celibacy was as misguided as the condemnation of Galileo for his espousal of heliocentrism. Both condemnations by church officials have been detrimental to the credibility of the church and its legitimate role as a teaching authority. The former, however, has proved far more disastrous in terms of personal and cultural suffering.

The idea that the state of celibacy is more perfect than the state of marriage is a theological figment, a rationalization in the service of male power, and has no relationship to spiritual reality. The Gospel dictum used to justify this reasoning is Matthew 19:21, "If you would be perfect, go sell what you have, give it to the poor and you will have treasure in heaven, afterward come back and follow me." The direct reference, of course, is to overreliance on material things, not on sex or sexual relationships. It is an appeal to the power of a lived belief in Jesus. Theologians have expanded this saying of Jesus to sexuality. In practice, sex, not faith, becomes the central concern and justifies celibacy as the essential element of the more perfect state, and indeed the cornerstone of the whole celibate/sexual system of the church. In reality, one may live in splendor and have the advantage of every material convenience and still be a participant in this superior state of perfection as long as one is male and nonmarried. The *practice* of celibacy is not even a requirement for incorporation into the state.

Only a gross misunderstanding and spiritualization of sexuality support a logic that holds that because Jesus was male, men are superior to women. Similar reasoning presumes that Jesus was celibate, and therefore celibacy is superior to marriage. Such reasoning does not stand critical examination, biologically, psychologically, or even theologically. The calamitous potential of a system that constructs its edifice on this cognizance has been proven, individually and institutionally. It is truly a house built on sand. Incomplete understanding of Jesus' sexuality, insofar as it has been translated into a celibate/sexual system, has been destructive and violent in the degree that it has been translated into systemic function and structure. If Jesus Christ were proven to be homosexual in orientation or sexually active in marriage, his life and message would not be altered; nor would it make homosexuality or marriage superior to heterosexual orientation or celibacy.

Technically, according to the current teaching of the church, every unmarried Christian is bound to the same sexual standard as the committed celibate—perfect chastity. Again, such concrete reasoning is of little help and is in fact destructive to those preparing for marriage and those preparing for celibacy. We all must learn to love and relate; no orientation or state has a superior claim in and of itself.

The current sexual crisis in the church will not destroy the reality or practice of celibacy. The crisis, however, will force us to clarify its essence, support its process, and refine its spiritual potential for a new age and divorce it from the denigration of women and the arrogance of religious superiority. Protestantism did not reject celibacy because it was being practiced with honesty and vigor. It rejected a power system intrinsically aligned with a law it preached and for the most part did not practice.

The youth of our time are having a similar reaction, and in addition they are rejecting all church teaching about sex. They cannot give credence to a system that they experience as unreasonable and essentially dishonest. Young people and the future are the greatest casualties in the current crisis in the church. Some effects of former crises over celibacy have been permanent. The nearly complete rejection of celibacy as a religious practice has to a degree impoverished Protestant spirituality, again because celibacy is part of the natural biosexual diversity of the human species and in its own way, based on radical self-knowledge, translates an awareness of the reality of the transcendent and the value of altruism into love and service. As Gandhi pointed out, the world—life—is in need of a certain number of people who practice celibacy.

We are a people of God. Love, in full conformity with the mind and heart of Christ, is open to the married as well as the celibate. To hold otherwise denigrates spousal, parental, and every love that informs the myriad ways we serve one another.

Those of us who care deeply about the celibate tradition of the church do not promote it by parading it under false colors. Celibacy can be a valuable way to contribute to life, love, and culture—if it is honestly lived. We cannot hide behind systems or ideals, no matter how exalted. We, celibate and married—as well as all lovers—will ultimately be judged on the reality of our lived existence. We are all one and equal before the throne of Life and Love. Each of us should approach the reality of love with the clear knowledge that we need each other and a humility that rejects false claims to superiority.

What of real value will remain if we reject a celibate/sexual power structure based on categories of superiority, and in turn demand personal application of the gospel message—a universal call to love? Won't the religious world fall apart? Won't chaos reign? No. Celibacy will persist—celibate love—and the process of celibacy genuinely entered into and honestly pursued. Marital love equally will remain, integrated and enhanced. The value of sex and its responsible use will be enhanced. Life will be more greatly treasured.

# BIBLIOGRAPHY

Abbott, W. M. (Ed.). *The Documents of Vatican II*. New York: America Press, 1966.

American Psychiatric Association. *Diagnostic and Statistical Manual of Mental Disorders, 4th ed.* Washington, DC: Author, 1994.

Angelica, J. C. *A Moral Emergency: Breaking the Cycle of Child Sexual Abuse*. Kansas City, MO: Sheed & Ward, 1993.

Anonymous. *The Cloud of Unknowing*. London: Underhill, 1946. (Original manuscript circa 14th century.)

Armstrong, K. *Holy War: The Crusades and Their Impact on Today's World*. New York: Anchor Books, Doubleday, 1991.

Aschheim, S. E. *The Nietzsche Legacy in Germany, 1890–1990*. Berkeley: University of California Press, 1994.

Athanasius. *The Life of Antony and the Letter to Marcellinus* (R. C. Gregg, Trans.). New York: Paulist Press, 1980.

Augustine, Saint. *Confessions* (H. Chadwick, Trans.). New York: Oxford University Press, 1991.

Balducelli, R. The decision for celibacy. *Theological Studies*, 1976, 36, 219–242.

Barry, W. A., Birmingham, M., Connolly, W. J., Fahey, R. J., Finn, V. S., Gill, J. J. Affectivity and sexuality: Their relationship to the spiritual and apostolic life of jesuits. *Studies in the Spirituality of Jesuits*, 1978, X(2 & 3), March–May.

Bass, E., & Davis, L. *The Courage to Heal*. New York: HarperPerennial, 1994.

Baumann, P. An incarnational ethic listening to one another. *Commonweal*, 1994, 28 January.

Bellah, R. N. *Beyond Belief: Essays on Religion in a Post-Traditional World*. Berkeley: University of California Press, 1991.

Benedict. *The Rule of St. Benedict*. Collegeville, MN: Liturgical Press, 1981.

Berlin, F. S. Pedophilia: Diagnostic concepts, treatment, and ethical considerations. *American Journal of Forensic Psychiatry*, 1986, 7(1), 13–30.

Bernanos, G. *The Diary of a Country Priest*. New York: Macmillan, 1966.

Berry, J. *Lead Us Not into Temptation: Catholic Priests and the Sexual Abuse of Children*. New York: Doubleday, 1992.

Biffi, G. La presenza della virgine. *L'Osservatore Romano* (Rome, Italy), 1989, 23 December. Also *Washington Post*, 1989, 23 December.

Bloom, H. *Ruin the Sacred Truths.* Cambridge, MA: Harvard University Press, 1989.

Boas, F. *Race, Language, and Culture.* Chicago: University of Chicago Press, 1988.

Booth, L. *When God Becomes a Drug: Breaking the Chains of Religious Addiction & Abuse.* Los Angeles: Tarcher/Perigee, 1991.

Bornemann, A. Editorial. *The Jeffersonian* (Baltimore, MD), 1994, 19 January.

Boswell, J. *Christianity, Social Tolerance, and Homosexuality.* Chicago: University of Chicago Press, 1981.

Boswell, J. *Same-Sex Unions in Premodern Europe.* New York: Villard, 1994.

Bowman, J. *Bending the Rules: What American Priests Tell American Catholics.* New York: Crossroads, 1994.

Brown, J. C. *Immodest Acts: The Life of a Lesbian Nun in Renaissance Italy.* New York: Oxford University Press, 1986.

Brown, P. *Augustine of Hippo.* London: Faber & Faber, 1969.

Brown, P. *The Cult of the Saints.* Chicago: The University of Chicago Press, 1981.

Brown, P. *The Body and Society: Men, Women and Sexual Renunciation in Early Christianity.* New York: Columbia University Press, 1988.

Brown, P. *Society and the Holy in Late Antiquity.* Berkeley: University of California Press, 1989.

Brown, P. *Power and Persuasion in Late Antiquity Towards a Christian Empire.* Madison: University of Wisconsin Press, 1992.

Brown, R. E., Fitzmyer, J. A., Murphy, R. E. *The Jerome Biblican Commentary.* Vol. I: The Old Testament. Vol. II: The New Testament and Topical Articles. Englewood Cliffs, NJ: Prentice-Hall, 1968.

Burkett, E., & Bruni, F. *A Gospel of Shame: Child Sexual Abuse and the Catholic Church.* New York: Viking, 1993.

Campbell, J. *The Inner Reaches of Outer Space.* New York: Harper & Row, 1988.

Canadian Bishops. *From Pain to Hope: Report from the CCCB Ad Hoc Committee on Child Sexual Abuse.* Ottawa, 1992, June.

Canon Law Society of America. *Code of Canon Law.* Washington, DC: Author, 1984.

Cantor, N. F. *Inventing the Middle Ages.* New York: Morrow, 1991.

Capra, F. *The Tao of Physics: An Exploration of the Parallels Between Modern Physics and Eastern Mysticism.* 3rd ed., updated. Boston: Shambhala, 1991.

Carnes, P. J. *Out of the Shadows: Understanding Sexual Addiction.* Minneapolis, MN: CompCare Publications, 1983.

Carnes, P. J. *Don't Call It Love: Recovery from Sexual Addiction.* New York: Bantam Books, 1991.

Carey, R. P. *Psychosexuality and the development of celibacy skills.* Paper presented at the National Catholic Educational Association 89th Annual Convention, St. Louis, MO, 1992, 21 April.

Cass, V. C. Homosexual identity: A concept in need of definition. In J. P. DeCecco & M. G. Shively (Eds.), *Origins of Sexuality and Homosexuality.* New York: Harrington Park, 1985.

Cassian, J. *On Chastity* (T. G. Kardong, Trans.). Richardson, ND: Assumption Abbey Press, 1993.

Chaucer, G. *Canterbury Tales* (J. U. Nicolson, Trans.). Garden City, NY: Doubleday, 1934.

Church of England. *Issues in Human Sexuality*. London: Church House, 1991.

Clark, K. *An Experience of Celibacy*. Notre Dame, IN: Ave Maria Press, 1982.

Cline, S. *Women, Passion & Celibacy*. New York: Carol Southern Books, 1993.

Coate, M. A., Dowell, S., Kimmerling, B., Malone, M., McGinn, B., O'Keefe, J., Orchard, G., Schneiders, S., Sheldrake, P., Toolan, D., Woodgate, F. Celibacy. *The Way Supplement*, 1993.

Cochini, C. *Origines apostoliques du célibat sacerdotal*. Paris: Editions Lethielleux, 1981.

Cochini, P. C., *Il Sacerdozio e il Celibato nei Padri e nella Tradizione della Chiesa*. Rome, 1993, 26 May.

Collins, R. F., Coote, N., Cosstick, V., Dunstan, P., Fisher, A., Gallagher, R., Kelly, K., O'Sullivan, B., Rist, J. & A., Williams, D. The church and sexuality. *Priests and People*, 1993, August-September.

Congregation for Institutes of Consecrated Life and Societies of Apostolic Life. *Fraternal Life in Community*. Rome, 1994.

Congregation for the Clergy. *Directory on the Ministry and Life of Priests*. Libreria Editrice Vaticana, 1994.

Consultation on Homosexuality, Social Justice and Roman Catholic Theology. *Homosexuality and Social Justice*. San Francisco, 1986.

Daly, M. *Pure Lust*. Boston: Beacon Press, 1984.

Daly, M. *Beyond God the Father*. Boston: Beacon Press, 1985.

Davis, N. Z., & Farge, A. *A History of Women in the West: III. Renaissance and Enlightenment Paradoxes*. Cambridge, MA: Belknap Press of Harvard University Press, 1993.

Dawkins, R. *The Selfish Gene*. New York: Oxford University Press, 1989.

Dawkins, R. *The Extended Phenotype: The Long Reach of the Gene*. New York: Oxford University Press, 1992.

Degler, C. N. *In Search of Human Nature*. New York: Oxford University Press, 1991.

Delumeau, J. *Sin and Fear: The Emergence of a Western Guilt Culture 13th–18th Centuries*. New York: St. Martin's Press, 1990.

Demause, Lloyd. *Foundations of Psychohistory*. New York: Creative Roots, 1982.

Demause, L. The universality of incest. *Journal of Psychohistory*, 1991, 19(2), 123–164.

De Nike, L. Struggling with Celibacy. *Towson Times* (Towson, MD), 1994, 19 January, pp. 20–22.

Dennett, D. C. *Consciousness Explained*. Boston: Little, Brown, 1991.

Didascalos. Charism of celibacy: A priest's personal story of liberating discovery. *Tablet*, 1994, 9 July, pp. 856–858.

Dinshaw, C. *Chaucer's Sexual Poetics*. Madison: University of Wisconsin Press, 1989.

Dourley, J. P. *Love, Celibacy and the Inner Marriage*. Toronto: Inner City Books, 1987.

Dreese, J. J. The other victims of priest pedophilia. *Commonweal,* 1994, 22 April.

Duby, G. *The Knight, the Lady, and the Priest: The Making of Modern Marriage in Medieval France.* New York: Pantheon, 1983.

Dulles, A. *Models of the Church.* Garden City, NY: Doubleday, 1974.

Dworkin, A. *Woman Hating.* New York: Dutton, 1974.

Dworkin, A. *Pornography: Men Possessing Women.* New York: Putnam, 1981.

Dworkin, A. *Intercourse.* New York: Free Press, 1987.

Dyson, F. *Origins of Life.* Cambridge, MA: Cambridge University Press, 1990.

Eccles, J. C. *Evolution of the Brain: Creation of the Self.* London: Routledge, 1989.

Eckhart, M. *The Essential Sermons, Commentaries, Treatises, and Defense* (E. Colledge & B. McGinn, Trans.). New York: Paulist Press, 1981.

Eisler, R. *The Chalice and the Blade: Our History, Our Future.* San Francisco: Harper & Row, 1987.

Erikson, J. M. *St. Francis and His Four Ladies.* New York: W.W. Norton, 1970.

Facaros, D., & Pauls, M. *Tuscany and Umbria.* London: Cadogan Books, 1989.

Faller, K. *Child Sexual Abuse: Intervention and Treatment Issues.* Washington, DC: National Center on Child Abuse and Neglect, 1993.

Feister, J. How the church is confronting clergy sexual abuse. *St. Anthony's Messenger,* 1994, 101(9), 28–35.

Fenichel, O. *Collected Papers, First Series.* New York: W. W. Norton, 1953.

Ferder, F., & Heagle, J. *Your Sexual Self: Pathway to Authentic Intimacy.* Notre Dame, IN: Ave Maria Press, 1992.

Fichter, J. H. German women and married clergy. *America,* 1994, 16 April, pp. 12–15.

Fiorenza, E. S. *In Memory of Her: A Feminist Theological Reconstruction of Christian Origins.* New York: Crossroad, 1992.

Fisher, H. E. *Anatomy of Love: The Natural History of Monogamy, Adultery, and Divorce.* New York: W. W. Norton, 1992.

Foucault, M. *The Archaeology of Knowledge and the Discourse on Language.* New York: Pantheon, 1972.

Foucault, M. *The History of Sexuality.* Vol. 1: An Introduction. New York: Pantheon, 1978.

Foucault, M. *Discipline and Punish: The Birth of the Prison.* New York: Vintage Books, 1979.

Foucault, M. *The Use of Pleasure.* Vol. 2 of *The History of Sexuality.* New York: Vintage Books, 1986a.

Foucault, M. *The Care of the Self.* Vol. 3 of *The History of Sexuality.* New York: Pantheon, 1986b.

Foucault, M. *Politics, Philosophy, Culture: Interviews and Other Writings 1977–1984* (L. Kritzman, Ed.). New York: Routledge, 1988.

Foucault, M. About the beginning of the hermeneutics of the self. Transcript by M. Blasius & T. Keenan. *Political Theory,* 1993, 21(2), May, 198–227.

Fox, R. L. *Pagans and Christians.* New York: Knopf, 1987.

Fox, T., & Berry, J. As a nation discusses pedophilia, even pope admits it's a problem. *National Catholic Reporter,* 1993, 2 July, 2–3.

Fraad, Harriet. Children as an exploited class. *Journal of Psychohistory*, 1993, 21(1), Summer, 37–51.

Fraisse, G., & Perrot, M. *A History of Women in the West: IV. Emerging Feminism from Revolution to World War*. Cambridge, MA: Harvard University Press, 1993.

Fraser, B. G. A glance at the past, a gaze at the present, a glimpse at the future: A critical analysis of the development of child abuse reporting statutes. *Chicago-Kent Law Review*, 1978, 54(3), 641–686.

Freud, A. *The Ego and the Mechanisms of Defense*. New York: International Universities Press, 1974.

Freud, S. Three Essays on the Theory of Sexuality. In *Complete Psychological Works, Vol. 7 (1901–1905)*, pp. 125–248. London: Hogarth Press, 1953.

Freud, S. Group Psychology and the Analysis of the Ego. In *Complete Psychological Works, Vol. 18 (1920–1922)*, pp. 67–145. London: Hogarth Press, 1955a.

Freud, S. Beyond the Pleasure Principle. In *Complete Psychological Works, Vol. 18 (1920–1922)*, pp. 3–66. London: Hogarth Press, 1955b.

Freud, S. Group Psychology and Other Works. In *Complete Psychological Works, Vol. 18 (1920–1922)*, pp. 67–145. London: Hogarth Press, 1955c.

Freud, S. Fetishism. In *Complete Psychological Works, Vol. 21 (1927–1931)*, pp. 149–159. London: Hogarth Press, 1961a.

Freud, S. The Future of an Illusion. In *Complete Psychological Works, Vol. 21 (1927–1931)*, pp. 3–58. London: Hogarth Press, 1961b.

Freud, S. Civilization and Its Discontents. In *Complete Psychological Works, Vol. 21 (1927–1931)*, pp. 64–148. London: Hogarth Press, 1961c.

Freud, S. Introductory Lectures on Psycho-analysis. In *Complete Psychological Works, Vol. 16–17 (1915–1917)*, pp. 243–476. London: Hogarth Press, 1963.

Furlong, M. A sense of rejection. *Tablet*, 1987, 10 October.

Gabbard, G. *Sexual Exploitation in Professional Relationships*. Washington, DC: American Psychiatric Press, 1989.

Gaboury, D., & Burkett, E. The secret of St. Mary's: Sex abuse and the church. *Rolling Stone*, 1993, 11 November, pp. 48–87.

Galdston, I. *The Interface Between Psychiatry and Anthropology*. New York: Brunner/Mazel, 1971.

Gallagher, J. *How to Survive Being Human*. Westminster, MD: Christian Classics, 1988.

Gallagher, M. P. Science with prayer, *Tablet*, 1993, 15 May, p. 630.

Garfinkel, H. *Studies in Ethnomethodology*. Oxford: Blackwells Polity Press, 1989.

Gay, P. *Freud: A Life for Our Time*. New York: W. W. Norton, 1988.

Gay, P. *The Cultivation of Hatred*. New York: W. W. Norton, 1993.

Gazzaniga, M. S. *Mind Matters: How Mind and Brain Interact to Create Our Conscious Lives*. Boston: Houghton Mifflin, 1988.

Gil, E. *Treatment of Adult Survivors of Childhood Abuse*. Walnut Creek, CA: Launch Press, 1990.

Gilbert, A. N. Buggery and the British Royal Navy 1700–1761. *Journal of Social History*, 1976, 10, 72–76.

Gilligan, C. *In a Different Voice: Psychological Theory and Women's Development.* Cambridge, MA: Harvard University Press, 1993.

Glass-Gurri, M. E., & Glass-Gurri, G. E. *Using Psychometric Testing to Identify Sexual Abuse by Clergy.* Unpublished paper, 1994.

Godin, A. *The Psychology of Religious Vocations: Problems of the Religious Life.* New York: University Press of America, 1983.

Goergen, D. *The Sexual Celibate.* New York: Seabury Press, 1975.

Goergen, D. *Being a Priest Today.* Collegeville, MN: Liturgical Press, 1992.

Greeley, A. M. *The Cardinal Sins.* New York: Bernard Geis, 1982a.

Greeley, A. M. *Thy Brother's Wife.* New York: Bernard Geis, 1982b.

Greeley, A. M. *Ascent into Hell.* New York: Bernard Geis, 1983a.

Greeley, A. M. Priests, celibacy and *The Thorn Birds. TV Guide,* 1983b, 26 March, pp. 4–6.

Greeley, A. M. *Virgin and Martyr.* New York: Warner Books, 1985.

Greeley, A. M. *Angels of September.* New York: Warner Books, 1986.

Greeley, A. M. *Confessions of a Parish Priest: An Autobiography.* New York: Pocket Books, 1987.

Greeley, A. M. *Clerical Culture and Pedophilia.* Unpublished paper, 1992.

Greeley, A. M. A view from the priesthood. *Newsweek,* 1993, 16 August, p. 45.

Green, R. *Sexual Science and the Law.* Cambridge, MA: Harvard University Press, 1992.

Greene, G. *The Power and the Glory.* New York: Bantam Pathfinder Editions, 1972.

Griffiths, P. A. Mathematics—from servant to partner. *Notices of the American Mathematical Society,* 1993, 40(6), July/August, 594–600.

Groeschel, B. J. *The Courage to Be Chaste.* New York: Paulist Press, 1985.

Gross, M. L. *The Psychological Society: A Critical Analysis of Psychiatry, Psychotherapy, Psychoanalysis and the Psychological Revolution.* New York: Random House, 1978.

Grubman-Black, S. D. *Broken Boys/Mending Men: Recovery from Childhood Sexual Abuse.* New York: Ivy Books, 1990.

Guggenbühl-Craig, A. *Power in the Helping Professions.* Dallas: Spring Publications, 1986.

Gunzel, R. J. *Celibacy: Renewing the Gift, Releasing the Power.* Kansas City, MO: Sheed & Ward, 1988.

Hamer, D. H., Shu, S., Magnuson, V. L., Hu, N., & Pattatucci, A. M. A linkage between DNA markers on the X chromosome and male sexual orientation. *Science,* 1993, 261, 321–327.

Hamilton, W. D. Altruism and related phenomena, mainly in social insects. *Annual Review of Ecology and Systematics,* 1972, 3, 193–232.

Hamman, A. *How to Read the Church Fathers.* New York: Crossroad, 1993.

Hann, R. R. Commitment, theology, and the dilemma of religious studies at the state university. *Horizons,* 1992, 19/2, pp. 263–276.

Hardy, A. *The Divine Flame.* London: Collins, 1966.

Harpham, G. G. *The Ascetic Imperative in Culture and Criticism.* Chicago: University of Chicago Press, 1993.

Hartmann, H. *Essays on Ego Psychology.* New York: International Universities Press, 1964.

Hastings, A. The origins of priestly celibacy. *Hielthrop Journal*, 1983, XXIC, 171–177.

Heaney, R. P. Sex, natural law and bread crumbs. *America*, 1994, 26 February, p. 12.

Hebblethwaite, P. *Paul VI: The First Modern Pope*. Mahwah, NJ: Paulist Press, 1993.

Hemrick, E., & Wister, R. *Readiness for Theological Studies: A Study of Faculty Perceptions on the Readiness of Seminarians*. Washington, DC: Seminary Department of the National Catholic Educational Association, 1993.

Hengel, M. *The Pre-Christian Paul*. Philadelphia: Trinity Press International, 1991.

Hermand, P. *The Priest: Celibate or Married*. Baltimore-Dublin: Helicon, 1965.

Hoffman, R. J. Vices, gods, and virtues: Cosmology as a mediating factor in attitudes toward male homosexuality. In J. P. DeCecco & M. G. Shively (Eds.), *Origins of Sexuality and Homosexuality*. New York: Harrington Park, 1985.

Hoge, D. *Evening News*. CBS. 1990, 11 August.

Hoge, D. R. *Research on Men's Vocations to the Priesthood and the Religious Life*. Washington, DC: National Conference of Catholic Bishops, 1984.

Hunter, M. *Abused Boys: The Neglected Victims of Sexual Abuse*. New York: Fawcett Columbine, 1990.

Ignatius, St. *The Spiritual Exercises*. St. Louis: Institute of Jesuit Sources, 1978.

Ignatius of Loyola. *A Pilgrim's Journey*. Collegeville, MN: Liturgical Press, 1991.

James, W. *The Varieties of Religious Experience: A Study in Human Nature*. New York: Penguin Books, 1985.

John Paul II. *Pastores Dabo Vobis*. Rome: Vatican Press, 1992.

John Paul II. *Veritatis Splendor*. Rome: Vatican Press, 1993.

Jurgens, W. A. *The Priesthood: A Translation of the Peri Hierosynes of St. John Chrysostom*. New York: Macmillan, 1955.

Kaufman, P. *Why You Can Disagree . . . And Remain a Faithful Catholic*. New York: Crossroad, 1991.

Kaufmann, W. *Nietzsche*. Princeton, NJ: Princeton University Press, 1974.

Keller, E. F. *Reflections on Gender and Science*. New Haven, CT: Yale University Press, 1985.

Kellert, S. R., & Wilson, E. O. *The Biophilia Hypothesis*. Washington, DC: Island Press, 1993.

Kelly, J. N. D. *The Oxford Dictionary of Popes*. New York: Oxford University Press, 1986.

Kennedy, E. C., & Heckler, V. J. *The Catholic Priest in the United States: Psychological Investigations*. Washington, DC: United States Catholic Conference, 1972.

Ker, I. *John Henry Newman: A Biography*. New York: Oxford University Press, 1988.

Kern, S. *The Culture of Love: Victorians to Moderns*. Cambridge, MA: Harvard University Press, 1992.

Kerr, M. E., & Bowen, M. *Family Evaluation: An Approach Based on Bowen Theory*. New York: W. W. Norton, 1988.

Keuls, E. C. *The Reign of the Phallus: Sexual Politics in Ancient Athens*. Berkeley: University of California Press, 1985.

King, T. M., & Gilbert, M. W. (Eds.). *The Letters of Teilhard de Chardin and Lucile Swan*. Washington, DC: Georgetown University Press, 1993.

Kinsey, A. C., Pomeroy, W. B., & Martin, C. E. *Sexual Behavior in the Human Male*. Philadelphia: W. B. Saunders, 1948.

Kinsey, A. C., Pomeroy, W. B., Martin, C. E., & Gebhard, P. H. *Sexual Behavior in the Human Female*. Philadelphia: W. B. Saunders, 1953.

Klapisch-Zuber, C. *A History of Women in the West: II. Silences of the Middle Ages*. Cambridge, MA: Belknap Press of Harvard University Press, 1992.

Klein, F., Sepekoff, B., & Wolf, T. J. Sexual orientation: A multi-variable dynamic process. *Journal of Homosexuality*, 1985, 11, 35–49.

Konstan, D. *Sexual Symmetry: Love in the Ancient Novel and Related Genres*. Princeton, NJ: Princeton University Press, 1994.

Kotze, V. T. *Stress Among Roman Catholic Clergy in South Africa*. South Africa: privately published, 1991.

Kotze, V. T. Letters. *Tablet*, 1994, 19 March, p. 320.

Krafft-Ebing, R. V. *Psychopathia Sexualis*. Brooklyn, NY: Physicians and Surgeons, 1934.

Kraft, W. *Sexual Dimensions of the Celibate Life*. Kansas City, MO: Andrews & McMeel, 1979.

Kramer, H., & Sprenger, J. *Malleus Maleficarum*. New York: Dover, 1971.

Kristeva, J. *Powers of Horror: An Essay on Abjection*. New York: Columbia University Press, 1982.

Kuhn, T. S. *The Structure of Scientific Revolutions*. Chicago: University of Chicago Press, 1962.

Küng, H. *Global Responsibility: In Search of a New World Ethic*. New York: Crossroad, 1990.

Küng, H., & Kuschel, K.-J. *A Global Ethic: The Declaration of the Parliament of the World's Religions*. New York: Continuum, 1993.

Laeuchli, S. *Power and Sexuality: The Emergence of Canon Law at the Synod of Elvira*. Philadelphia: Temple University Press, 1972.

Laqueur, T. *Making Sex: Body and Gender from the Greeks to Freud*. Cambridge, MA: Harvard University Press, 1990.

Leach, W. *True Love and Perfect Union: The Feminist Reform of Sex and Society*. Middletown, CT: Wesleyan University Press, 1989.

Lederman, L. *The God Particle: If the Universe Is the Answer, What Is the Question?* New York: Houghton Mifflin, 1993.

Leishman, K. Heterosexuals and AIDS. *Atlantic Monthly*, 1987, February, 259, pp. 39–48.

Lerner, G. *The Creation of Patriarchy*. New York: Oxford University Press, 1986.

Lerner, G. *The Creation of Feminist Consciousness: From the Middle Ages to Eighteen-seventy*. New York: Oxford University Press, 1993.

Lestapis, de S. *Birth Regulation: The Catholic Position*. London: Burns & Oates, 1963.

LeVay, S., & Hamer, D. H. Evidence for a biological influence in male homosexuality. *Scientific American*, 1994, 270, pp. 44–49.

Lever, M. *Sade: A Biography* (A. Goldhammer, Trans.). New York: Farrar, Straus & Giroux, 1993.

Lévi-Strauss, C. *Totemism.* Boston: Beacon Press, 1963a.

Lévi-Strauss, C. *Structural Anthropology.* Basic Books, 1963b.

Lévi-Strauss, C. *The Jealous Potter.* Chicago: University of Chicago Press, 1988.

Lew, M. *Victims No Longer: Men Recovering from Incest and Other Sexual Child Abuse.* New York: HarperCollins, 1990.

Lewes, K. *The Psychoanalytic Theory of Male Homosexuality.* New York: Simon & Schuster, 1988.

Lindberg, D. C., & Numbers, R. L. *God and Nature: Historical Essays on the Encounter Between Christianity and Science.* Berkeley: University of California Press, 1986.

Lukács, G. *The Theory of the Novel.* Cambridge, MA: MIT Press, 1987.

Lumsden, C. J., & Wilson, E. O. *Genes, Mind, and Culture: The Coevolutionary Process.* Cambridge, MA: Harvard University Press, 1981.

Lumsden, C. J., & Wilson, E. O. *Promethean Fire: Reflections on the Origin of Mind.* Cambridge, MA: Harvard University Press, 1983.

Mahoney, D. T. *Touching the Face of God: Intimacy and Celibacy in Priestly Life.* Boca Raton, FL: Jeremiah Press, 1991.

Malinowski, B. *Sex and Repression in Savage Society.* Chicago: University of Chicago Press, 1985.

Mann, J. M. *AIDS in the World.* Cambridge, MA: Harvard University Press, 1992.

Mann, J. M. *Infectious Disease Challenges in AIDS.* Participant Workbook. New York: SCP Communications, 1993.

Marcus, G. E., & Fischer, M. M. *Anthropology as Cultural Critique: An Experimental Moment in the Human Sciences.* Chicago: University of Chicago Press, 1986.

Marcus, I. M., & Francis, J. J. *Masturbation: From Infancy to Senescence.* New York: International Universities Press, 1975.

Marcuse, H. *Eros and Civilization: A Philosophical Inquiry into Freud.* Boston: Beacon Press, 1974.

Mbuy Beya, B. Ways to liberate the women of Africa. *Tablet,* 1994, 14 May, pp. 591–592.

McAllister, R. J. *Living the Vows: The Emotional Conflicts of Celibate Religious.* San Francisco: Harper & Row, 1986.

McFague, S. *The Body of God: An Ecological Theology.* Minneapolis: Fortress Press, 1993.

McGovern, J. J. *Catholic Pocket Dictionary and Cyclopedia.* Chicago: Extention, 1906.

McHugh, P. R. Psychiatric misadventures. *American Scholar,* 1992, 61(4), Autumn, 497–510.

McHugh, P. R. Psychotherapy awry. *American Scholar,* 1994, 63(1), Winter, 17–30.

McNeill, J. J. *The Church and the Homosexual.* Kansas City, MO: Andrews & McMeel, 1976.

Medawar, P. *The Threat and the Glory.* New York: HarperCollins, 1990.

Meissner, W. W. *Psychoanalysis and Religious Experience*. New Haven, CT: Yale University Press, 1984.

Meissner, W. W. *The Psychology of a Saint: Ignatius of Loyola*. New Haven: Yale University Press, 1992.

Menninger, K. *Whatever Became of Sin?* New York: Hawthorn Books, 1973.

Miles, M. R. *Practicing Christianity: Critical Perspectives for an Embodied Spirituality*. New York: Crossroad, 1990.

Miles, M. R. *Desire and Delight*. New York: Crossroad, 1992.

Miller, A. *Banished Knowledge: Facing Childhood Injuries*. New York: Doubleday, 1986.

Miller, A. *The Untouched Key*. New York: Doubleday, 1988.

Miller, A. *Thou Shalt Not Be Aware: Society's Betrayal of the Child*. New York: Meridian, 1990.

Miller, D. *How Little We Knew*. Lafayette, LA: Prescott Press, 1993.

Miller, J. *Assault on Innocence*. Albuquerque, NM: B&K Publishers, 1988.

Money, J. Bisexuality and homosexuality. *Sexual Medicine Today*, 1984, 24 February.

Money, J. *Lovemaps: Clinical Concepts of Sexual/Erotic Health and Pathology, Paraphilia, and Gender Transposition in Childhood, Adolescence, and Maturity*. New York: Irvington, 1986.

Montini, G. B. *The Priest*. Baltimore-Dublin: Helicon, 1965.

Mooney, C. F. Theology and science: A new commitment to dialogue. *Theological Studies*, 1991, 52, 289–329.

Mooney, C. F. *Evolution and Theology*. Unpublished working papers, 1992.

Moore, G. *The Body in Context: Sex and Catholicism*. London: SCM Press, 1992.

Mosteller, R. P. Child abuse reporting laws and attorney-client confidences: The reality and the specter of lawyer as informant. *Duke Law Journal*, 1992, 42(2), 203–225.

Mott, M. *The Seven Mountains of Thomas Merton*. Boston: Houghton Mifflin, 1984.

Murphy, S. *A Delicate Dance: Sexuality, Celibacy, and Relationships Among Catholic Clergy and Religious*. New York: Crossroad, 1992.

Nash, J. *Stress, ego identity, and disclosure of homosexual orientation among midlife transition male Roman Catholic professionals*. Unpublished doctoral dissertation, Pacific Graduate School of Psychology, Menlo Park, CA, 1990.

Nash, J., & Hayes, F. The parental relationships of male homosexuals: Some theoretical issues and a pilot study. *Australian Journal of Psychology*, 1965, 17, 35–43.

National Center on Child Abuse and Neglect. *Child Abuse Prevention and Treatment Act, as Amended*. Alexandria, VA: U.S. Department of Health and Human Services, 1992, November.

National Child Abuse and Neglect Data System. *Working Paper 2: 1991 Summary Data Component*. Washington, DC: National Center on Child Abuse and Neglect.

National Conference of Catholic Bishops. *Spiritual Renewal of the Catholic Priesthood*. Washington, DC: Author, 1973.

National Conference of Catholic Bishops. *The Program of Priestly Formation*. 3rd ed. Washington, DC: Author, 1981, 30 November.

National Conference of Catholic Bishops. *Norms for Priestly Formation.* Washington, DC: Author, 1982, December.

National Conference of Catholic Bishops. *Spiritual Formation in the Catholic Seminary.* Washington, DC: Bishops' Committee on Priestly Formation, 1984.

National Conference of Catholic Bishops. *The Health of American Catholic Priests: A Report and a Study.* Bishops' Committee on Priestly Life and Ministry, 1985.

National Conference of Catholic Bishops. *Human Sexuality: A Catholic Perspective for Education and Lifelong Learning.* Washington, DC: United States Catholic Conference, 1990.

Nietzsche, F. *Thus Spake Zarathustra.* New York: Modern Library, 1980.

Nelson, J. B., & Longfellow, S. P. *Sexuality and the Sacred.* Louisville, KY: Westminster/John Knox Press, 1994.

Newman, J. H. *Loss and Gain: The Story of a Convert.* New York: Oxford University Press, 1986.

Newman, J. H. *Apologia Pro Vita Sua: Being a History of His Religious Opinions.* Oxford: Clarendon Press, 1990.

Noble, D. F. *A World Without Women: The Christian Clerical Culture of Western Science.* New York: Oxford University Press, 1992.

Noonan, J. T., Jr. Development in moral doctrine. *Theological Studies,* 1993, 54, 662–677.

Nordeen, E. J., & Yahr, P. Hemispheric asymmetries in the behavioral and hormonal effects of sexually differentiating mammalian brain. *Science,* 1982, 218, 391.

Norris, K. The virgin martyrs: Between "point vierge" and the "usual spring." In P. Elie (Ed.), *A Tremor of Bliss: Contemporary Writers on the Saints.* New York: Harcourt Brace, 1994.

O'Connor, J. M. St. Paul: Promoter of the ministry of women. *Priests & People,* 1992, August–September, pp. 307–311.

O'Malley, J. W. *The First Jesuits.* Cambridge, MA: Harvard University Press, 1993.

Ong, W. J. *Hopkins, the Self, and God.* Toronto: University of Toronto Press, 1986.

Ong, W. J. *Fighting for Life: Contest, Sexuality, and Consciousness.* Amherst: University of Massachusetts Press, 1989.

Oraison, M. *The Celibate Condition and Sex.* New York: Sheed & Ward, 1967.

O'Toole, J. M. *Militant and Triumphant.* Notre Dame, IN: University of Notre Dame Press, 1992.

Ovesey, L. *Homosexuality and Pseudohomosexuality.* New York: Science House, 1969.

Pantel, P. S. *A History of Women in the West: I. From Ancient Goddesses to Christian Saints.* Cambridge, MA: Harvard University Press, 1992.

Peacock, J. L. *The Anthropological Lens: Harsh Light, Soft Focus.* New York: Cambridge University Press, 1991.

Penrose, R. *The Emperor's New Mind: Concerning Computers, Minds, and the Laws of Physics.* Penguin Books, 1991.

Peterson, M. R. *At Personal Risk: Boundary Violations in Professional-Client Relationships.* New York: W. W. Norton, 1992.

Peterson, M., Doyle, T., & Mouton R. *Confidential Report to the American Bishops.* Private publication, 1985.

Pettersen, A. *Athanasius and the Human Body.* Los Angeles: Bristol Press, 1990.

Pfliegler, M. *Celibacy.* London: Sheed & Ward, 1967.

Poling, J. N. *The Abuse of Power: A Theological Problem.* Nashville: Abingdon Press, 1991.

Posner, R. A. *Sex and Reason.* Cambridge, MA: Harvard University Press, 1992.

Rabelais. *Gargantua and Pantagruel.* New York: Modern Library, 1944.

Raguin, Y. *Celibacy for Our Times.* St. Meinrad, IN: Abbey Press, 1974.

Redondi, P. *Galileo Heretic.* Princeton, NJ: Princeton University Press, 1987.

Reid, W. H. *The Psychiatric Times,* 1988, April.

Renner, G. Celibacy and sexual abuse. *Hartford Courant,* 1993, 28 March, 1–6.

*Report of the Commission on Obscenity and Pornography.* Washington, DC: U.S. Printing Office, 1970.

Rievaulx, A. *Dialogue on the Soul.* Kalamazoo, MI: Cistercian, 1981.

Rosenberg, A. *The Myth of the Twentieth Century: An Evaluation of the Spiritual-Intellectual Confrontations of Our Age.* Torrance, CA: Noontide Press, 1982.

Rossetti, S. (Ed.). *Slayer of the Soul.* Mystic, CT: Twenty-Third Publications, 1990.

Rossetti, S. J. *Parishes as Victims of Child Sexual Abuse.* Unpublished paper, 1994.

Rossetti, S. J., & Meyer, C. *St. Luke Institute Psychosexual Interview.* Unpublished paper, 1992.

Rousseau, J.-J. *The Confessions of Jean-Jacques Rousseau.* New York: Heritage Press, 1955.

Ruether, R. R. *Sexism and God-Talk Toward a Feminist Theology.* Boston: Beacon Press, 1983.

Ruggiero, G. *The Boundaries of Eros: Sex Crime and Sexuality in Renaissance Venice.* New York: Oxford University Press, 1985.

Sammon, S. D. *An Undivided Heart: Making Sense of Celibate Chastity.* New York: Alba House, 1993.

Sánchez, J. T. (Ed.). *Solo per Amore: Riflessioni sul celibato sacerdotale.* Rome: Edizioni Paoline, 1993.

Schetky, D., & Green, A. *Child Sexual Abuse: A Handbook for Health Care and Legal Professionals.* New York: Brunner/Mazel, 1988.

Schillebeeckx, E. *Celibacy.* New York: Sheed & Ward, 1968.

Schoenherr, R. A. *Full Pews and Empty Altars: Demographics of the Priest Shortage in United States Catholic Dioceses.* Madison: University of Wisconsin Press, 1993.

Shafer, I. H. *Eros and the Womanliness of God: Andrew Greeley's Romance of Renewal.* Chicago: Loyola University Press, 1986.

Shafer, I. H. *Andrew Greeley's World: An Anthology of Critical Essays, 1986–1988.* New York: Warner Books, 1989.

Shengold, L. *Halo in the Sky: Observations on Anality and Defense.* New York: Guilford Press, 1988.

Shengold, L. *Soul Murder: The Effects of Childhood Abuse and Deprivation*. New Haven, CT: Yale University Press, 1989.

Shweder, R. A., & LeVine, R. A. *Culture Theory: Essays on Mind, Self, and Emotion*. New York: Cambridge University Press, 1984.

Shweder, R. A. *Thinking Through Cultures: Expeditions in Cultural Psychology*. Cambridge, MA: Harvard University Press, 1991.

Sipe, A. W. R. Sexual aspects of the human condition. In P. W. Prayser (Ed.), *Changing Views of the Human Condition*. Macon, GA: Mercer University Press, 1987.

Sipe, A. W. R. *A Secret World: Sexuality and the Search for Celibacy*. New York: Brunner/Mazel, 1990a.

Sipe, A. W. R. Newfoundland report: A church reform manifesto. *National Catholic Reporter*, 1990b, 21 September, p. 24.

Sipe, A. W. R. Education for celibacy: An American challenge. *America*, 1991, 18 May, pp. 539–548.

Sipe, A. W. R. A house built on sand. Viewpoint. *Tablet*, 1992a, 12 September, p. 1118.

Sipe, A. W. R. Double-talk on celibacy. *Tablet*, 1992b, 16 May, pp. 605–606.

Sipe, A. W. R. Sex and celibacy. *Tablet*, 1992c, 9 May, pp. 576–577.

Sipe, A. W. R. A step toward the prevention of sexual abuse. *Human Development*, 1993a, 14(4), Winter, 27–28.

Sipe, A. W. R. To enable healing. *National Catholic Reporter*, 1993b, 17 September, pp. 6–7.

Sipe, A. W. R. Celibacy and imagery: "Horror story" in the making. *National Catholic Reporter*, 1993c, 2 July, p. 5.

Sipe, A. W. R. Celibacy in law and life. Viewpoint. *Tablet*, 1993d, 12 June, p. 742.

Sipe, A. W. R. The celibacy question. *Tablet*, 1993e, 5 June, pp. 737–738.

Sipe, A. W. R. Victims of clergy abuse achieve rightful status. *Bread Rising*, 1994, 4(1), pp. 2–3.

Sipe, A. W. R., & Gruman, H. *Behind the Minister's Black Veil*. In press.

Sipe, A. W. R., & Lamb, B. C. *Reading Andrew Greeley*. In press.

Spradley, J. P., & McCurdy, D. W. *The Cultural Experience: Ethnography in Complex Society*. Chicago: Science Research Associates, 1972.

Stahel, T. One pastoral response to abuse. Interview with Joseph P. Chinnici. *America*, 1994, 170(2), pp. 4–8.

Stearns, G. B., Baggerley-Mar, K., Merlin, E., Bonner, D., & Higgins, R. *Report to Father Joseph P. Chinnici, O.F.M. Provincial Minister, Province of St. Barbara*. Independent Board of Inquiry Regarding St. Anthony's Seminary, 1993, November.

Steinberg, L. *The Sexuality of Christ in Renaissance Art and in Modern Oblivion*. New York: Pantheon/October Books, 1983.

Stern, K. *The Flight from Woman*. New York: Farrar, Straus & Giroux, 1965.

Stewart, C. Radical honesty about the self: The practice of the desert fathers and its heirs. *Subornost*, 1990, 12(1), pp. 25–39, 143–156.

Stewart, C. *The Monastic Journey According to John Cassian*. Petersham, MA: St. Bede's Publications, 1993, pp. 29–40.

Stickler, A. (Ed.). *Guide to the Vatican, Museums and City.* Rome: Cita del Vaticano, 1986.

Stocking, G. W., Jr. *Observers Observed: Essays on Ethnographic Fieldwork.* Madison: University of Wisconsin Press, 1985.

Stocking, G. W., Jr. *The Ethnographer's Magic and Other Essays in the History of Anthropology.* Madison: University of Wisconsin Press, 1992.

Stoller, R. J. *Observing the Erotic Imagination.* New Haven, CT: Yale University Press, 1985.

Suenens, L. J. *Love and Control.* Westminster, MD: Newman Press, 1962.

Suleiman, S. R. *The Female Body in Western Culture.* Cambridge, MA: Harvard University Press, 1986.

Swaab, D. F., & Fliers, E. A Sexually Dimorphic Nucleus in the Human Brain: Hypothalamus and Sex Differences. *Science,* 1985, 228, 1112–1115.

Swerdloff, R. S., & Gorski, R. Effect of androgens on the brain and other organs during development and aging. *Psychoneuroendocrinology,* 1992, 14(4), 375–383.

Tannahill, R. *Sex in History.* London: Scarborough House, 1992.

Teilhard de Chardin, P. *The Phenomenon of Man.* New York: Harper & Row, 1961.

Teilhard de Chardin, P. *The Future of Man.* New York: Harper & Row, 1964.

Teilhard de Chardin, P. Comment je crois. *Oeuvres.* Vol. 10. Paris: Seuil, 1969.

Thébaud, F. *A History of Women in the West: V. Toward a Cultural Identity in the Twentieth Century.* London: Belknap Press of Harvard University Press, 1994.

Theisen, J., Power, authority, and charism in the church. In F. A. Elgo (Ed.), *The Spirit Moving the Church in the United States, Proceedings of the Theology Institute of Villanova University.* Villanova, PA: Villanova University Press, 1989, 63–95.

Theweleit, K. *Male Fantasies: Vol 1. Women, Floods, Bodies, History.* Minneapolis: University of Minneapolis Press, 1987.

Theweleit, K. *Male Fantasies: Vol 2. The Male Body: Psychoanalyzing the White Terror.* Minneapolis: University of Minneapolis Press, 1989.

Thomas, J. L. Book review of R. Grinder, *Sex and Sin in the Catholic Church. National Catholic Reporter,* 1975, 12, p. 11.

Tinder, G. *The Political Meaning of Christianity.* Baton Rouge: Louisiana State University Press, 1989.

Tolstoy, L. *The Kingdom of God Is Within You.* Lincoln: University of Nebraska Press, 1984.

Trible, P. *God and the Rhetoric of Sexuality.* London: SCM Press, 1992.

Tribe, L. H. *Abortion: The Clash of Absolutes.* New York: W.W. Norton, 1990.

Turner, V. W., & Bruner, E. M. *The Anthropology of Experience.* Chicago: University of Illinois Press, 1986.

Turner, W. J. *Homosexuality, Type 1: An Xq28 Phenomenon.* Unpublished paper, 1992.

Turner, W. J. Comments on discordant MZ twinning in homosexuality (T.B.P.). *Archives of Sexual Behavior,* 1994, 23 February.

United States Catholic Conference. *Letter to the Bishops of the Catholic Church on the Pastoral Care of Homosexual Persons.* Rome: Sacred Congregation for the Doctrine of the Faith, 1986, 1 October.

Ursano, R. J., McCaughey, B. G., & Fullerton, C. S. *Individual and Community Responses to Trauma and Disaster: The Structure of Human Chaos.* Cambridge, MA: Cambridge University Press, 1994.

Vivelo, F. R. *Cultural Anthropology Handbook.* New York: McGraw-Hill, 1978.

Vogels, H.-J. *Celibacy—Gift or Law?* Kansas City: Sheed & Ward, 1993.

Von Bertalanffy, L. System, symbol and the image of man. In I. Goldston (Ed.), *The Interface Between Psychiatry and Anthropology.* New York: Brunner/Mazel, 1971.

Wadsworth, B. J. *Piaget's Theory of Cognitive and Affective Development.* London: Longman, 1989.

Wagner, R. *Gay Catholic Priests: A Study of Cognitive and Affective Dissonance.* San Francisco: Institute for Advanced Study of Human Sexuality, 1980.

Weakland, R. G. Herald of Hope: The Church's Passover. Reprint from *Catholic Herald,* Milwaukee, WI, Easter 1993.

Weinberg, S. *The First Three Minutes: A Modern View of the Origin of the Universe.* New York: Basic Books, 1988.

Weinberg, S. *Dreams of a Final Theory.* New York: Pantheon, 1992.

Weininger, O. *Sex and Character.* New York: G. P. Putnam's Sons, 1909.

Wells, M. *Canada's Law on Child Sexual Abuse.* Ottawa: Department of Justice, 1990.

Whitehead, A. N. *Science and the Modern World.* New York: Free Press, 1967.

Whitehead, E. E., & Whitehead, J. D. *A Sense of Sexuality: Christian Love and Intimacy.* New York: Doubleday, 1990.

Wiener, N. *The Human Use of Human Beings: Cybernetics and Society.* Garden City, NY: Doubleday, 1954.

Williams, W. I. *The Spirit and the Flesh: Sexual Diversity in American Indian Culture.* Boston: Beacon Press, 1986.

Wilson, E. O. *The Insect Societies.* Cambridge, MA: Belknap Press of Harvard University Press, 1971.

Wilson, E. O. *Sociobiology: The New Synthesis.* Cambridge, MA: Belknap Press of Harvard University Press, 1975a.

Wilson, E. O. Human decency is animal. *New York Times Magazine,* 1975b, 12 October, pp. 38–50.

Wilson, E. O. *On Human Nature.* Cambridge, MA: Harvard University Press, 1978.

Wilson, E. O. *Biophilia.* Cambridge MA: Harvard University Press, 1984.

Wilson, E. O. *The Diversity of Life.* Cambridge, MA: Belknap Press of Harvard University Press, 1992a.

Wilson, E. O. The return to natural philosophy. *Harvard Divinity Bulletin,* 1992b, 21(3), 12–15.

Winter, G., O'Flahery, F., Kenny, N. P., MacNeil, E., & Scott, J. A. *The Report of the Archdiocesan Commission of Enquiry into the Sexual Abuse of Children by Members of the Clergy.* Vol. 1. Archdiocese of St. John's Newfoundland, 1990a.

Winter, G., O'Flahery, F., Kenny, N. P., MacNeil, E., & Scott, J. A. *The Report of the Archdiocesan Commission of Enquiry into the Sexual Abuse of Children by Members of the Clergy*. Vol. 2. Archdiocese of St. John's Newfoundland, 1990b.

Winter, G., O'Flahery, F., Kenny, N. P., MacNeil, E., & Scott, J. A. *The Report of the Archdiocesan Commission of Enquiry into the Sexual Abuse of Children by Members of the Clergy: Conclusions and Recommendations*. Archdiocese of St. John's Newfoundland, 1990c.

Wojcik, J. Church scandals prompt action. *Business Insurance*, 1994, 2 January, p. 1.

Wolf, J. G. *Gay Priests*. San Francisco: Harper & Row, 1989.

Wright, N. T. *The New Testament and the People of God*. Minneapolis: Fortress Press, 1992.

Young, D. *Origins of the Sacred: The Ecstasies of Love and War*. New York: St. Martin's Press, 1991.

# NAME INDEX

# SUBJECT INDEX

214